Additional Praise for
CRM at the Speed of Light

"The ability to successfully manage customer relationships can be a decisive advantage in today's competitive world. *CRM at the Speed of Light* provides an industry insider's view of the business applications that can create this advantage for your business."

—Craig Conway,
President and CEO,
PeopleSoft, Inc.

CRM at the
Speed of Light

CRM at the Speed of Light

Capturing and Keeping Customers in Internet Real Time

Paul Greenberg

Osborne/**McGraw-Hill**

Berkeley ► New York ► St. Louis ► San Francisco ► Auckland ► Bogotá
Hamburg ► London ► Madrid ► Mexico City ► Milan ► Montreal ► New Delhi
Panama City ► Paris ► São Paulo ► Singapore ► Sydney ► Tokyo ► Toronto

Osborne/**McGraw-Hill**

2600 Tenth Street
Berkeley, California 94710
U.S.A.

For information on translations or book distributors outside the U.S.A., or
to arrange bulk purchase discounts for sales promotions, premiums, or
fund-raisers, please contact Osborne/**McGraw-Hill** at the above address.

*CRM at the Speed of Light: Capturing and Keeping Customers in Internet
Real Time*

1234567890 DOC DOC 019876543210

ISBN 0-07-213337-6

This book was composed with QuarkXPress 4.11 on a Macintosh G4.

My dedications never change. They are to those who are everything to me and to whom I am devoted and dedicated well beyond this book. This book is to my mom, Helen Greenberg; my dad, Chet Greenberg; my brother, Bob Greenberg; my sister-in-law, Freyda Greenberg; my niece, Sara Greenberg; and, of course, to my beloved wife, Yvonne Greenberg. Their acts of grace and goodness are not extraordinary—they are ordinary: continuously giving is part of their lives day in and day out, which makes them even more extraordinary people. We are all Greenbergs and I am blessed.

Contents

Foreword

The influence of technology on business is undeniable. In this century, we've seen communications evolve from hand-carried messages to a global network that lets individuals reach one another instantly almost anywhere on the globe. People who were forced to base important business decisions on limited, dated information now have immediate access to a tremendous amount of real-time data. Correspondingly, computing has evolved to the point where individuals now have immediate and personal access to computational power unavailable at any cost just a few years earlier. The most dramatic evidence of this is the Internet, where computing and communications have converged to provide global individual empowerment on a scale never seen before.

Less than five years ago, it was common to hear comments such as, "The Internet is a fad—it won't last," or "People won't buy online." Today, these comments are laughable, as the Internet has become the catalyst driving the most sweeping changes in the business world this century. Not only has the Internet fostered new business models, such as collaborative marketplaces aggregating suppliers and customers, it has fundamentally changed the relationship between business and consumers. Empowered with access to more information and competitive choices than ever before, customers are approaching business with higher expectations than ever before.

Businesses are being forced to react. Satisfy your customer's expectations or lose them to a competitor lurking a single mouse click away. Drive revenue growth and profitability in the face of greater competition. Sustain competitive advantage in the face of product commoditization. Relationships between your business, your customers, and your suppliers are the one constant that emerges. This underscores the critical need to improve the way these relationships are managed and fostered. Furthermore, these relationships are not isolated to those involving customers, as some vendors would lead you to believe. Every business enterprise includes customers, employees, and suppliers in a dynamic, constantly evolving network focused on the exchange of goods and services for money. The relationships linking customers, employees, and suppliers represent an opportunity for enterprises to build loyalty, profitability, and competitive advantage through their strategic and consistent management.

CRM applications necessarily involve the functions of marketing, sales, and service. However, the ability of the enterprise to practice good CRM and consistently transform the expectations of customers into positive experiences requires all parts of the enterprise working together with the benefit of insight and empowerment. The integration of business process and the seamless support provided by business applications can't stop at departmental boundaries or point-solution limitations. Any division between the front office and the back office interrupts the business process flow, and can jeopardize the customer experience. Integration of enterprise applications is essential to facilitate good CRM. Open integration lends flexibility and safety to implementation, and enables you to leverage legacy investments as you build out your e-business infrastructure.

Insight, derived from the ability to monitor and measure the entire business process, forms the foundation of strategic decision making. Without a true understanding of the business, the available options, and their corresponding tradeoffs, decisions will be inefficient and inconsistent. I believe accurate insight must be integrally coupled with operational applications for all people throughout the enterprise, so they can track their job performance, prioritize their actions, and ensure consistency with corporate goals. The ability to finally provide this empowerment to all people throughout the enterprise is now here, today, at PeopleSoft.

We are experiencing a landmark shift in business technology away from client/server applications to pure-Internet applications. Much as the business landscape shifted away from mainframe-based applications to the desktop a decade ago, this shift is being driven by reduced costs of deployment and maintenance, and also by the simplicity, ease of use, and accessibility the Internet provides. Today's dynamic business enterprise demands that applications be available to the entire enterprise, not just employees sitting at their desks. Only pure-Internet applications provide the ability for a business to extend insight and empowerment to customers, employees, and suppliers supporting the flexible, dynamic environments of today's businesses. PeopleSoft's CRM applications integrate to your business processes throughout the enterprise. They are insightful, providing measurement and analysis to enable continuous improvement of the processes. Finally, they are pervasive, enabling people to access them regardless of role, channel or device, or location.

I believe you will find Paul Greenberg's work to be informative and educational. In the crowded, confusing world of business applications, Paul's experience with both front-office and back-office systems comparison, implementation, and integration can assist you in identifying basic business needs and how application technology can help you address them. At the end of the day, it's all about people collaborating together to make business work.

Customers, Employees, and Suppliers—People Power the Internet.

—Craig Conway, president and CEO,
PeopleSoft, Inc.

Acknowledgments

Writing books is not just writing. It is often as much about project management as it is about being a creative scribe. Project management isn't usually fun. It involves dealing with others who are on the same deadline as you without the sense of urgency that you feel. Not a pleasant thing to try to rope in errant writers or whoever.

This book was fun because it didn't work that way. First, I did most of the writing. But second, those who also wrote and supported me were awesome people who met deadlines. I even had entire companies that met deadlines! PeopleSoft/Vantive, Interact Commerce Corporation, Onyx, and MicroStrategy, to be exact.

Equally as emotionally tasty, I met a number of remarkable people who will be lifelong friends. Not bad, being able to write a book that turned into a life experience!

Sections of this book were written by incredible stalwarts and excellent writers such as Charlie Sundling, CEO of Pipeline Software, and Jeff Brown, director of technology services for my company, Live Wire, Inc. Charlie did 95 percent of the chapter on the ASPs and contributed to another chapter, as did Jeff. Michael Simpson, chief marketing officer of Interact Commerce Corporation, gave of his time and company and writing skills to make this book work in a way that I didn't think was going to be possible. Pat Sullivan, CEO and president of Interact Commerce and a man voted one of the ten most significant people in CRM history, was always friendly, gracious and, in my eyes truly worthy of his designation as a top ten guy.

But it didn't stop there. Ted Hillestad of MicroStrategy worked tirelessly and on the same deadlines as me, setting up meetings and interviews for me at MicroStrategy with some of the good people quoted in this book, Mark LaRow and Christian Hernandez. These folks redefined helpful, moving it from CD-quality to DVD-quality.

Ed Schreyer is a busy man as the vice president of Strategic Marketing for PeopleSoft. Even so, in the midst of this nonstop schedule, he saw to it that everything showed up on time and I was kept informed. A great guy at a great company.

Mei Lin Fung is someone I didn't know a few months ago. She is a good person and a gifted economist and CRM specialist. I am indebted to her for her permission to use the "Primer on Customer Lifetime

Value" and for her help in putting that part of the book together. Greenberg Lifetime Value derived.

These are the people I didn't even know before this book began and now I do. Thus, a new group of friends and colleagues. That makes the book worth it regardless of anything else. I can't thank these folks enough without stretching the acknowledgments to about 1,200 pages, which would get my editor really mad. However, there is one person I do want to mention because she was pretty special. Stacy Hendricks is the PR manager at Onyx Software. Not only did she jump to opportunities and work non-stop with her colleagues to help me meet my deadlines, even including a "until midnight Sunday at her office" stint, which was way above and beyond the call, but also she is one of best poets I've ever read. Real power in a great person.

But now, for those I did know. When I write, they remain with me at all times. Some are people I've met through business, and some I've known for my whole adult life (and, for some, even longer).

Paul McCauley—manager for the Deloitte & Touche account at Interact Commerce Corporation—a true friend, much more than just a business colleague and one person who, through his immeasurable help and support, has seen to it that there is a chance for this book to succeed. He is one of those people I met through business who transcend the circumstance.

Nachi Junankar—president of Live Wire, the company I work for. He is a young man who is bright and wise beyond his years and someone I value as a business colleague and, even more so, as a friend. He has been more than encouraging in my production of this often difficult volume. He has been totally supportive when he didn't have to be.

Craig Thompson, CFO—a good man with a great heart. Craig has been a guiding spirit and light for me for three years now. He is a direct participant in this book because his knowledge needs to be extended to a world beyond his normal audience. He's that smart. A great friend.

Scott Fletcher—I worked closely with Scott on my last book, when he was VP of Technology Services for PeopleSoft. He does well because he is someone who can match business expertise with a truly human touch. He's been there for me whenever I've needed him to be and I hope he can say the same of me.

Stella Ivanov—Siebel consultant. If it weren't for her, I wouldn't know the "technofunctional" insides of Siebel Call Center. She is a smart, kind person willing to put up with my ignorant questions.

Additionally, I truly appreciate the efforts that the various CRM leaders who wrote for Chapter 1 made. In addition to Scott Fletcher and Michael Simpson, both mentioned above, that includes Craig Conway, president and CEO, PeopleSoft, Inc.; Brent Frei, president and CEO, Onyx Software; Peter Keen, a man of great depth and humor and humanity, chairman, Keen Innovations; Ronni T. Marshak, senior vice president, Patricia Seybold Group; and Robert Thompson, president of Front Line Solutions, Inc., who contributed throughout the book in so many ways.

There was another group of people that were involved with this book who always are luminous to me. That's my family and near family. If I write a hundred books, those members of my family and extended family will be standing there holding me up for all hundred. That means my immediate family: Yvonne, my wife; my brother Bob; my mom, Helen and father, Chet; my sister-in-law, Freyda, and my niece Sara Rose. Check out my dedication for more on them. They give me unconditional love that, in good and bad moments, I needed throughout these months. Writing a book ain't easy.

And it means the Newfoundland branch of my family (my wife's side): my mother-in-law, Martha; my brothers-in-law and their spouses, Wayne and Carol, and Vernon and Bong; and my sister-in-law and her spouse, Ann and Byrne. They have been supportive beyond the norm, always there, always ready to help, always willing to be part of me. How much more could I really ask?

Editors are scary sometimes because you think that they are your critics and they are the ones who are going to cut you to shreds. True enough. They are your critics, but they cut your writing to coherence, not shreds. They are the ones who make it work and they are the ones who see to the book being on time. My editors, Laurie Stewart and Lunaea Weatherstone, are the best of the best. Certainly the best I ever had, and I suspect among the best on the planet. They maintained balance (mine) and still made me work at a feverish pace to fix what I wrote. That meant lots of work, which they tirelessly did. I'll put it this way: if I ever get to write for Osborne/McGraw-Hill again, I'm going to insist they are my editors again. I know other authors who think the same. We are all justified in that thought.

Are there others? Sure there are, but this isn't the Academy Awards and I'm not winning an Oscar, though I wouldn't mind, if the Academy is reading this. There is, however, one other person I want to thank profusely: my managing editor and the editorial director at Osborne/McGraw-Hill, Roger Stewart. He is a delight, a superb professional, and one amazing human being. He is funny, supportive, and smart, and he knows how to get the best out of me. I'm happy to know him, book or no book. Writing a book is not always fun, but Roger always is.

There's no more to say and I've probably left some people out for which I apologize, but enough of this—read on, Macduff!

Introduction

There is a sea change in business. It doesn't mean that the temperature of the oceans is increasing or that NOAA has been brought in to monitor business. It means there's been a revolution in how you and your colleagues and competitors see customers and, more importantly, how the customers see you and themselves. Until the last couple of years, the customer was the person or persons who purchased commodities or services from your company. It seemed to be pretty simple. But globalization began moving at warp speed in the 1990s with the entry of the Internet into the mainstream. Customer demand superseded product demand. The customer was no longer just a commodity purchase machine.

What did the customer morph into? Who are customers, really? They are your employee, your partner, or your commodity or services purchaser. They are your supplier. It is anyone or any entity you have a relationship with that involves business in any way. There is no longer a true distinction in what constitutes a customer, only how you treat different groups of customers. When you work with your employees to see that they are happy in the workplace, that effort defines them as your customer. You are providing a service or commodity of value to them in return for value—their labor. When you develop a strategic alliance partner who actually may have software that fills a hole in your offering and vice versa, they are your customers. Each of you has a potentially useful value proposition for the other. This is not an entirely new idea.

Now the customer is the controlling force. No longer is the customer molded and shaped to the product. It has been entirely reversed and has become more of a continuous, real-time process than a fixed plan. How often have you heard that the need for a business to be flexible is vital for survival and growth in the New Economy? That's flexible with the *customers*. When customer demand shifts, so must the enterprise, just to survive, much less flourish.

Okay, enough of this. So, you ask, what is CRM? What is the purpose of this book on CRM technology and the Internet? The more substantial definition of CRM is being left to Chapter 1. However, I'll throw in a short, distilled, filtered definition (120 proof) of CRM to begin to satisfy your terminological blood lust. CRM is a complete system that (1) provides a means and method to enhance the experience of the individual customers so that they will remain customers for life, (2) provides both technological and functional means of identifying, capturing, and retaining customers, and (3) provides a unified view of the customer across an enterprise. There are many books in the marketplace that claim to be about CRM. Some are primarily books on reinvented marketing methodologies. Some are actually on CRM as a system. This book is neither. It is about the technology of CRM.

The subject of this book is the technological wrapper for the system. The focus of the book is on the Web-based technologies available for implementing a CRM system. I'll show you how to use that technology to provide you with the tools to make your customers, however you define them, happy. CRM provides you with a tangible return—when done well.

For Clarity's Sake

What constitutes the CRM system is a complex, constantly shifting almost liquid set of definitions, concepts, and methodologies that change according to the principles of customer real-time demand (in other words, a closed infinite loop) and dramatically shifting market conditions. Thus, CRM needs to provide a wrapper that is as fluid as its parent. This book is focused on giving you a glass for the fluid—providing shape and substance for CRM technology. If I accomplish what I set out to do, by the end of the book you'll have enough information to make an informed business decision on implementing CRM in your company along with a CRM strategy. The book is not meant to provide you with a new CRM method. The strategies out there are either better than adequate or adequate to do so. CRM has one-to-one marketing and permission marketing methodologies already embedded in a good deal of its functionality.

This book will tell you what CRM strategies and philosophies are out there, who the major players in the CRM world are, the different flavors of CRM, what technologies are available for your business, and the difference between CRM and eCRM. There is one as surely as there are differences between parents and their children. While some of the CRM stalwarts will be dated by the time of this book's publication, the vast majority of kings, queens, princes, and princesses of CRM will still be around and flourishing. Please contact me if you want to be on top of all this. My contact information is at the end of this Introduction.

Who Is This Book For?

How does CRM work? Does it have importance to your business even though you personally never talk to your customers or you're not an information technology company? Maybe you think you're too small for this high-tech stuff, or you may be so large that you have tens of millions or even hundreds of millions in investment in legacy systems that you simply don't want to throw away. This book is designed to show you not only how important CRM is to you, but also what kinds of technology are there to support this extremely important system. The book is for the executive or staff member of any company, large or small, the internal information systems manager, the rookie or experienced IT consultant who is looking for a new IT career or simply wants to get grounded in what CRM is. It is designed for the CRM power user who is looking to improve his/her knowledge of what technology is available. It is for those executives who are considering how they are going to implement CRM. Really, it's for anyone who has even a passing interest in the CRM world.

How This Book Is Organized

The book is organized to provide you with a continuous overview of CRM, but also to allow you to read each chapter separately and independently—once you've read Chapter 1. Chapter 1 is what CRM is. Not only what I think it is, but what industry leaders think it is. You will have the benefit of the wisdom of the "been there, done that" CRM crowd.

Once you've accomplished this formidable task, you can then begin to read in order or skim through to the chapters that interest you. In the largest sense, this book covers the CRM technologies: what makes them valuable to you, how to get them into your company, and what the future holds. Basically, this is your (I hope very readable) CRM primer.

What This Book Isn't

This book is not a how-to guide to managing your customer relationships. There are dozens of contemporary books available on that subject, such as *Loyalty.com*, by Fred Newell, *Customers.com*, by Patricia Seybold, the *One-to-One Marketing* series, by Martha Rogers and Don Peppers, and *Permission Marketing*, by Seth Godin. One-to-one and permission marketing are the embedded core of much of CRM. CRM reshapes the entire way a business does business by making it customer-centric rather than the product-centrism of most of the twentieth century. The stereotypical used-car salesman of the 1950s—and its late twentieth century media derivative, the infomercial—are not only no longer appropriate, but downright reactionary. They are examples of the extremes of product-focused marketing—classic cases of attempting to create demand for a product, instead of what are rightfully *au courant* design strategies for long-term customer retention. Do you think the Thighmaster people are aiming at getting their customers to buy a Thighmaster twice? How many thighs do you have to master?

What else isn't this book? It is not a technical manual. The book isn't written for technofunctional gurus to help them implement CRM better. Given the range of applications and services for CRM in the marketplace, that would be an impossible task, however needed it is. So this may not be the book for you if you're looking to implement Siebel or Clarify, Vantive or E.piphany, in particular. Chapter 14 will go through a typical midlevel CRM implementation, and there will be references throughout the book to some of the hows for implementing CRM. Just don't expect to find your particular package's specific instructions.

What This Book Is

With the wild growth of the Web frontier and its maturation to the heartland of world enterprise, it has become the way to do business, not an enhancement of business. The lightning speed of business conductivity with the high bandwidths of T1, T3, cable modem, and DSL for Internet access gives the customer a substantial flexibility in determining what they want and getting it from whom they want. Geographical and access speed restrictions are gone, and the competitive activity fostered by the Web is intense. E-business evolution works at warp speed. In the space of two years, extranets, which were the supply/value chains that linked vendors, enterprises, and customers, evolved to e-procurement sites in early 1999. Companies began to bid their services and materials to interested buyers in digital marketplaces in late 1999. Hundreds of buyers interact with hundreds of sellers peddling their RFP-responsive wares. The year 2000 brought a derivative private marketplace where individual enterprises selectively procure goods and services from handpicked, individually approved sellers enveloped in a very secure technical environment, which is a significantly more advanced level of the 1998 extranet. Most interesting is that each step on this evolutionary scale has hundreds of businesses and tens of millions of dollars. Whole industries grew from each of these steps. The speed of evolution is only overtaken by the speed of opportunity seized.

Customers are now driving this demand, and the demand sometimes changes overnight. It isn't easy to keep a customer happy for long these days. I will provide you with a look at the technology that is available to make your customer life cycle immersive for the customer and for you. What CRM will provide is the foundation for the integration of the customer into your corporate ecosystem. But please remember the cardinal rule of CRM: it's a system to increase the interactivity of the customer and the company so that the company can retain the customer in a long-term lucrative relationship, with everyone made happy. It isn't technology-focused, though technology is what makes CRM interesting. Otherwise it's just a selling or marketing or customer service system, not CRM.

The Corporate Ecosystem

What in the world is a corporate ecosystem? Actually, it does deal with the environment—the business environment of your company. Speed to market and customer-determined responsiveness are creating the conditions that are forcing businesses to rely increasingly on their suppliers' and vendors' speed and responsiveness *and* to be attuned to their customers in almost real time. This means that the interconnectivity of the company, its suppliers and vendors, and its customers is a contemporary requirement of business. The corporate ecosystem takes the integration a step further and, through the use of the Internet, ties the organizations and groups the enterprise depends on into a virtual single entity that depends on each unit functioning integrally with the others. If customers need something, they can get it through you almost immediately because of your ability to order their goods from your Palm on the spot through your suppliers via your intranet, extranet, or portal. In fact, through your portal, your customers can order from your suppliers directly, if that's the way you choose to establish your ecosystem.

An Aerobic Theme: Running Through the Book

Central threads run throughout the book. First, in order to give you a comprehensive technological picture of CRM, I will examine CRM solutions that are provided by a handful of companies in depth. Keep in mind, my prejudices are in this book. The companies I like due to their products and attitude are the ones I like. However, I've tried to be fair to all companies in this book. Keep in mind, too, that my likes and dislikes aren't uninformed opinion. They are well-researched concepts that were founded in the forge of Internet and print reading, interviews with principals at many companies, conversations with industry pundits, and hands-on experience with several of the products. Am I possibly wrong? Sure. I'm like anyone else. I have opinions that are created by something I do every day or on occasion. Are there people who disagree with me? Certainly.

Chapter 10 will provide a look at some of the top companies and reference some of the broader matrices out there so that you are not company-deprived, though you might get information-overloaded. Most chapters will discuss the most important of the CRM vendors according to their specific solutions. You'll get an in-depth look at CRM technology as well as a broad spectrum of the available possibilities, giving you the freedom to make your own informed judgments.

The second theme is equally as transparent. This is about the technology, not the system. However, they are interconnected as surely as your suppliers are connected to you. Without CRM the System, there is no CRM. Without CRM the Technology, CRM is costly, awkward, and evolutionary. With it, it is sleek, sexy, and revolutionary. On with the revolution!

For more information on CRM (or on N.Y. Yankee baseball and other intellectual pursuits), please email me at paul-greenberg @home.com or call me at (703) 980-9060, my cellphone.

Chapter 1

What Is CRM, Really?

Most of the readers of this book, while perhaps not all that familiar with Customer Relationship Management (CRM), are familiar with the Frank Capra classic Christmas movie, "It's a Wonderful Life." It is the story of George Bailey, played by Jimmy Stewart, a banker's son who takes over the family Building and Loan business, even though he has a restless soul and wants to see the world. What is commonly remembered about the movie is the timeless terrific theme that we all make an important difference as individuals. However, there is a CRM sub-theme that I'm sure Frank Capra wasn't particularly thinking about when he made the movie. It not only reflects the American social consciousness of the 1930s and 1940s, but is also an important reflection of precisely what the twenty-first century Internet-speed economy is going through.

If you remember, Henry F. Potter (as played by Lionel Barrymore) is the town's miserly, nasty, always-dressed-in-black banker. His life's mission was to make money for his bank and to squeeze that money from the townspeople who he saw as "rabble." As a result of his success, he was "the richest man in town." George Bailey, as the head of Bailey Building and Loan, on the other hand, saw that because the townspeople were his customers, his responsibility was to serve them with the best possible personal customer service. Mr. Potter followed the strict rules of the bank. If the rabble wanted to borrow money, they did it on the bank's terms or not at all. George Bailey lent the hardworking townspeople the money at reasonable, flexible rates during what seemed to be the depression years because that's the service they needed. He was a participant in their lives, even though, in the strictest sense, they were his customers. But they were also his neighbors. He gave personalized service to each of the townspeople and made it a point to actually know them. If he were not there, the townspeople would be forced to deal with the bank-centric Mr. Potter, who engendered a cynical customer versus company business policy due to the heartlessness of the company. It was no coincidence that when George Bailey was removed from the equation in the more famous sequences of the movie, the town's name went from Bedford Falls to Pottersville and became a heartless, cold, adversarial place. The final scene of the movie shows the townspeople coming to George Bailey's rescue by providing him with money to restore missing dollars that Mr. Potter falsely accused him of stealing, with each of the donors citing a time where George Bailey had rescued them from some difficulty. Heartwarming, indeed.

Putting it simply, who would you want to bank with—George Bailey or Henry F. Potter?

Let's fast-forward to the twenty-first century. There is a commercial on television for lendingtree.com that shows a couple sitting at a table with a banker. The banker says something to the effect of "Are you interested?" The couple says, "Can't you lower the rates a little?" The banker says, somewhat insistently, "This is a good package." The couple, unexpectedly, laughs and says, "Sorry to have taken up your time. Next!" Another banker comes in and sits down as a voiceover explains how bankers will bid for the privilege of lending you money at lendingtree.com. The customer controls the interaction between the borrower and the lender, something entirely new to traditional commercial lending hierarchies. Customer-focused, customer-controlled interactivity via the Web.

But Customer Relationship Management (CRM) seems to be a relative newcomer that appeared on business radar no more than perhaps two years ago, as enterprise resource planning (ERP) began its 1998 spin out of control and extended ERP (XRP) replaced it briefly as an acronym. This took place just prior to the recognized emergence of CRM and other front-office and middleware applications in early 1999. CRM then begat electronic Customer Relationship Management (eCRM), which popped out as something of importance from the Web-enabled egg of its CRM mother in late 1999. How is all of this any different from the "George Bailey principle" of customer loyalty and retention? Or is it any different?

What Is a Customer?

While retaining customer loyalty has been a sales principle since the beginning of time (even Adam needed to retain Eve's loyalty despite immense pressure from his competitor, the Snake), CRM is actually a tremendous step forward in creating a system that can provide a means for retaining individual loyalty in a world of nearly 6 billion souls. In order to understand CRM, we have to look at the changing nature of the customer because customers aren't what they used to be.

While "the customer is king" has been a mantra since the 1940s, its content has changed fundamentally over the past decade. What is interesting to begin with is what is defined as a customer.

When I worked with IBM back in the early 1990s, I remember being a bit puzzled by a designation their departments used with each other. When department 1 did work for department 2, they charged department 2 fees and expenses. Department 1 staff members specifically referred to this process as charging internal "customers." At the time, I was surprised, thinking, how could customers be employees of the same company even if they work for different departments? Aren't they fellow employees, friends, and such? Nope. They were (and are) customers—even if they are fellow employees and friends. It seems to be nitpicking and perhaps just for bookkeeping, but they are customers. Why? Because you are providing a service to them for a fee of some sort. Additionally, the department has the right to get bids on the services from both internal departments and outside consulting firms. You could be competing within and without!

This led me to investigate what exactly the concept of "the customer" was becoming. At that time, I distinguished between what is now called the business-to-consumer (B2C) "customer" and the business-to-business (B2B) "client." Department stores had customers. IBM had clients. Or so I thought.

After a substantial number of discussions with my colleagues and friends who were also in the business world, I came to the conclusion that the division between traditional customers (people who were sold your products outside the realm of the store) and internal customers (a department or division or team or employee) was becoming murky. In fact, all of them were customers that were sold to. IBM even had the bookkeeping to deal with it. It may have been going on for years. I didn't know. I just knew that my definition of customer had changed.

How Do We Define CRM? Let Me Count the Ways

A decade later, I began to write this book with the idea that it would be strictly about eCRM, which in my naïve way, I thought was *very* different than CRM. It wasn't and isn't. I plugged into the debates that are constantly being fought over what exactly CRM is. There is a standard industry rote response that says what it isn't: it isn't a technology. As you will see, that's true, but not strictly. I also heard that it was a "customer-facing" system. That it is a strategy and/or a set of business processes. A methodology. It is all of the above or whichever you choose. The Knowledge Capital Group defines CRM as a subset of something they call enterprise relationship management (ERM), which involves customers, suppliers, partners, and employees. They've developed a number of (useful) new terms such as "sphere of expertise" and "channels of execution" to help define it.

The buzz is very loud in this debate. It occurred to me that what better way to try to define CRM than to get some of the significant names in the industry to tell me. So that's what you are going to see in this chapter. These are the people in the CRM industry who make it the blockbuster industry it is.

The Heavyweights Define CRM

These folks (listed below in alphabetical order by their last names) were chosen because of their influence in the CRM world and because they represent a variety of CRM opinions that matter in the information technology world. There is the CEO of a company that owns a CRM product that handles large enterprise activity. There is the CMO of a company that specializes in CRM for the midmarket. There is the CEO of a company that has a portal-based CRM product. There is the president of a company that specializes in partner relationship management (PRM) consulting and one that has a vertical CRM product for federal government contractors. And there is the president of a company who specializes in CRM management consulting. They characterize a wide variety of Muhammad Alis. The definitions of CRM that follow each biography of the individual are written in their own words. Check them out; they're good.

Craig Conway, President and CEO, PeopleSoft, Inc.

Craig Conway joined PeopleSoft in 1999 as president and chief operating officer, and was promoted to chief executive officer in September 1999. He oversees all PeopleSoft business operations, including sales, marketing, professional service, customer support, development, finance, and administration.

Mr. Conway was president and chief executive for OneTouch Systems, a leader in the field of interactive broadcast networks. Previously, he served as president and chief executive for TGV Software, Inc., an early developer of IP network protocols and applications for corporate intranets and the Internet. Mr. Conway also spent eight years at Oracle Corporation as executive vice president in a variety of roles, including marketing, sales, and operations.

DEFINITION

Every time a customer approaches your business, they arrive with an expectation. It may be a service need, or a new product interest, but in every case, they have an expectation that accompanies their interest in your business. What happens next will form an experience that shapes their behavior. A good experience may increase their loyalty and tendency to purchase again. A poor experience may transfer their business to your competitor. The ability to recognize this process and to actively manage it forms the basis for Customer Relationship Management, or CRM.

The ability to ensure that the enterprise will act with unity of purpose to ensure experiences that exceed every expectation is a monumental task. Customers interacting with employees, employees collaborating with suppliers—every interaction is an opportunity to manage a relationship. Only recently has technology advanced to support interactions with any role through any channel, to any touch point across the extended enterprise. Building this requires applications that can seamlessly support business processes as they span the enterprise, deliver information, empowerment, and insight to every individual, wherever they are, and continually monitor, measure, and improve the process.

We are on the verge of the most significant transformation in the business landscape since mainframe applications migrated to the desktop a decade ago. The Internet blends computing and communications into a platform-independent, globally accessible, and universally usable medium. To date, the Internet's impact on business has been substantial, creating new channels for commerce, driving new market models and enabling collaborative business-to-supplier relationships. This change is only the tip of the iceberg. The most significant benefit for business will be leveraging the Internet to support the very fabric of the enterprise. Delivering pure Internet applications directly to browsers will empower a global workforce to know, to do, to measure, and to improve their jobs in support of a common, customer-oriented strategy. This is the promise of CRM.

We experience CRM ourselves every day. Dining at a favorite restaurant or taking our car in for service is an interaction with a business that leaves us with an experience. If you recall pleasant or unpleasant memories of these experiences, think about how those feelings affect your propensity to return to those businesses again. Have you enjoyed special treatment as a regular customer at some establishments? Have you complained about poor service and vowed never to go back? Your experiences shape your buying patterns, significantly influencing your lifetime value as a customer.

Loyal, repeat customers can form a significant competitive advantage for a business in many ways. Truly loyal customers form a market share base that is unassailable to the competition. The cost of sales for existing customers is far less than the cost of generating market awareness, acquiring new customers, and establishing a business relationship with them. None of this should be particularly surprising. Savvy business managers have been always catered to their most valued customers because they understand the importance it holds for their business.

The issue is not whether CRM is important for business, but how best to apply it. CRM can be a personal undertaking of small business owners and merchants who do a majority of their trade face to face, and on a scale permitting them to know and understand their customers, their business, and their partners personally. Good CRM becomes much more challenging to maintain as business scales up, and as technological and behavioral trends put distance and anonymity between the business manager and their customers.

As businesses scale, it becomes impossible for one person to know and personally manage relationships with all of the business's valued customers. Initially, large enterprises attempted to address this by implementing distribution channels and an organizational hierarchy modeled after the military chain of command. By such a structured approach, business managers were still able to personally manage the few relationships that they were directly responsible for. At every level of the organization, people were able to personally optimize the business process and priorities for their "customers" and consistency was implemented via the top-down organizational structure.

Traditional businesses are now moving toward more direct interaction with their end consumers, and Internet-based businesses are experiencing growth rates unimaginable just a few years ago. These trends make it impossible for individuals to personally and consistently manage all business relationships across the enterprise. In addition, they are unlikely to conduct their interactions in alignment with an overall enterprise strategy. The sheer one-to-many employee-to-customer ratio may make it impossible for a single person to manage, let alone support, the growing number of ways in which a customer can and will attempt to interact with a business.

What's even more problematic is ensuring consistent behavior across all of the people in your enterprise. This becomes apparent when viewed from the customer's perspective. The customer's interactions with your business are now handled by a variety of employees in different roles and situations. Not only are the people involved different, with different skills, backgrounds and motivations, they often have no knowledge of the other interactions the customer has had. What's worse is that they may also be unaware of a global strategy or desired service level for handling the particular customer. You may not have visibility and knowledge of inconsistent experiences being created for your customers, but your customers are acutely aware, and will behave with correspondingly inconsistent results.

One of the most dramatic influences on business today is being driven by technology. Technology is driving change at an unprecedented pace. One change that is significantly altering the traditional business landscape is how technology empowers consumers, who are now beginning to enjoy the upper hand in their relationships with businesses. The shift of power creates opportunities for smart businesses to increase their market share and competitive advantage, and also presents the potential for disaster on a far greater scale for businesses that choose to ignore the issue.

Technology has empowered consumers with the ability to conduct business with a variety of alternatives to the traditional face-to-face contact. In addition it has given consumers access to far more information and choice than they have ever enjoyed before. This increased awareness, combined with increasing demands on personal time, creates consumers that are informed and impatient. Meeting their increased expectations is essential, perhaps critical.

Consumer-to-business interaction started at the distance of a handshake. It began to move farther apart with the invention of the phone. Once thought to be an invention of dubious value, the telephone is now the most significant customer interaction channel for most businesses. Almost all businesses today have a primary telephone contact number, and in many cases it leads to a sophisticated call center, with advanced skill set routing, escalation, and tracking systems that optimize the ability to deal with the customer. Growing in significance are the e-business channels: email, Web, and wireless. Growing consumer familiarity and comfort with these technologies is driving their growth as a medium for business interactions, creating additional challenges for businesses trying to maintain good CRM in the face of this increasing complexity.

Online commerce is maturing rapidly, shaped by changes in technology, consumer behavior, and innovation in business models. Even in its early stages, some fundamental consumer behaviors have emerged. The easy, immediate access to a wealth of information afforded by the Internet made it very convenient for comparison shopping. Consumers can get much more information about the products that interest them in a much shorter amount of time. They can also identify a greater variety of businesses with which they could potentially get what they want. The informed consumer is much less likely to settle for an inferior product, price, or service, and consequently has greater expectations. The Internet's immediacy and the growing demands on people's personal time are reducing their threshold of impatience. Customers are not as content to wait in line and are placing greater value on time. The buying pattern of browse by Internet, order by phone, and ship overnight satisfies the consumer's desire to get the best deal and ensures that the purchase transaction is correctly handled and that the wait to receive the benefit is minimized.

The problem for businesses arises from the reduction in personal contact they have with the customer. They may not even be aware of a potential customer traversing their website comparison shopping, and thus miss the opportunity to assess the prospect's value and attempt a corresponding level of service and sales. The order, if received, is handled by an anonymous agent in a call center, or perhaps automatically by the website. The order gets transferred to a fulfillment system optimized for efficiency and cost reduction, not for ensuring consistent customer experiences.

All is fine when there are no glitches, but the test of CRM comes when the customer calls wondering where the product is. Can your business identify the customer, treat them according to the service level they deserve, find their order no matter if it was placed by mail, phone, fax, email, or Web, and track it through the supply chain? If "find the customer's order" gives you images of disconnected processes, employees shrugging and saying "I don't know" as a manual foxhunt spreads across several departments, buildings, individuals, and computer systems, then you have a serious CRM problem. Your customer couldn't care less about the struggles your organization endures—they just expect their needs to be met.

Another significant change businesses are experiencing is the waning ability to rely on traditional forms of differentiation for competitive advantage. Customers used to endure poor CRM because a business offered a significantly better product, happened to be geographically convenient, or could offer better pricing. These competitive advantages are being eroded by the changes technology is creating in the business landscape.

The oldest form of competitive advantage is location. Economic theory maintains that in the absence of other factors, customers prefer to travel the shortest distance to tender a transaction with a business. Businesses use this advantage with the local customers who won't bother to look further to meet their needs. This advantage is dissolving with the growth of the Internet and global express shipping. Now customers are much more aware of equivalent or better business opportunities on a global basis, and can receive fulfillment of their transactions with overnight shipping. The "best deal" may not be with the business across the street, but with the business across the ocean. Internet distance is measured by mouse clicks, and this virtual proximity is eliminating geographical advantage for business.

Size is the next traditional competitive advantage to suffer in the new economy. The advantage of size manifests itself in awareness, and in pricing advantages that result from economies of scale. Bigger companies have been able to leverage better pricing. Again the new, electronically linked economy is eroding this advantage. New online marketplaces aggregate supply and demand, enabling businesses of all sizes to benefit from economies of scale. The dynamic, interconnected Web of business-to-business e-commerce enables collaboration on supply, fulfillment, and even production, eliminating the need for a business to build and own it all themselves. Aggressive investment, often significantly in advance of any hope of profitability, enable new market entrants to pose competitive challenges to established business, both in terms of awareness and more disturbingly in terms of unprofitable business models permitting them to compete on price, at least temporarily.

Awareness and presence are also becoming easier to generate, regardless of size. Skillful use of the Internet can create the impression that a business is much larger than it physically is. Again the reach of the Internet, coupled with global logistics, even allows a small company in a single location to pose a competitive threat to a larger business with a larger geographic footprint.

Perhaps the most startling transformation is the shift away from product-driven differentiation to service-based differentiation. As product cycles continue to be driven shorter, the lifespan of any individual product advantage declines. This is particularly evident in the technology sector, but almost any product you can imagine is being driven toward commoditization. Consider a highly sophisticated, expensive, complex piece of machinery—the jet engine.

Would an aircraft manufacturer select an engine supplier on the basis of a 10 percent improvement in power or fuel economy? If that improvement came at the cost of decreased reliability or quality? Not a chance. In fact, the value of the supplier-to-business relationship—reliable delivery, service, support, and flexibility—may weigh significantly more than the individual product characteristics in driving purchase decisions.

In the face of all of these dramatic changes, relationships continue to maintain their value in determining customer behavior. As other traditional forms of competitive differentiation erode, relationships are growing in importance in determining whether businesses succeed or fail. In fact, they are one of the few remaining areas where a business can proactively manage and control their destiny. A business can't control the pace of technology, it can't control the economy, it certainly can't control its competitors, but it can control they way it manages interactions with its customers.

Given that the process of transforming expectation to experience is inevitable, what's available to assist businesses in implementing good CRM? Early CRM products were focused on automation and cost savings. These centered on a single isolated department or business function, such as support or sales. The effectiveness of these "islands of automation" was limited, as their reach did not extend past the department. As CRM products evolved into "suites," they linked the traditional customer-interfacing roles of marketing, sales, and support within a single system. The two major shortfalls of front-office suites are their limited effectiveness across the enterprise, and the need to measure, analyze, and optimize the system on an ongoing basis.

CRM suites are more effective than a collection of disparate, isolated systems, but in reality the "island of automation" is just bigger than it was before. For CRM to be truly effective, it must integrate with and support the business processes that create customer experiences. These business processes span the enterprise, involving back-office functions like accounting, purchasing, production, and logistics in addition to the traditional front-office functions of marketing, sales, and support. Customers expecting the same great treatment they received from marketing and sales may be in for a bad surprise when they connect with the call center to resolve a billing mistake. If the agent has no ability to access the billing system, they may need to wait while internal process and communication find, verify, and fix the issue. They may just get transferred to the accounting department and an individual who has no idea who the customer is, how important they are, or how they need to be treated. If the customer tries to use the Web to solve this problem, they may be out of luck if the website can't link to billing history and order status. If your most valued customer calls your 800 number requesting a change in billing information for an order they placed via your website 30 minutes ago, can your enterprise guarantee they get what they need? For CRM to be truly effective, it must be integrated to the business processes spanning your enterprise.

Good CRM must be able to help people throughout the enterprise make smarter decisions faster. Workflow or process without the ability to measure, analyze, and improve its effectiveness simply perpetuates a problem. Similarly, gaining true insight into the value of customers is based on the ability to analyze complete information, which also spans the enterprise. For example, assessing customer value might be based on how much they have purchased. This is an inaccurate indication of value when you consider that the same customer may not be a candidate for any near term purchases, and there may be others who are on the verge of purchasing significant amounts. This still doesn't give a truly accurate reflection of value until you factor in the associated costs of serving the customers. Often, marquee customers have customized support arrangements or service level agreements, making them much more costly to serve than other customers. Now we must truly have an accurate representation of customer value and how best to implement good CRM, right? Not if we also consider their current satisfaction level. Good CRM might focus more energy on the unhappiest high-value customer in an effort to retain them than the high-value customers who are already very happy and at less risk of abandonment.

Good CRM must also be accessible to every person in your enterprise that is involved in processes that shape customer experiences. It doesn't help to have a wonderful system that nobody uses. Technologies like wireless PDAs and cellphones enable your mobile workforce to access your CRM system from virtually anywhere they need to be. Technologies like pure Internet applications enable everyone in your enterprise—even your suppliers and partners—to access your system with just a browser and the right authorization. This type of pervasive access to CRM ensures that everybody who can influence customer experiences has the right information about the customer, their value, and their needs, and is empowered to ensure a positive experience for the customer.

I believe successful CRM must be integrated, insightful, and pervasive. Integrated CRM allows your entire enterprise to align around the common goal of exceeding the expectations of your customers. Insightful CRM enables you to truly understand which customers your efforts should focus on, and how to continually optimize your enterprise to meet their needs. Pervasive CRM applies technologies such as pure Internet applications to enable everyone who makes your enterprise work—your customers, your employees, and your suppliers—to easily access applications and analysis, wherever they may be. Together, these abilities will foster a successful CRM program that transforms expectations into great experiences, forming the foundation of competitive advantage, growth, and profitability.

Scott Fletcher, President and COO, epipeline

Scott Fletcher joined epipeline in 2000 as president and chief operating officer. He oversees all epipeline business operations, including sales, marketing, customer support, product development, finance, and administration. epipeline is the first comprehensive online service dedicated to streamlining the process of developing business with the government.

Mr. Fletcher was vice president of worldwide services for Annuncio Software, a leader in the field of e-marketing platforms. Previously, he served as vice president of PeopleSoft's Professional Services Group, a world leader providing e-business applications.

DEFINITION

The hype surrounding Customer Relationship Management (CRM) has been pervasive within the business, technology, media, and academic communities since early 1997. Because of this hype, and the numerous constituents that contribute to it, there are as many definitions and interpretations of CRM as there are self-purported CRM gurus. Much like the hype surrounding Business Process Reengineering (BPR) and Total Quality Management (TQM) in the late 1980s and early 1990s, there is a tremendous value proposition hidden beneath all this. Businesses must move beyond the hype, though, to best position their enterprise to be successful CRM practitioners.

At its core, CRM is an enterprise-wide mindset, mantra, and set of business processes and policies that are designed to acquire, retain, and service customers. Broadly speaking, CRM includes the customer-facing business processes of marketing, sales, and customer service. CRM is not a technology, though. Technology is a CRM enabler. So why has CRM become so pervasive recently? Hasn't the primary goal of business always been to acquire, retain, and service customers? Why is CRM such a "novel" concept?

The answer to these questions is that advances in technology serve as the primary catalyst to the CRM bonanza. The rise of the Internet as a means to transact business, increasing and affordable bandwidth, and advances in computing power are all driving CRM. These technology advances greatly empower customers and position them to more easily access information on products, services, and competitors. In short, customers are in control more than ever before. For innovative and proactive companies that readily embrace this new customer-powered paradigm, the situation is great. By adopting customer-centric business processes and leveraging technology, these companies better serve their customers by developing improved products and services and delivering personalized service. For laggard companies, though, the customer-empowered new world order is nightmarish.

Fortunately, the confluence of technology advances, empowered customers, and an increasing competitive environment has given rise to a variety of technology-based CRM offerings to help businesses just catching the CRM wave. These CRM offerings consist primarily of sales force automation (SFA), marketing automation, customer service, and, to a certain extent, partner relationship management (PRM) software. These packages serve primarily to automate the various customer touch points within an enterprise. Whether automating an email marketing campaign, allowing a sales representative to configure and price a product *on the fly*, or allowing a customer to update their billing address via the Web, these offerings serve primarily to automate processes. While this automation does enrich the customer experience and allows an enterprise to better serve customers, it is not enough. To best acquire, retain, and service customers, enterprises must intimately know their customers. Enterprises must possess extensive knowledge of customer buying patterns, channel preferences, and historical contact information. This requires collecting and analyzing data to provide a comprehensive, cohesive, and centralized view of a customer.

The need and importance of this global customer view explains the rise in data-warehousing and business intelligence software vendors. By tapping into the wealth of data collected by the SFA, marketing automation, customer service, and PRM applications with business intelligence tools, companies are better positioned to execute their CRM strategies and serve customers. Thus, the CRM technology landscape today consists primarily of sales, marketing, and customer service software vendors coupled with data-warehousing and business intelligence vendors.

So what does this mean in the real world? What business interactions are examples of effective CRM? Effective CRM is allowing a customer to update her account information online and enabling your customer care, sales, and marketing organizations to have instantaneous access to that information. Effective CRM is providing a personalized online shopping experience to a customer by analyzing her past online and offline interactions and delivering product and service recommendations based on that data. Effective CRM is having the ability to determine which customers are most profitable, determining what drives that profit, and ensuring that customer-specific business processes and practices maintain or increase that customer profitability. Effective CRM is also having the ability to know what customers are not profitable, why they are not profitable, and being able to change tactics to ensure future profitability. In short, CRM is about knowing your customers. It's about creating and growing relationships with your customers. It's about remembering customer preferences and forging long-term relationships with them by delivering exceptional service and product offerings tailored to them.

Brent Frei, President and CEO, Onyx Software

Brent Frei is president, CEO, and co-founder of Onyx Software, a leading provider of customer-centric e-business software solutions. Since the company's inception in 1994, Onyx has grown exponentially. In 1999, Onyx Software was named a Deloitte & Touche "Fast 500" company, and the 10th fastest-growing high-tech company in America, with a 21,051 percent revenue growth rate from 1994 to 1999. Under Mr. Frei's leadership, the company has grown to more than 500 employees worldwide, winning several prestigious awards for fostering an outstanding corporate culture. The company has established offices throughout the United States, in Australia, France, Germany, Hong Kong, Singapore, and the United Kingdom, as well as an impressive network of software, hardware, services, and distribution partnerships worldwide. Onyx's award-winning products have been licensed to more than 500 global customers in a variety of industries, including financial services, high technology, health care, manufacturing, and telecommunications. The company became publicly traded on NASDAQ under the symbol ONXS in February 1999.

As a leader, Mr. Frei has been recognized as a "Pioneer in Technology" by the Smithsonian Institute and was recently among an exclusive handful of global CEOs selected to represent the technology industry at the Technology Pioneers' session of the 2000 World Economic Forum in Davos, Switzerland. In June 2000, Mr. Frei was the sole recipient of Dartmouth College's Thayer School of Engineering Fletcher Award for lifetime achievement.

Prior to co-founding Onyx, Mr. Frei was a programmer analyst with Microsoft Corporation, where he was the primary architect of an integrated, international Customer Relationship Management system that is used for sales, marketing, customer service, and product support by Microsoft's international subsidiaries and that is still in use today. Before his tenure at Microsoft, Mr. Frei received patents for several of his cellular system designs as a mechanical engineer at Motorola. He received a Bachelor of Engineering degree from Dartmouth's Thayer School of Engineering and his AB in Engineering Sciences from Dartmouth College.

DEFINITION

What is CRM? It is a comprehensive set of processes and technologies for managing the relationships with potential and current customers and business partners across marketing, sales, and service regardless of the communication channel (see Figure 1-1). The goal of CRM is to optimize customer and partner satisfaction, revenue, and business efficiency by building the strongest possible relationships at an organizational level. Successful CRM requires a holistic approach to every relationship with the entire organization sharing and contributing to that view.

But before companies can implement a CRM system or even begin to assess the validity of a CRM system to address their needs, some very fundamental truths must first be underscored and communicated.

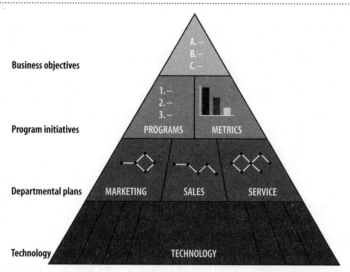

Figure 1-1: Onyx view of building a business that will use CRM (Copyright 2000, Onyx Software. All rights reserved.)

Business objectives outlining two- to five-year strategic goals should be clearly defined. These can include revenue, market share, and margin goals. They might also dictate corporate style such as "be a customer-centric company" or "differentiate on service levels." These should then drive the next level of business fundamentals: program initiatives.

Program initiatives are typically one to one and a half years in scope. They are the near-term game plans intended to move the company another step toward the long-term objectives of the company. They take the form of directives such as "build out the direct sales force in a vertical market," "focus on expansion within the customer base," and "improve customer satisfaction by five points." These initiatives are then associated with specific measurements that will be the clear indications of successful forward progress. Underlying these program initiatives are the specific departmental plans.

Departmental plans are the processes and behavior that form the fabric of every day work within the organization. Examples include deploying an automated email response system, enabling customer self-help on a website, or streamlining the call center processes to answer customer inquiries in shorter time frames. There are often dozens of major processes within a department and many that cross departments. Organizations range in ability or desire to coordinate and integrate these process pieces. The three layers of business operations are then supported by technology.

Technology is used to automate and enable some or all of the business processes and initiatives. Organizations use either many separate best-of-breed solutions or larger, integrated platform solutions to achieve the goals of technology-enabled business. The technology strategy is generally a reflection of the coordination, or lack thereof, of the organization.

Organizations tend to execute their technology strategies in one of four levels, which are indicative of how coordinated the organization is top to bottom and side to side, and how effectively and efficiently it is executing. The levels can be classified as (1) functional, (2) departmental, (3) partial CRM, and (4) CRM. The future of CRM is at least one level beyond these, to what we call the Business Relationship Network. A company that operates as a Level One, or functional, organization is characterized by the compartmentalization or granularity of its independently managed business processes. This is typical of Fortune 500 companies that have extremely large operational infrastructures. Intra-team coordination and cooperation is challenging, and inter-departmental coordination and cooperation is nearly impossible. Process and the technology to support it are executed in very granular pieces. Examples of this would be sales forecasting, automated email response, and Web self-help as stand-alone technical solutions.

Return on investment in this model is typically only possible in very large companies where economies of scale make it feasible. This is one of the reasons very large organizations become increasingly inefficient as they expand. The technology deployed in this environment usually provides benefits only into the bottom layer of the operational structure, helping to manage the departmental plans. Since the technology tends to be fragmented and only benefits the specific departmental processes, large data warehouse, and large integration and synchronization projects are common. These become the technologies necessary to serve the top two layers of the operational structure.

A company that operates as a Level Two, or departmental, organization is characterized by intra-departmental synchronization by implementing coordinated processes and deploying technology across an entire department. Cross-departmental process and technology is sparse. Typical examples of structures on this level are sales force automation, call centers, and channel management. This is possible in all sizes of companies.

Return on investment in this model is typically two to five times the initial and ongoing investment. The technology deployed in this environment usually provides benefits through the bottom layer and into the middle layer of the operational structure, helping to make an entire department more efficient and effective. Rarely does this structure account for a dramatic increase in customer loyalty or revenue because the company does not treat the customer holistically. This type of organizational structure might allow an individual or a single department to serve a client better, but it does not create an affinity for the company at large.

A company that operates as a Level Three, or partial CRM, organization builds upon previous processes, still honing intra-departmental synchronization with coordinated processes and departmental technology. This level, however, does benefit from cross-departmental process and technology coordination characterized, for example, by sales and marketing sharing a customer database or synching up strategies. In this model, multiple master customer databases still exist. This model is increasingly possible as you go down in company size. Return on investment in this model is typically four to seven times the initial and ongoing investment. The technology deployed in this environment generally provides benefits through the bottom layer and into the middle layer of the operational structure, helping to make several arms of the business more efficient and effective.

A company that operates as a Level Four, or full CRM, organization has achieved a single master customer database upon which the whole organization coordinates process and strategy. This model is very difficult for large organizations as it requires significant operational coordination and process.

Return on investment in this model is typically five to ten times that of the initial and ongoing investment. The technology deployed in this environment typically provides benefits through all layers of the operational structure, helping to make all arms of the business more efficient and effective. Technologies like data warehouses are less common and less necessary in this model.

This level is characterized by:

- ▶ A single, universally shared customer instance and data

- ▶ Coordinated departmental strategies and processes

▶ Closed loop reporting and real-time analytics

▶ Internet-based and traditional processes woven together into a single CRM mosaic

Only by creating this environment within a business can you begin to develop and nurture customer fidelity to the entire business rather than just the individual serving the client. Businesses who have deployed Level Four CRM operating systems across the entire organization have seen far greater revenue growth, margins, customer satisfaction, and customer loyalty than businesses deploying partial CRM systems.

As an illustrative example, consider the customer relationship in the home building industry. An individual architect who provides an exceptionally high level of service will stand above those who don't. He or she will create a level of customer satisfaction that will generate substantially more referrals than his or her peers. However, that referral stream is for the individual architect alone who will quickly become overbooked with clients. If, however, that service level and satisfaction can be extended across the architect's entire firm and the client feels that the whole firm is working for them, then the relationship moves from an individual to an organizational relationship, and now the firm will get the referrals even if the individual architect is unavailable.

This is the difference between organizational effectiveness and creating a competitive advantage for the business as opposed to individual effectiveness. This difference presents itself in almost every industry. Ever been in a company where a salesperson takes his customers with him when he leaves the company? This happens because the relationships didn't extend from the individual to the company. Level Four CRM prevents this by creating competitive advantage at the company level in addition to the individual.

The future of CRM is to extend this relationship strength another step further—beyond Level Four and into other parts of the customer's relationship (service) network.

Let's say the architecture firm does a lot of work with a specific general contractor. If the general contractor and the architect interact with the customer only within their own silos and don't communicate with each other on the customer's behalf, the customer will quickly get frustrated at the inefficiencies of repeating the same conversation over and over. And the customer's satisfaction with both parties will go down very quickly even if they are both providing high levels of service independently. If, on the other hand, the architect and contractor share the right information at the right time every time, the customer will feel everyone is working together to best serve him or her, and satisfaction with both parties will be even higher than that generated by the parties independently.

This relationship network continues from the contractor to the subcontractors, interior designers, landscapers, and the like. Almost every industry operates in some likeness to the home building industry, with customer information passing from one entity to another and collaboration among entities being desired if not required. In the mortgage industry, the mortgage broker works with the realtor, wholesale lender, underwriter, escrow agent, title agent, and appraiser, among others. In the enterprise software industry, the software company works with the management consulting firm, systems integrator, hardware company, database vendor, and other software partners. In the sports industry, the franchise owner works with the league, arena, concessions vendor, merchandiser, and opposing franchise.

Within every industry there is a network of people and organizations that need to work together to better serve each individual customer. This is the future of CRM. Businesses that can serve the customer seamlessly across the broadest network will be those with the highest margins, most loyal customers, strongest partnerships, and greatest revenue acceleration.

So, how does a company go about creating a relationship network for its customers?

To create relationship networks, companies must develop Level Four CRM for each customer-focused business unit, and extend that system to other customer units and organizations within the customer's entire relationship network. Full CRM is the building block for relationship networks and is required to participate in this world of distributed Customer Relationship Management, which we call the Business Relationship Network. The goal is to extend the full CRM approach beyond the traditional four walls of the organization to other people and entities within the particular relationship network of every customer. Businesses that can serve the customer seamlessly across the broadest relationship network will be the market leaders in their respective industries and will create significant barriers to entry for companies not in the network.

Peter Keen, Chairman, Keen Innovations

Peter Keen is the founder and chairman of Keen Innovations (formerly the International Center for Information Technologies). He has served on the faculties of Harvard, MIT, and Stanford, with visiting positions at Wharton, Oxford, Fordham, the London Business School, Stockholm University, the Technical University of Delft, and Duke University. In 1994, he was profiled by *Forbes* magazine as the "consultant from Paradise." In 1988, he was named by *Information Week* as one of the top ten consultants in the information technology field.

His research, writing, education, and public speaking all focus on helping firms make a management difference in their deployment of information technology as a business resource and on bridging the gap in understanding, language, and planning between business decisions and technology choices. When all leading firms in an industry have access to the same technology, the competitive edge comes from fusing people, process, and technology. The management challenge is for business managers to lead IT, without having to know the details of the technology but understanding and enacting the key decisions about policy, infrastructures, and funding that enable their technical professionals to design, implement, and operate the platform. That integrated platform is an essential base for business innovation in just about every industry today and vital for coordinating operations in a global environment.

A prolific writer, Peter Keen is the author of many books that have strongly influenced the business-technology dialogue, starting with *Decision Support Systems* (1978), which introduced the concept of IT as a support to managerial judgment, *Competing in Time: Using Telecommunications for Competitive Advantage* (1986), the first book to anticipate the immense impact of telecommunications on the basics of business, and *Shaping the Future: Business Design Through Information Technology* (1991), a book addressed to senior executives that has been translated into many European and Asian languages. *The Process Edge: Creating Value Where It Counts* (1997) looks at business processes as invisible financial assets and liabilities to be managed as a portfolio of capital investments targeted at increasing shareholder value. His most recent books all address the management side of electronic commerce and the Internet economy. *The eProcess Edge* (2000) focuses on sourcing process capabilities and *From .com to .profit* (2000) zeros in on the value imperatives that

drive effective business models. Earlier books are *Trust by Design,
Business Internets and Intranets,* and *On-Line Profits.*

He has worked as a consultant on a long-term basis as an adviser to
top managers in helping them fuse business choices and technology
decisions. Examples of companies with which Mr. Keen has worked in
this mode include British Airways, British Telecom, Citibank, Glaxo,
IBM, MCI Communications, Royal Bank Of Canada, Cemex (Mexico), Sweden Post, Unilever, World Bank, IATA, CTC (Chile), HP, and
many others. His work with these companies has generally included
the development and delivery of senior management education programs for action (rather than just "awareness") as a lever for taking
charge of change and making IT part of everyday planning and management thinking. He is on the advisory boards and boards of directors of several Internet companies, including e-Credit, WebIQ, and
Celosis.

DEFINITION

I wish we could get rid of the term CRM, but it's established and
there's no point in trying to change it and add yet another piece of
jargon to the IT vocabulary. I'd prefer CREE—customer relationship
experience enhancement—instead of Customer Relationship Management. My objection to CRM comes from a "here we go again"
feeling. You don't "manage" customers; you enhance their relationships with your company. The information you collect and how you
use it should be targeted at the customer experience, from the customer perspective.

IT people largely think in terms of structure and control and
leave out the reality of the human as human. We first had "user
involvement"—turning colleagues, clients, and collaborators into
an abstraction. Then we had office "automation" and "reengineering"—"Hi, we're the BPR brigade and we're here to reengineer you."
CRM largely began as "data-warehousing," as if information about
customers and their interactions with the company are just boxes of
records stored in the attic. In the CRM arena, there's now plenty of
talk about "sales force automation." That's an interesting view of
what sales representatives do and why.

CRM—I'll stay with the term—runs the danger of becoming a
way to view customers from a distance as a statistical database of
information that can be used to segment markets, target promotions, identify niches, and customize and personalize websites. All

these are valuable, but they look at the customer from the company's viewpoint and they ignore many elements of the customer experience. Here are my three tests of a company's real, as opposed to well-intentioned but merely espoused, commitment to enhancing the customer relationship:

▶ Has your company put in place the combination of software, processes, and accountability mechanisms to ensure that every customer email gets an answer from a qualified source within 12 to 36 hours? That source may be an automated service, but when the customer has a "problem" it's more often a crisis that requires human judgment. If your firm is like well over half the companies surveyed on this topic, the email disappears into the electronic ether. So much for "relationship."

▶ Are personalized financing options a core part of your CRM database and data warehouses? No? But the core of any commercial relationship is financing.

▶ Is 25 percent of executive bonus compensation based on some metric of customer relationship satisfaction? If not, then clearly the customer relationship is secondary to meeting budgets, filling quotas, and the like.

With this as background, here is my personal definition of CRM as I hope it will be:

Customer Relationship Management is the commitment of the company to place the customer experience at the center of its priorities and to ensure that incentive systems, processes, and information resources leverage the relationship by enhancing the experience.

In terms of technology, CRM is the design, communication, and use of information to ensure that customers grow more and more confidence, trust, and sense of personal value in their relationship with the company.

Ronni T. Marshak, Senior Vice President, Patricia Seybold Group

Ronni T. Marshak is a senior vice president and principal consultant/analyst with the Patricia Seybold Group. She is a principal consultant in the firm's Customers.com consulting practice, which specializes in jump-starting, improving, and/or salvaging business-to-business and e-business initiatives. This parallels the winning formula outlined in Patricia Seybold's best-selling book, *Customers.com*, by identifying how to "make it easy for customers to do business with you."

Ms. Marshak served as editor and coauthor of *Customers.com*. The book is a *Business Week, Wall Street Journal, USA Today*, BN.com, and amazon.com best seller.

Ms. Marshak is also the customer value practice leader in the firm's Customers.com Strategic Planning Service. This practice area focuses on developing and implementing strategies for being in a positive and profitable relationship with customers. She has consulted for such vendors as IBM, Microsoft, Lotus, Digital, and Hewlett Packard as well as user organizations such as the International Monetary Fund, Blue Cross/Blue Shield, the American Cancer Society, and the Commonwealth of Massachusetts. Her research has appeared in such publications as *Fortune, Network World*, and *Computerworld*.

Ms. Marshak is the author of *Word Processing Packages for the IBM PC* and coauthor of *Integrated Desktop Environments and Database Software for the IBM PC: The Desktop Generation*, both published by McGraw-Hill as part of the Seybold Series on Professional Computing. She has appeared as a speaker at such industry events as AIIM, Groupware '9x, the Workflow Conference, Comdex, Windows-OS/2 Conferences, UnixExpo, Unisys Open Forum, and the Office Automation Conference.

Ms. Marshak holds a Bachelor's degree from the University of Massachusetts and an MEd from Northeastern University.

Definition

CRM has become the new buzzword of e-business. And it seems that there are almost as many definitions for CRM as there are vendors promoting products for getting closer to customers.

We propose that establishing and managing customer relationships is first and foremost a strategic endeavor, not a technology category. Just as your company established goals, strategies, plans, and objectives, you need to determine how your customer relationships are being served at each step.

Technology fits only at the tactical level—as the tools with which you implement your plans to support your strategies.

On the technology side, we have identified two different types of technologies that support your customer relationship strategy (CRS): CRM, the customer-facing, interaction systems, such as support, campaign management, and sales force automation; and Customer Intelligence (CI), which provides tools to capture, store, process, access, organize, and analyze/model customer data. The results of this analysis are typically put into action via the CRM systems.

Remember the old commercial, "It's a breath mint." "No, it's a candy mint." "Why, it's two, two, two mints in one!" (Or for "Saturday Night Live" fans, "It's a floor wax." "No, it's a dessert topping!") So goes the ongoing debate over Customer Relationship Management. Is CRM the customer-facing applications of customer service/support and sales, or is it the back-office applications of customer data interpretation?

I believe that this question misses a crucial point, and that is that managing customer relationships—which is, after all, what CRM is all about—is not simply a group of applications, nor should we be focused on technology.

Establishing and maintaining long-term, mutually beneficial relationships with your customers is something that must be at the core of your organization's *raison d'etre*. Your executives must mandate it. Your employees must embrace it. It must become a core value of your company. You have to feel it in your gut!

That has nothing to do with technology.

So, here I am, espousing motherhood and apple pie. You all know that customers are vital to every business. You know that relationships with your customers are the key to your success. But with the advent of new and exciting technologies that focus on customer interactions and analyzing customer information, we've gotten caught up in the inner workings of CRM technologies. We are now able to perform customer-related processes over organizational boundaries in real time! We can be in constant touch with our customers. The technology is exciting (and confusing), and we are spending all our time trying to figure out which products to implement rather than determining how we want our customer relationships to look and feel. We've lost sight of the bigger picture—the strategic importance of our customer relationships.

Let's look at it another way. Every company's game plan includes what I call the "G-SPOT." (See Figure 1-2.) This stands for Goals, Strategies, Plans, Objectives, and Tactics. Here's how it breaks down for CRM:

> **Goals** Every business has clearly defined goals. At the most basic level, these include things like profitability, worldwide recognition, and high stockholder value.

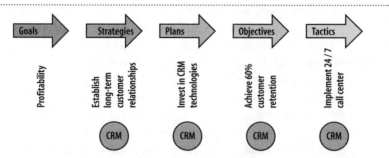

Figure 1-2: The CRM G-SPOT: In this example, the goal of profitability (which, of course, breaks down into many strategies) is supported by a CRM strategy and implemented using CRM tactics (Copyright 2000, Patricia Seybold Group. All rights reserved.)

Strategies To achieve your goals, you establish strategies, such as designing innovative products, focusing on international markets, and establishing long-term relationships with customers.

Plans Executing strategies requires plans. For example, to design innovative products you might implement a plan of hiring top product engineers; to focus internationally you might develop a public relations plan that targets worldwide press; and to establish customer relationships you might determine to measure customer satisfaction and behavior and to invest in technology to support customer interactions.

Objectives These are the measurable goals of each plan, such as maintaining a 60 percent customer retention rate or lowering product return rates to less than 20 percent.

Tactics Tactics are how you achieve the objectives that are part of the plans to implement the strategies to achieve the goals (whew!). For example, you might establish a 24/7 call center or create a data warehouse that consolidates all customer information.

I'm sure you've noted that CRM topics and technologies fit in almost every area (see Figure 1-2). Customer relationships are, in themselves, a strategic concern. The plans lay out how to establish the relationships. The objectives indicate how to recognize (via measurements) successful customer relationships. And CRM technologies are implemented at a tactical level in support of the strategy.

Now that we've positioned technology in the strategic planning and implementation process, we can go back to the original question: is CRM the customer-facing applications of customer service/support and sales, or is it the back-office applications of customer data interpretation?

Basically, we see two dimensions of CRM technology: customer-facing applications and company-facing applications.

Customer-facing applications are fundamentally those that customers actually experience. These might also be considered customer interaction applications, wherein customers interact with your employees, your website, and/or your systems.

The old standby CRM applications—the ones originally featured at all the CRM trade shows—fall primarily into the customer-facing category:

Sales force automation (SFA) Epitomized by Siebel Systems, SFA applications include such capabilities as lead tracking, opportunity management, contact management, and (more recently) aspects of partner relationship management.

Customer service and support Led, again, by Siebel (after its Scopus Technology acquisition) and PeopleSoft (which acquired Vantive), these customer-facing applications include areas such as call center management, online help facilities, internal helpdesk, and expert knowledge-based systems for problem resolution.

Marketing automation The automation of marketing functions encompasses a wide variety of capabilities, some of which are customer facing, such as automated email response systems, campaign management/execution tools, surveys and contest management, and the management and distribution of marketing materials (both hard copy and online) to salespersonnel and partners.

Marketing automation, however, is the primary culprit in the confusion between customer-facing and company-facing applications. While the execution of campaigns, the customer engagement capabilities (such as surveys and contests), and direct customer research (soliciting feedback from customers) all involve interacting with customers, the major portion of marketing responsibilities are actually handled within the organization. Thus, these should be called customer-facing. At the Patricia Seybold Group, we call these applications Customer Intelligence.

The Customer Intelligence process (described by Lynne Harvey in her July 13, 2000, report, "How to Provide Customer Intelligence," http://www.psgroup.com/) consists of four steps:

1. Gathering customer data.

2. Analyzing that data.

3. Formulating a strategy based on the analysis in order to recognize customer value.

4. Taking action based on the strategy.

There are six different categories of tools to achieve Customer Intelligence (as Ms. Harvey described in her August 10, 2000, report, "The Customer Intelligence Landscape," http://www.psgroup.com). These are tools for:

► Gathering customer information

► Storing customer information

► Processing customer data

► Accessing customer information

► Organizing customer data

► Modeling and analyzing customer data

The line between customer-facing and company-facing applications is very blurry, however. This is because the customer-facing products are typically the solutions used to gather customer data (from call center databases, contact managers, and so on) and, similarly, the action taken as the fourth step of the CI process is usually delivered via customer-facing systems (offers in a campaign, new loyalty programs, and so on).

Further adding to the confusion is that vendors that offer solutions on both sides of the equation don't stop at the border! Sales systems, such as Siebel's, offer data capture, storage, and analysis. Analysis systems, such as E.piphany's, offer campaign management and execution.

The key difference is in the purpose of the two types of solutions. CI is an internal process for truly understanding who your customers are and what they want from you. The customer-facing applications, which I continue to call CRM, are all about being in touch with customers, getting their input into your databases, and giving them ways to interact with you so that these interactions (and behaviors) can be captured and analyzed.

There is truly a symbiotic relationship between Customer Intelligence and Customer Relationship Management. But it helps everyone when we can attach more granular labels to the different technology areas.

Thus, I propose that we reserve the acronym CRM for the front-end, customer-interaction systems. The company-facing analysis and strategizing should be called Customer Intelligence.

Both are implemented in support of a customer relationship strategy. And thus, heretical as it may seem, I propose that we call the strategic aspect (which is removed from all technology) CRS (see Figure 1-3).

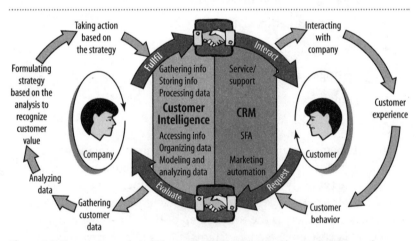

Figure 1-3: Your customer relationship strategy (CRS) is supported by two dimensions of technology: the Customer Intelligence products that act in support of the overall CI process (indicated with the arrows on the left) and the CRM products (Copyright 2000, Patricia Seybold Group. All rights reserved.)

Where does eCRM fit in? I've heard dozens of definitions for how eCRM is different than regular old CRM, such as it is the Internet-based stuff; it is the automated stuff (no person is involved, such as automated email responses); it is the different customer touch points (website, phone center, email), and so on.

The term "eCRM" was first coined by people who were communicating with customers in new ways, typically referring to using the Web as the interaction point. But since then the term has expanded into irrelevance. Most, if not all, CRM solutions now have Web-based components (or will soon have them). And using the Internet has become a standard way of doing business, not something new and innovative.

Marketeers still use eCRM as a PR play. I find it an arbitrary distinction. If a CRM product doesn't provide some or all of the many eCRM functions, it won't be around for long.

In spite of my emphatic insistence that we clearly differentiate CRS, CRM, and CI, the definition of CRM will continue to encompass just about every technology or strategic initiative that even mentions the word customer. Vendors will continue to position products that are clearly in the Customer Intelligence space as CRM for a couple of reasons. First, as mentioned, CRM technology is often the beginning and end point for the CI process. Second, CRM, as a concept, is hot! Customers and the press are paying attention.

If you take away only one message from this perspective, it's that your relationships with your customers need to start at the strategy level. You must establish and be committed to a comprehensive customer relationship strategy. The CRM and CI technologies are there to be implemented in support of the strategy. Remember, when you implement a sound strategy, you can achieve your corporate goals.

Michael Simpson, CMO, Interact Commerce Corporation

With more than 14 years of experience in the software industry, Michael Simpson has often been recognized as a leading marketing and industry strategist. As chief marketing officer for Interact Commerce Corporation, Mr. Simpson has contributed to their position as the leading mid-market CRM provider and helped further the growth of the best-selling contact manager, ACT!

Prior to joining Interact Commerce Corporation, Mr. Simpson worked for Novell, Inc., where he last served as director of strategic market planning. He joined Novell in 1992 and is widely credited with engineering the core positioning and marketing strategy for their directory services business that helped power a turnaround at Novell, the world's fifth-largest software company. Before Novell, he was general manager of a network integration and consulting firm.

Mr. Simpson has been a guest speaker on industry direction in more than 20 countries and has appeared in the global business and industry press, including *US News & World Report*, the *Washington Post*, CNN, and CNBC.

In addition to contributing to this book, he has collaborated on a Knowledge Management book due out in 2001.

DEFINITION

What is CRM? Well, I guess the answer to that is usually determined by the person you are asking, and what they get out of having a customer relationship managed. Therefore, it is important to look at it from the perspective of the different participants. We'll get to that in due time, but we first must lay some groundwork to measure those perspectives.

Most people and businesses look at CRM as a combination of software and business process to accomplish a particular set of goals, usually centered on growing top-line revenue. The component milestones, or methods, around the base revenue objectives are often disputed. And, in fact, I would argue they morph a bit along the edges for each company even after initial implementation depending on the current condition of the business. But there should be some absolutes that are fundamental constants.

There are the obvious basics that may or may not be necessary to mention, but I'm doing it anyway. First of all, CRM should not be totally self-serving in its individual methods of implementation, meaning it needs to assist your customer, but it had better benefit the top and bottom lines of the company as its ultimate goal. After all, you're not in business to implement cool technology—you're in it to make money, plain and simple. What smart companies understand—well, actually, any company that has survived their own business or market's initial growth period and subsequent reality—is that your level of understanding and effort toward your customers' experience in dealing with you versus your competitors is the primary determining factor of future revenues. And, of course, your ability to retain customers is a major determining factor in what your bottom line looks like because the cost of acquiring new customers is exponentially greater than selling to existing ones.

So, the elements of CRM that need to be understood must start with what the essence of a relationship is. A lot of people are fond of saying that relationships are based on trust, but frankly, that's a crock. Certainly, positive and mutually "enjoyable" relationships are based on trust as a major factor, but that is not required for a relationship to be mutually beneficial, thus justified, and even relatively solid. If you strip away all the hype around how to "do" relationships, you are left with one simple concept. The real essence of a relationship is simply a memory of past interactions.

Think about it. Once you have an interaction with an individual, bi-directionally, you carry that memory into your next interaction. But you don't start over from scratch each time unless maybe it's your 103-year-old grandmother you're talking about—you build on those past interactions. How you constantly recall and apply past interactions to present ones defines the quality of your relationships. I know this sounds like a bunch of philosophical mumbo-jumbo, but understanding this foundational truth is paramount to building a filter for every effort you make in the world of CRM.

When you have a relationship with an individual, you would be pretty frustrated if every time you spoke to that person they had no recollection of your previous conversation. If every time you were forced to start from scratch, you would, in short order, realize that your relationship wasn't going anywhere, was too frustrating and time consuming with very little return, and you would avoid that person completely. In fact, you would likely even be angry enough to let others know about your negative experience with that person.

Well, when you have a relationship with one of your customers, you may think about the individual as a component of their overall account; but that is rarely the case from your customer's perspective. Whether you sell through partners or direct sales, if the salespeople represent themselves as you, your customer thinks they have a relationship with *your* company because they have a relationship with a representative. Whether that customer is truly an individual, or an individual in a business that's a customer, they think of your company as a single entity. Freud might have been comfortable dividing people into their ids, egos, and superegos, but most of us consider ourselves to be single entities. And that's how customers view our companies, too. That goes for your websites as well.

This highlights one of the greatest objectives of CRM: to create a consistent customer experience. Your relationship with a customer should be thought of as an ongoing conversation without end. Regardless of who your customer talks to, whether your accounts receivables person, customer service rep, salesperson, or in receiving a call from telemarketing, a direct marketing letter, or even returning to your website, they expect that you have some collective consciousness. Fail to demonstrate that collective consciousness and they'll believe you just don't appreciate them or their business. The result is that your relationship is vulnerable to the next price war or marketing program from a competitor. You could be just a click away from starting over with that customer, but doing it from the doghouse, a disadvantage a competitor who has no history with your customer is free from. That's right, the history of your relationship with your customer could very well be the thing that makes you vulnerable if you don't take it seriously.

So how do you create this collective consciousness? Well, CRM is obviously the solution, but although software is a necessary component, there is more to it than that. Getting people to use the software is the key—and that requires some business process, a clear understanding of the value it provides the individuals, some pretty serious efforts in internal evangelism, and clear, measurable returns.

You must build an infrastructure that links a history of your customer interactions together in a common data source. Yes, you can connect your customer-facing sales teams, support, marketing, back office, and Web presences so that you can get everybody sharing a common understanding of that customer. And you should mold the solution to the way your people and your customers work—not the other way around. Whether wireless, Web, remote, or in the office, they need to be completely informed to be effective.

CRM is about creating a consistent customer history so you can create a consistent customer experience. This enables accountability and team-based assistance in managing that customer. It enables potential and existing customers to feel cared for, deepening their loyalty, resulting in increased sales.

When you think about what CRM is for you, think about what every participant in that management process needs to be successful—including your customer.

Robert Thompson, President, Front Line Solutions, Inc.

Robert Thompson is founder and president of Front Line Solutions, Inc., an independent CRM consulting and research firm specializing in the emerging field of partner relationship management (PRM).

Through his groundbreaking research in PRM requirements and best practices, he has earned a reputation as the industry's leading PRM consultant.

In January 2000, Mr. Thompson founded CRMGuru.com (http://www.crmguru.com/), which has become the largest and fastest-growing CRM portal, with more than 35,000 members worldwide. CRMGuru.com unites a worldwide community of business managers who want to learn about CRM and exchange ideas and perspectives with others.

Mr. Thompson is frequently quoted in industry publications such as *InformationWeek, Computerworld, Computer Reseller News*, and *Sm@rt Reseller* and speaks at numerous industry conferences. In 2000, he was the chairman of the first two PRM conferences in the United States and will participate as chairman or keynote speaker at several conferences in 2001. Mr. Thompson writes a regular column for *VARBusiness* magazine, publishes the CRM e-newsletter *On the Front Line*, and is the moderator for CRM.Talk, the world's largest CRM email discussion list.

Throughout his career, Mr. Thompson has advised leading companies on the strategic use of information technology to solve business problems and gain a competitive advantage. Prior to starting his consulting firm in 1998, he had fifteen years of experience in the IT industry, including positions as business unit executive and IT strategy consultant at IBM, and as vice president of a large value-added reseller.

Mr. Thompson is a board member of the Northern California chapter of the CRMA, a professional association dedicated to the CRM industry. He earned a Bachelor's degree and an MBA from the University of California, Irvine.

Definition

CRM is a term that gained widespread recognition in the late 1990s. Market analysts say that billions of dollars will be spent on CRM solutions—software and services designed to help businesses more effectively manage customer relationships through all types of direct and indirect channels.

Yet even as the market for CRM technology expands, confusion reigns. The most common question asked at our CRM portal CRMGuru.com is simply: "What is CRM?"

A panel of CRM experts—the "gurus" working with CRMGuru. com—developed this answer:

> Customer Relationship Management (CRM) is a business strategy to select and manage customers to optimize long-term value. CRM requires a customer-centric business philosophy and culture to support effective marketing, sales, and service processes. CRM applications can enable effective Customer Relationship Management, provided that an enterprise has the right leadership, strategy, and culture.

So there it is, simple question and simple answer, right? Well, as many business executives and CRM project managers can attest, effective CRM is not all simple or easy. For starters, how exactly does a company create a "customer-centric business philosophy and culture?" Not with a software package, that's for sure.

As the pyramid diagram in Figure 1-4 shows, CRM must start with a business strategy, which drives changes in the organization and work processes, which are in turn enabled by information technology. The reverse does not work—a company cannot automate its way to a new business strategy. In fact, the majority of projects that focus on technology first, rather than business objectives, are destined for failure, according to extensive best practices research. However, a customer-centric business can reap significant benefits using CRM technology.

CRM as a business strategy is not a new idea. Savvy business executives have always understood that they should focus on customers with the best potential for sales and profits, and provide good service so they'll come back again and again. And technology is not required for effective CRM. Consider a successful small business. The business owner and the staff work hard to provide personal, high-quality service, building a loyal customer base over time. Computers are not necessarily required.

Why, then, has CRM become so popular? The bottom line: power has shifted to customers, due to the convergence of three powerful trends:

▶ ERP systems are no longer a source of competitive advantage for most companies. The back office is fully automated, now what?

▶ The cycle of innovation to production to obsolescence has accelerated, leading to an abundance of options for customers and a shrinking market window for vendors.

▶ The Internet has made it far easier for customers to decide which supplier to buy from and, if necessary, switch to another vendor at the click of a mouse.

CRM Is Not Just Software!

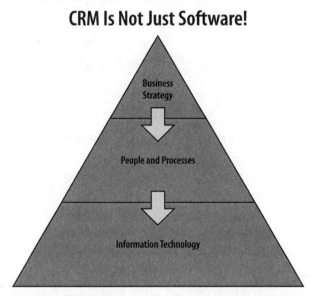

Figure 1-4: The CRM pyramid (Copyright 2000, Front Line Solutions, Inc. All rights reserved.)

With product advantages reduced or neutralized in many industries, the customer relationship itself has gained importance. For larger businesses, however, the neighborhood boutique approach doesn't work. CRM technology provides a more systematic way of managing customer relationships on a larger scale.

CRM applications support marketing, sales, commerce, and service processes, as shown in the CRM Solutions Map in Figure 1-5.

Traditionally, enterprise employees have been the primary users of CRM applications. Then, e-business or eCRM applications were introduced to allow enterprises to interact directly with customers via corporate websites, e-commerce storefronts, and self-service applications. Finally, starting in 1999, PRM applications hit the market, designed to support channel partners and other intermediaries between an enterprise and its end customers.

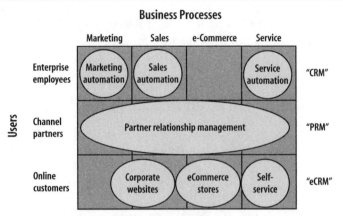

Figure 1-5: CRM Solutions Map (Copyright 2000 Front Line Solutions, Inc. All rights reserved.)

These applications support the following business processes involved in the customer relationship lifecycle:

Marketing Targeting prospects and acquiring new customers through data mining, campaign management, and lead distribution.

Sales Closing business with effective selling processes, using proposal generators, configurators, knowledge management tools, contact managers, and forecasting aids.

E-commerce In the Internet age, selling processes should transfer seamlessly into purchasing transactions, done quickly, conveniently, and at the lowest cost.

Service Handling post-sales service and support issues with sophisticated call center applications or Web-based customer self-service products.

In summary, CRM is a disciplined business strategy to create and sustain long-term, profitable customer relationships. Successful CRM initiatives start with a business strategy and philosophy that aligns company activities around customer needs. CRM technology is a critical enabler of the processes required to turn strategy into business results.

What Is CRM Technology?

You can see the confluences and the differences in the general definition of CRM as presented by these CRM champions. They all define
it as a disciplined business strategy. They acknowledge technology
as the driver of the strategy. This book is about the car and particularly the driver. So with that agreement, we now have to take it a tad
deeper. What is the technology of CRM? The industry standard definition of the components of CRM technology were expounded
upon by the META Group in "The Customer Relationship Management Ecosystem" (available for free after registering on their website
http://www.metagroup.com/).

Types of CRM Technology

There are three segments: operational, analytical, and collaborative.
The technological architecture is spoke-to-spoke between the operational and analytical. Operational CRM is the customer-facing
applications of CRM—the aforementioned sales force automation,
enterprise marketing automation, and front-office suites that encompass all of this simultaneously. The analytic segment includes data
marts or data warehouses such as customer repositories that are used
by applications that apply algorithms to dissect the data and present
it in a form that is useful to the user. The collaborative CRM, which
reaches across customer "touch points" (all the different communication means that a customer might interact with such as email, phone
call, fax, website pages, and so on) includes applications such as the
partner relationship management (PRM) software you will become
familiar with as you get through this book.

Operational CRM

This is the "ERP-like" segment of CRM. Typical business functions
involving customer service, order management, invoice/billing, or
sales and marketing automation and management are all part of this
bandwidth on the spectrum. This is perhaps the primary use of CRM
to date. One facet of operational CRM is the possibility of integrating with the financial and human resources functions of the enterprise resource planning (ERP) applications such as PeopleSoft and
SAP. With this integration, end-to-end functionality from lead management to order tracking can be implemented, albeit not often

seamlessly. In fact, CRM project failure rates, according to the 2000 study done by the META Group, are purported to be between 55 and 75 percent. A major reason for the project failure and sometimes the cause of problems even when the implementation is successful is the inability to integrate with the legacy systems.

Part of the operational CRM universe includes the customer call center, the subject of much discussion and debate in recent years. For more on this, see Chapter 9.

Analytical CRM

Analytical CRM is the capture, storage, extraction, processing, interpretation, and reporting of customer data to a user. Companies such as MicroStrategy, Inc., have developed applications that can capture this customer data from multiple sources and store it in a customer data repository and then use hundreds of algorithms to analyze/interpret the data as needed. The value of the application is not just in the algorithms and storage, but also in the ability to individually personalize the response using the data.

Collaborative CRM

This is almost an overlay. It is the communication center, the coordination network that provides the neural paths to the customer and his suppliers. It could mean a portal, a partner relationship management (PRM) application, or a customer interaction center (CIC). It could mean communication channels such as the Web or email, voice applications, or snail mail. It could mean channel strategies. In other words, it is any CRM function that provides a point of interaction between the customer and the channel itself.

CRM Technology Components

Besides the types of CRM that are available for you to choose from, there are components that make it up. What is the difference? Imagine operational, analytical, and collaborative CRM as the car models. The components are the under-the-hood things—some with chrome, some encrusted with grease, but all under the hood.

CRM Engine

This would be the customer data repository. The data mart or data warehouse is where all data on the customer is captured and stored.

This could include basic stuff such as name, address, phone number, and birth date. It could include more sophisticated information such as the number of times you accessed the Lands End website (I *know* you did) and what you did on the pages you accessed, including the amount of time you lingered over that cashmere sweater. It could include the helpdesk support and purchase history with Lands End.

Ultimately, the purpose is a single gathering point for all individual customer information so that a unified customer view can be created throughout all company departments that need to know the data stored in this CRM engine house.

Front-Office Solutions

These are the unified applications that run on top of the customer data warehouse (CDW). They could be sales force automation, marketing automation, they could be service and support and customer interaction applications. The important thing is that analytics, reports, and the easy instant access to this information are hallmarks of these solutions. In the client/server environment particularly, they provide employees with the information they need to make informed choices on what to do next with a customer—whether it is a sales opportunity closing or solving a customer complaint.

The more specific applications provide an element of self-service for the customer. For example, when you log into amazon.com with your personal ID and password, you get specific recommendations that are based on complex analytic algorithms interpreting what it sees as your preferences in a pretty sophisticated way. Nary a human soul touched your file. It was all automated. The self-service is your ability to act on the recommendations (that is, to purchase them).

Both types of applications are essential to a complete CRM system.

Enterprise Application Integrations (EAIs) for CRM

These sit between the CRM back office and front office. They also sit between the newly installed CRM system and the been-around-forever enterprise legacy systems. They also allow CRM-to-CRM communications. "They" are pieces of code and connectors and bridges that are called as a body EAIs, formerly known as middleware. EAIs will provide the messaging services and data mapping services that allow one system to communicate with disparate other systems, regardless of formatting. With the move of the Internet to the mainstream, it is hoped that the Extensible Markup Language (XML) will be the universal go-between, allowing one system to correspond with another. However, because of the current state of XML, with the evolution of vertical XMLs with different data descriptions particular to the vertical industry, XML universality is not quite there, though it continues to gain ground as the standard. The EAI connectors will remain powerful. The issue for them has always been price, with connectors that would link Siebel to SAP amounting to a cost of tens and potentially even hundreds of thousands to purchase and configure. More recently, though, companies like Scribe Systems have been producing reasonably priced, very effective connectors and interfaces for the multisystem interaction.

CRM in the Back Office

The analytic tools are the back-office applications for CRM. They are back office simply because they operate behind the scene and are utterly transparent to the customer and the user. However, they are used for personalization. In the example above, those analytic applications provide the slicing and dicing of the data for Lands End. They could produce demographic, geographic, or financial analysis. They could produce purchase history or an individual's preferences expressed by trips through different channels.

Customer Lifecycle

What about the customer? What about the customer lifecycle? Is the lifecycle what the customer rides to get him back to good health? Not exactly. You are going to see references to this throughout the book and an entire appendix (Appendix B) devoted to customer lifetime value (CLV). What the hell is all this about?

Pretty straightforward, really. It is far cheaper to retain existing customers than to acquire new customers. Therefore, presuming that this is the goal of most companies, the next thing to determine is the value of that customer to your company. A customer who is consistently losing money for you, while he has been with you for 40 years, is not valuable to you directly, though there may be some value to you in the marketing. But how do you figure out that? The lifecycle of the customer is the process the customer has been undergoing to be with you for all these years. This includes that customer's purchase history, among other things. To find out what is the expected revenue generated from that single customer over the anticipated lifetime of that customer's relationship with you is both the customer lifecycle and the CLV.

Customer Interaction

Some of the value that technology brings to the table in CRM is through increased customer interaction that doesn't necessarily occur with a human being. It is the convenience and the ability of the customer to get something they need without having to rely on a busy human being, or worse, a lazy human being. I would rather be able to act on a recommendation from the amazon.com personalization machine than have a human being suggest what to read—unless that human being was someone I already trusted. Big difference. The psychology of this automated interaction is interesting. If I see a recommendation to buy *CRM at the Speed of Light: Capturing and Keeping Customers in Internet Real Time*, and I'm interested in CRM, I'm going to give it a look and perhaps purchase this worthy title. If a salesperson recommends it to me, unless I asked him to recommend a good CRM title, I'm going to think he is telling me to buy something so he can get a commission. I'm always going to be a tad suspicious that he is pushing overstock (heaven forbid!) or a book that has his agenda behind it, not my interest. Oddly, if it is a book suggested by my reading habits, the very nature of the suggestion—impersonal, analytic—is going to make me more inclined to look. It's more my agenda, under my control. Yet, I haven't spoken to a single human throughout the transaction. Hmmm.

As you'll see in Chapter 9, what used to be helpdesks or customer service calls can often be taken care of on the Internet with the customers helping themselves to an answer. The early "interaction" was document fax back. Now it is far more sophisticated, with both service information instantly available to the customer service representative (operational) and service without service representatives but with customer interaction available.

This interaction is a critical component of CRM—especially the online variety.

I think that we're ready to move on. CRM defined. Now to eCRM.

Chapter 2

Putting the "e" in eCRM

There's a lot of debate over whether eCRM is a real designation or just a marketing ploy by CRM companies trying to distinguish themselves in the burgeoning morass of CRM pretenders. It is a real designation, but it isn't a revolutionary new system or set of processes. eCRM is CRM online. Period. Beginning of story.

The reason I say beginning of story is that eCRM, CRM online, implies an additional means of communication and level of interactivity with the customer. Where it really differs is the technology and its architecture. It allows for increased interactivity and self-service for the customer. It also is cool.

CRM and eCRM: What's Different?

Check out the screen shot in Figure 2-1. Note the designation "WebTicket." That's eCRM. Being able to take care of your customer via the Internet. Or the customers being able to take care of themselves online. That's the difference between CRM and eCRM. That implies a myriad of issues, questions, approaches, technologies, and architectures that are different from client/server-based CRM. Many of them are general issues related to the Internet. Others are general issues related to the creation of applications for the Internet. The third group is related to eCRM directly and its actual value to business.

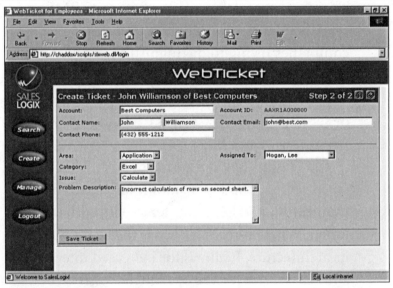

Figure 2-1: Online customer service support ticket (Copyright 2000, Interact Commerce Corporation. All rights reserved. Reprinted with permission of Interact Commerce Corporation.)

Why the move to online CRM? Can't we just do things the old way (client/server CRM being the "old way")? Nah. The use of the Internet as a main business artery is why there is an eCRM. As the U.S. population becomes increasingly comfortable using the Internet *securely*, it is increasingly likely that more of the standard business transactions that are done on the phone or even in person will be done via the Internet. The initial popular trust of online business activity is coming through America's favorite pastime: shopping.

This is reflected in a Roper/AOL Cyberstudy conducted in early 2000 about online purchasing habits. It showed an increase from 31 percent of the Internet community purchasing something online in 1998 to 42 percent of the same group purchasing semi-regularly online in 1999. The increases were due to more women getting involved. In 1998, 24 percent of the purchasers were women; in 1999, that same gender hit 37 percent of the total. This same behavior is expected to drive the percentages even higher this year because studies done in mid-2000 indicate that, for the first time, Internet users are primarily women (52 percent). In fact, by 2004, according to the Forrester Group, the business-to-consumer (B2C) market is estimated to be $184 billion.

This is nothing by comparison to the potential for the business-to-business (B2B) market. The $184 billion is dwarfed by Forrester's estimate of $2.7 trillion in B2B business—and they are the pessimists! The Gartner Group for the same time period is estimating $7.3 trillion!

Estimates notwithstanding, what is significant is that the evolution of secured trust in engaging in commercial activity online is increasing dramatically. What does this mean for CRM? How does translating to the Web mean something either better or at least significantly, usefully different for a business?

The Web Experience

As hokey as it may sound, there *is* a "Web experience." It is a complex set of relationships between the Web surfer and the person(s) (either anonymous or known) at the other end of the Internet line with the Internet being the channel that the parties use to communicate with each other. The relationships between the parties and the interactions (key word, here) between them are very different from other forms of interaction. For example, how often have you decided to email a friend rather than call him? The thought behind it is that it is easier to do that than call. Is that the reason? Let's take a quick peek. You're emailing them a four-paragraph note on something that happened to you at work. You'd, of course, like their comments on it. You then feel compelled to comment on their comments. *Ad infinitum.* The total time was about ten minutes of typing and sending the email. If no response is necessary, five minutes max. A phone call, especially if they were on speed dial, was probably two minutes, or five minutes total with responses. But doing it the email way stripped out the other things that go on in phone conversations (including nuance and tone), could be done at your leisure (meaning no particular block of time was roped off to do it), sent at your leisure, and responded to and from at your (and your correspondent's) leisure. Additionally, there were no distractions in the discussion. The subject matter written was the subject matter referenced. No more, no less. The interaction was there without the interaction being actually there. No baggage, no emotion, and no complicated thought process. It was what it was—and it didn't save you a bit of time. It just seemed that way because you had more individual control over the process.

That reflects what is both good and peculiar about the Web experience. Why peculiar? It is a social interaction done in isolation that creates as many problems as it solves. There is never actually a substitute for human interaction, but there is also no way an individual human can cover all bases all the time with a customer. For example, if you are a salesperson making a call to a customer site and meeting with the executive vice president of a company, it would be helpful to know that the EVP had emailed to the site with a customer service question to a different division a week before. He had also spent time studying the Web pages that were concerned with your expenses-tracking software and your ERP financial package. Additionally, he watched a demo and downloaded a white paper on the integration of CRM and the back office. All this information related to the EVP's Web experience was captured by the various site tools and centralized in a customer repository. It was analyzed through various analytic algorithms that were then compiled into a report you access using your laptop or Palm, depending on what eCRM software you use. By the time you reach the EVP's office, you are armed and ready (with the information, that is). The website he logged into promoted your products very well. He was able identify your financial package as the one he wanted. He also enjoyed the look and feel of the website and the sophistication of the demonstrations. This gave him more subliminal faith in your product's sophistication, your company's professionalism, and thus your ability to deliver your application successfully.

By the way, for a product that can actually create this kind of ambiance, check out the Eloquent Presenter ActiveX control for something to view those online streaming demos with. To see this baby in action, check out the Siebel website product demonstrations at http://www.siebel.com/. Just be ready for a call from a Siebel representative within 24 hours of your signing up to see the demos— loaded with the information about you they need to take the call to the level of a thumbs-up qualified lead or a thumbs-down no go. They *are* good and the Eloquent Presenter is that impressive.

The EVP's transactions are a small segment of the Web experience. What is the purpose of the Web experience in the CRM world? It is to identify a customer, derive the value of the customer, and interact with the customer. This is so whether it is a single individual who buys more frequently than other individuals or a corporation that is doing more business (or less) with you than any other customer. Its odd nature makes innovation necessary to make that the identification, derivation, and interaction happen to the benefit of your customer and your company.

eCRM's value comes from giving a customer that "total experience" on the Web. Traditional CRM channels can't do that because it is based on applications that may not be amenable to giving the customer direct access to the interfaces and functionality. Ordinarily, CRM provides a set of tools that, while possibly Web enabled, aren't designed from the ground up for the Web. It is more for the corporate department or the individual employee to do his customer-related intelligence, marketing, and service more effectively. It isn't a ground-up creation or redevelopment so that all functions, external and internal, are entirely Web based. For example, personalization tools (see Chapter 6 for a detailed discussion of personalization) are more appropriate to Web customer experiences. Personalization tools have little value if used in a purely client/server environment. However, this doesn't guarantee that eCRM is entirely wonderful. Brent Frei, president and CEO of Onyx Software, provides this caution:

> eCRM is the customer-facing Internet portion of CRM. It includes capabilities like self-service knowledge bases, automated email response, personalization of Web content, online product bundling and pricing, and so on. eCRM gives Internet users the ability to interact with the business through their preferred communication channel, and it allows the business to offset expensive customer service agents with technology. So the value is largely one of improved customer satisfaction and reduced cost through improved efficiency. However, an eCRM

strategy deployed alone can also backfire and actually result in decreased customer satisfaction. If the customer's interactions through electronic channels are not seamlessly integrated with those taking place through traditional channels, the customer is likely to become extremely frustrated. Also, if the basis for the content being served up to the customer doesn't consider all the data gathered by the rest of the business, the customer is likely being served in the wrong way. Therefore, it's imperative that eCRM be installed in conjunction with traditional CRM and that the two are tightly integrated. Otherwise, the value of eCRM might actually be negative.

The Features of eCRM

The technology of the "e" is probably the most debated facet of the eCRM versus CRM debate. It is the one place where the difference is paramount. If you look at the philosophical, methodological, systemic, and process functional differences between CRM and eCRM, they are minimal. But the engines and architectures for their execution are very different because the communications media are different.

The Machinery: Rebuilt Engine or New Engine?

Some CRM companies have Web-enabled their existing application and called it "Internet ready." Others have redesigned it from the bottom up so that it is a Web application, rather than a client/server application that can be viewed on the Web. These are fundamental architectural differences. Mere accessibility from a browser does not make a CRM application into eCRM. For the technology to fulfill its true promise of making the desired customer activity possible, the invisible technical details really do matter. For example, do you want to have an application that is optimized for Internet activity—meaning it uses HTML; is accessible from your desktop, your Palm, or your laptop; can be accessed securely using Internet security protocols; is reachable via TCP/IP; and so on? Or would you rather have something that works from a more standard client/server architecture and can be accessed in a more kludgy fashion via a browser but is only half as functional as the pure eCRM application? (Pardon my biases here.)

Application servers drive the pure Internet CRM applications. The applications servers that are often found in three-tier architectures are not created just for the Internet—client/server architecture is, in fact, why the three-tiered approach was fashioned. But they are the best contemporary architecture for the Internet. The applications servers provide preconstructed Web pages to a Web server that delivers them to the users through their Web browsers. This model preserves the fundamental value of the Internet as a communications medium—common, platform-independent access to data anytime, anywhere. There is no program or application code that needs to reside on the user's PC, therefore users gain immediate access to the application with the right URL and security authorization. It's just like using your Web browser to view any other Web page: click the right link and you see the information. PeopleSoft/Vantive CRM 8.0 is a good example of this.

The PeopleSoft Internet Architecture consists of the following principles. Applications are based on standard Internet protocols and languages such as HTTP and HTML. Internet applications can easily be accessed from a Web browser. The Internet applications user experience is maintained through the Web look, feel, and usage paradigm. It is not "Windows 98 on the Web."

Here is where there is a key difference. No client software is installed with pure Internet applications—the browser is the client. The architecture is a true multitier, server-centric model, featuring separation of presentation, business logic, and data management functionality. If you're not familiar with Internet-centric applications, think of what you assume about the loading of the application and interface when you open Microsoft Word 2000. I presume the answer is nothing at all. It's just a routine thing that you do and it is simply like walking. It happens. There is nothing interesting or special about it. Think about that when you load Internet Explorer 5.5 to get onto the Web. You think about the fact that you are loading up your Internet connection. It is not part of the desktop. With Internet-centric applications, the browser is no different than the Word 2000 interface. It is just part of the desktop. No modem, no special anything. Like walking. Part of the landscape, not separate from it. This works particularly well when you have a broadband Internet connection such as a T1 or T3 line, cable modem, or DSL that allows you to be up and running on the Internet 24 hours a day, 7 days a week. With a ground-up eCRM application, it is as ubiquitous as the desktop is from wherever you are connected.

By contrast, CRM Web-accessible applications are not nearly the same level of business utility because they are not purely data driven. These systems rely on application code—applets or controls that must be downloaded and installed on users' systems to enable them to communicate with the CRM database. This can defeat platform independence and present logistical challenges to the anywhere-anytime promise afforded by the Internet. Requiring code to be installed on each user's system is invasive. It increases the challenge and cost to manage and maintain, and it may not even be feasible to do in all cases. If your vacationing sales director forgot to bring a laptop along (it's a vacation, after all), the sales director may not be able to convince the Internet café in the area to allow the download and installation of a specific applet needed to view the latest pipeline. Your partners, too, may not appreciate having to install "your system" on their system to work with you.

If it's important to you to be able to connect your employees with customers, partners, and suppliers, it's important to understand the limitations that "Windows 98 on the Web" can impose on your business processes. Can you imagine having to install a special application on your PC to read a newspaper or trade stocks over the Web? Like any other purchase, *caveat emptor*.

Ultimately, the difference is in:

Occupied real estate The pure Internet application usually rests on the server with the browser as client. The Web-enabled client/server application needs downloaded applets and applications to the desktop to carry out a specific function.

The "feel" With the browser as the client, it is easy to feel that access anywhere and anytime is true because all functions are accessible transparently. When you load and unload applets each time you need a specific function, you feel less in control of your Internet CRM destiny.

The backend code While CRM is considered a front-office technology, meaning that the applications are both available to the customer (customer-facing) and impact the customer, there is a backend to the front office. In other words, to put the "e" in eCRM, the development tools for the Web have to be used. Such tools as Java, Enterprise Java Beans (EJB), Perl, and CGI are the groundwork for the "webification" of CRM.

eCRM and Portals

Before the Internet, enterprise portals were space-time continuum holes that Star Trek's flagship went through. With the emergence of the Internet, enterprise portals took on a whole different meaning. They became the gateways to entire Web-based communities and customer activity.

A *portal* is a gateway to an array of services or, optimally, a community. It is a centralized entry point, usually centered on a Web server that links multiple information and interactivity sources and allows a personalized view of any or all of the services according to the user who is entering. The personalization is accessible through a password and user ID. Each different user has a different view of the array of information, goods, and services available to them. This is an easygoing concept that maximizes the control of the viewer. Each person using the portal personalizes the view. Yet the collection of goods, services, and information is universal and available on multiple servers sitting behind the portal doors. This way, thousands of users can get what they need, with all things available to all people and with the workflow and security built in. Probably the best example of a portal-building product is Plumtree Software's Corporate Portal 4.0 tool, released at the end of 2000. Plumtree's tools allow the creation of interlinked portals combined with "gadgets"—portal add-ins in multiple locations, through the use of their Massively Parallel Processing Engine (MPPE). This adds superpower to portals by letting a portal user access multiple portals, increasing the selection of goods, services, information, and communities by manifolds.

How would you deploy a portal? What benefit do they have to your company? Onyx's Frei has some advice:

> A good CRM portal aggregates all relevant customer information within a single application or desktop in a format that is customized and personalized for the department or individual interacting with the data. An ideal portal doesn't just provide access to customer data, but becomes a knowledge base that is tailored to the needs of each different audience, culling together Web content, third-party applications, reference materials, detailed customer information—anything within or outside of the enterprise that customer-facing groups can utilize to enhance their understanding of a customer's experience and needs.

Several things are important for a highly successful CRM portal strategy:

▶ The system should be architected around the customer, instead of around specific job functions. By putting the customer at the application's core, no matter who is viewing, using, or sharing the information, companies are assured a seamless customer interaction process.

▶ Deploying a CRM portal solution only in one department or one business unit will not yield the same results as an enterprise-wide solution that gives every front-office employee access to the critical customer data and knowledge base.

▶ A thin-client or Web-based portal system saves millions of dollars in time, employee turnover, and other costs by greatly reducing system implementation and management time. While there is still a need for client/server technology, and Onyx still supports it, the future is on the Web where installations, upgrades, and expansions can be managed from one location, on one server, and all end users need to gain access is a Web browser.

▶ Different audiences require different views and different types of information, making it absolutely necessary to tailor content and structure to each. Onyx has broken these into three main buckets: customer, employee, and partner. These three main audiences can then be segmented further into departments, divisions, job function—even down to the individual so that every person interacting with the CRM system is viewing only the information relevant to them, in the format that makes the most sense for them and with rules in place that make the most efficient use of their time.

Onyx

Onyx has taken a creative and distinctive approach to building its CRM application suite. Portals are the centerpieces for all its CRM functionality, whether through a client/server platform or online. They are more advanced than the typical CRM application because Onyx provides multiple elements of Web-based self-service for customers, partners, and employees, all of whom could be called, with a little stretching, customers.

Onyx Employee Portal

The Onyx Employee Portal is an enterprise-wide Web solution that combines CRM functionality with third-party applications and relevant Internet content. Its purpose is to maximize the efficiency of marketing, sales, and service teams, which it does very well.

There are several CRM functions that the Employee Portal provides:

Sales can review an account's complete history, manage sales pipelines and opportunities, forecast deals, and review win-loss data.

Marketing can create customer and prospect lists, conduct marketing campaigns, and manage leads, via fax, email, or postal mail.

Customer service can resolve service inquires as well as seamlessly manage service queues and monitor customer satisfaction.

Relevant Internet content links to Internet sites that are integrated directly into the interface, giving employees instant access to company profiles, stock quotes, competitive research, maps, sales coaching, and such.

Third-party applications integrate into a single interface so employees no longer have to open and close multiple applications to access the information they need.

Onyx Customer Portal

Onyx doesn't stop with employee portal access. The Customer Portal is a personalizable, Web-based product line application that markets to, sells to, and services prospects and customers across multiple channels. E-marketing capabilities enable companies to tailor their marketing efforts to the individual needs of distinct customer segments. Some of the functionality provided includes:

Online catalog that helps customers thoroughly research products by accessing all the information they need.

Lead capture and profiling that captures prospect information on your website and lets you leverage that information for follow-up.

Online surveys gather preference information. This can be used for qualifying prospects.

Literature fulfillment provides automatic fulfillment of prospect and customer literature requests by email, fax, or postal mail.

Email marketing enables personalized, outbound email messages based on prospect profile information.

The Customer Portal also provides e-commerce capabilities to streamline a customer's buying experience and strengthen your company's sales effectiveness. These features include:

Online product configuration enables customers to design and configure a product to meet their unique requirements.

Online order processing makes information from online transactions available to sales and service employees for cross-selling, up-selling, and improved customer service.

Finally, and perhaps, most importantly for eCRM, the e-service capacity offers customers options for self-service and interaction using the most convenient channel. This is where the self-service features that are essential for proper eCRM become apparent:

Web self-help empowers customers to solve problems themselves, 24/7, using an online knowledge base of solutions.

Online service allows customers to submit and track service and support incidents over the Web.

Email management automatically routes, prioritizes, and escalates inbound emails from customers.

Profile management allows customers to update profile information themselves.

Product registration enables customers to register products online, quickly and easily.

ONYX PARTNER PORTAL

Through its powerful portal applications, Onyx forgets no one. There are strong PRM elements embedded in the Partner Portal Capabilities, including:

Collaborative selling Onyx collaborative selling capabilities enable partners to become virtual members of your sales team by providing the following functions:

Lead entry gathers detailed information from partners about new sales opportunities.

Lead distribution assigns leads to partners, using rules-based routing and escalation.

Pipeline management manages and monitors channel sales processes for improved planning and forecasting.

Online catalog handles partner requests for self-service training.

Collaborative e-commerce Onyx collaborative e-commerce features are interesting. They aren't just aimed at alliance partners; they are aimed at channel partners. A channel partner sells your product or services and, in return for that, makes money and gets some serious discounts and extra help. They are often value-added resellers (VARs) because they can sell the product and, frequently, can provide specialized services to enhance the value of the product for the customer. The value to the vendor is that the channel can sell more than half their product sales in a given year with far less overhead than maintaining a sales force to do that. Note that several of the features that are available to the channel partners are also available in a slightly different format, but with the same technology, to the customers. With that, take a look:

Literature fulfillment enables partners to order sales and marketing collateral from the Web.

Online product configuration empowers partners to configure custom products for customers online.

Online order processing allows partners to easily place orders with you over the Web.

Collaborative service Again, Onyx's collaborative service is an advanced use of eCRM online capabilities. This involves a version of employee or customer self-service: partner self-service. The features include:

Web self-help allows partners to solve their customers' problems.

Online service allows partners to submit and update customers' service incidents using the Web or email.

Customer surveys allow partners to submit preference information on behalf of their customers.

Customer product registration and order history enable partners to register products online and research order history on behalf of customers.

ONYX E-BUSINESS ENGINE

The Onyx e-Business Engine—the backbone of Onyx 2000—powers all of these portals. Four elements of the Onyx e-Business Engine work together to deliver scalable, enterprise-wide customer management:

e-Business data center provides a single repository for all customer information, with enterprise-wide access. What is intriguing here is that the data center is accessible through the portals. This makes Onyx's product different than others on the market.

e-Business process technology enables a consistent customer experience. It takes all CRM-related sectors including marketing, sales, and service and unifies the view of the customer. It does it through a workflow that consolidates all reporting functions including the consolidated view of tasks, data and events in all the sectors, and it routes appropriately so that they can be managed or escalated if necessary.

e-Business integration framework integrates Onyx with enterprise applications, including ERP applications, telephony systems, Internet content, and Web applications. An integration framework is vital to any eCRM application because if the application can't link to the legacy systems or future enterprise systems, the use value declines dramatically. Integration is the knottiest problem in the CRM world. It is elegantly solved here.

Universal interface framework creates convenient, custom interfaces for your employees, partners, and customers, and combines multiple applications into one user interface. Again, this is a valuable feature because it provides individual views of the universal customer view. The ability to easily customize what you see when you log in with your Internet Explorer 5.5 is something with inestimable value. Why should you be looking at the marketing funds allocations for the class of customers labeled "young and restless" when you are the account manager for the Lockheed Martin account and you need the prospective sales figures for the quarter? It's nice to be able to look at whatever you need to and eliminate superfluous information and mouse clicks to get to the pertinent stuff.

Is eCRM Really Separate?

There is an ongoing debate now being waged by camps of analysts and pundits. Is eCRM a separate discipline from CRM? For example, the Knowledge Capital Group, a group of analysts, in their fascinating report, "KCG Marketview: CRM Redefined" (available for free on the Onyx website, http://www.onyx.com/) call the "e" a "fatal distraction" in the following sentences:

> ...the danger is that companies will attempt to optimize the "e" channel—the Web channel—at the expense of all others. CRM, however, is inherently a multi-channel strategy. Customer relationships transcend the Internet.

Good point. I will continue to use the "e," unlike the KCG, until all CRM is Web integrated. But using the Internet for CRM is now a necessary strategy, not a market edge. The vendors that don't optimize their CRM applications for the Web are the vendors who are out of business very soon. eCRM is actually CRM twenty-first century style.

The implications of that, technologically and practically, were addressed throughout this chapter. Without much further commentary, suffice it to say, eCRM is CRM and CRM must become eCRM.

Chapter 3

Sales Management versus CRM

This is not a long chapter. It is here to do one thing—give you a brief definition of the difference between sales management and CRM. If you haven't figured out what you think CRM is after Chapters 1 and 2, then the apocalypse is upon us. This chapter is just a final mop-up so that we can get on to more substance in the book.

CRM Is Not Sales Management

Traditionally, sales management is what it sounds like—the things that you do to find sales opportunities and close them. That can include contact management, prospecting, lead qualification, opportunity management, and account management. If you are a sales manager, it also includes managing the sales process. That means forecasting and pipeline management (that is, the tracking of stages of deal closure and probabilities related to that). The facets I've just described resemble a subset of CRM called sales force automation (SFA), a topic I cover thoroughly in Chapter 4, so I won't go into it right now. Suffice it to say, this differs from CRM.

However, there are things that involve sales management that don't involve CRM, such as managing the other salespeople on your sales teams (for example, training sales people in techniques to close deals) or developing a sales-oriented culture. CRM isn't part of the human resources issues involving salespeople. It doesn't concern itself with recruiting salespeople or creating mentoring programs for the younger salespeople. Though it does concern itself with the compensation of those salespeople, CRM primarily concentrates on tracking commissions and management by objectives (MBOs). In other words, CRM is concerned with the variable compensation that is directly or indirectly related to the sales deal and not, ordinarily, the recording, analyzing, setting, or identifying of fixed compensation, such as salaries.

There are distinct differences between sales management and CRM's sales force automation, too. Look at this description of IBM Global Service's sales force in a recent Sales & Marketing Management Top Sales Force Awards chart from the November 2000 website:

> As the IT consulting and services arm of IBM, Global Services salespeople have to be well-trained in how to sell to high-level executives and use e-commerce. The education has obviously paid off: This is Big Blue's fastest growing division.

CRM doesn't concern itself with the salesperson's ability to sell to high-level executives, just the results of the attempts to sell to high-level executives. If an IBM Global Services salesperson went to speak with the executive vice president mentioned in the example in Chapter 2, CRM applications would provide the salesperson with the information on that EVP from the customer database repository. CRM applications would allow the salesperson to add to that repository by tracking the results of the meeting and the level of influence this EVP had. It wouldn't provide the training for high-level executive pitches; that's sales management.

CRM is a business strategy with technology being a critical component. It involves the measurement of the lifetime value of a customer so that weight can be given to attention to each customer. CRM also encompasses analytical, operational, and collaborative functions. It involves not just sales, but also partnerships, marketing, and customer service. In other words, sales management pales by comparison when it comes to attempting to ensure that customers have a lifelong relationship with companies. In its classically narrow definition, sales management concerns itself with maintenance and improvement of that part of the customer relationship that involves the sale itself. Customer acquisition and retention are secondary considerations to the sale. That is a narrow definition and I'm sure there are those who would dispute this one, but that's okay. That said, let's now move on.

Contact Management: Not Your Father's (or Mother's) CRM

Another easy source of confusion is CRM and contact management. I've often been asked a question something like this: "Doesn't ACT! do that?" (ACT! being one of the leading contact management software applications available today). On occasion, my answer has been yes. But even then, the context is very different and the power is too. It's the equivalent example of seeing a lion in your house and saying, "Oh, that's a nice kitty, isn't it?" ACT! and Goldmine up to version 4.0 were often assumed to be what was meant by CRM. They are not. They are contact managers. Goldmine, with the release of version 5.0 and a name change to Goldmine Front Office 2000, has made a transformation that brings them closer to being a sales force automation tool. In 2000, Goldmine became a division of Frontrange Solutions, they added a customer call center product called Heat, and pushed into wireless eCRM with the late 2000 announcement of Goldmine Everywhere Server. This has brought them considerably closer to broad CRM functionality, removing them from the world of contact management.

However, contact managers are essentially only an evolutionary step up from personal information managers. Don't get me wrong. Contact managers (especially ACT! 2000) have real value. Small businesses can often use them in lieu of CRM. They have many of the features that are defined by sales force automation packages, but they are not SFA. They are certainly not CRM. Table 3-1 points out a few of the differences between the two packages.

Table 3-1: Some Differences Between Contact Managers and CRM Applications

Contact Management	CRM Applications
Functionality limited to contacts and some associated sales functions.	Functionality encompasses sales, marketing, customer service, and analytics.
Some sales processes embedded. No (or limited) customization possibilities.	Embedded best practices and sales processes that are also entirely customizable to fit.
Views limited to contact related with tabs such as notes/history, opportunities associated with the contact, and so on.	Views nearly unlimited and customizable to any degree of complexity.
Limited data synchronization, if any.	Data synchronization for both the desk-bound and the mobile sales professional.
No real integration with legacy systems. Primarily standalone.	Integration through native hooks or through powerful third-party tools.
Can be Web ready, but not often built for Web. Multiple users tend to be client/server based.	Frequently built from ground up for Web.
Not too scalable. Even the network versions are focused on the very small office. Not designed for more than a few handfuls.	Can be scaled to tens of thousands of users or down to less than ten.

Really, that's all there is to say about it. Sales management and CRM are different. Contact management and CRM are different. That is the end of the matter. On to CRM and its offshoots!

Chapter 4

Sales Force Automation: Good Products Aren't Enough

It used to be, back in the good old days, selling a product to a customer was enough to ensure success—if it was a good product. However, while that is generally still true, it is no longer enough. There are dozens of similar good products competing for markets that have worldwide scope and localized distribution needs. With the accession of the Internet to the mainstream, small and large companies compete to do business in the same marketplaces. It is no coincidence that customer retention has become one of the primary focuses of contemporary sales and marketing. It is easy to be lured away by Cathay's riches when the distance between you and Cathay is just a website away. No longer is Marco Polo necessary to bring back silk, gold, and gems. Get on the Web, order bullion and brocades, and get them via FedEx the next day by 2:30 P.M.

Suddenly sales process command and control, and tracking customers and potential customers, are high-powered necessities. For every Dell, there is a Hewlett Packard, Compaq, Gateway, and Micron lurking. For every Macy's, there is a Nordstrom selling the same merchandise at pretty much the same price. For each time you see a commercial for IBM, there is another one from Microsoft. What's a company to do?

Sales force automation (SFA), a candidate for father of CRM, is the answer to the salesperson's prayers. SFA is designed to help salespeople acquire and retain customers, reduce administrative time, provide robust (the industry's favorite word) account management, and, basically, to make salesperson activities something that earns them and their companies money.

Acquiring Customers Means Keeping Them

If there is anything that can blanch a sales manager's skin, it is the fear of losing customers. The process involved in getting a new customer is not only costly in pure financial terms, but it is also a psychic drain on sales teams. Retaining that same customer is far less costly and much more a matter of relationships—not products.

The cost of a Web commerce customer acquisition in pure dollar terms is often seen to be roughly 1.5 to 2.5 times the value of an average sale. For example, the online Gap retailer might spend between $100–120 to acquire a customer, who will then spend $75 on a clothing sale. What's the value? If he or she does it twice, the Web retailer's acquisition becomes profitable. Then the value of retention becomes obvious.

Shop.org, in a study released in late 2000 based on survey responses from 66 North American online retailers, showed that customer acquisition costs continue to decline from a high of $71 during Q4 1999, to $45 in Q1 2000, to $40 in Q2 2000. While that still isn't low, Shop.org thinks this is due, in part, to a shift away from relatively expensive television advertising to online advertising and marketing. I would venture to say that the use of more effective Web-based customer acquisition applications and methods have some bearing on this thankfully declining cost.

The bigger problem is that in the B2C and B2B markets, customer retention has never seemed to be high-priority until recently. For example, the online pure-play "e-tailer" (such as barnesandnoble.com) spends 76 percent of their revenues on acquiring customers and 3 percent on retaining them. That isn't necessarily bad or good, but it recognizes the cost of acquisition versus the cost of retention, not good or bad marketing decisions. In fact, according to a study published by *The Industry Standard* magazine in November 2000, it is *five times* more costly to acquire customers than to keep them.

Compounding the problem is that it is so much easier to switch from one product to another these days. A mouse click or two and a delete checkbox or three and you have switched merchants. The cost of customer switching is very, very low to the customer. It is compounded by the increasing similarity between products. What is the difference between ordering this book from amazon.com or from a brick-and-mortar Barnes and Noble bookstore? Well, there are some differences that can be outlined. But what's the difference between ordering from amazon.com or barnesandnoble.com? Actually, this question will be answered more than rhetorically in Chapter 6. But for now, let's leave it as a rhetorical question. For the customer, there is very little obvious difference at all.

Sales Force Automation: The Purpose

What is then expected of successful sales force automation? Not just the standard increases in revenue and margin. With the success of the "intangibles measurement" methodology represented by the Balanced Scorecard, there are means for quantifying measurements of customer satisfaction and sales force effectiveness that complement increases in the bottom line, as tangible as those increases are.

Increased Revenue

Needless to say, this is the *ne plus ultra* result for SFA: improvement in the bottom line. But a gross increase is not a sufficient answer for SFA success. Just as important are the increases in revenue per salesperson and in the gross profits per year. If you have an increase of 100 percent in sales revenues but your cost of sales has increased, or it came strictly as a result of your increased sales force, your SFA implementation failed.

Cost Reduction in Cost of Sales

Interestingly, this is a key parameter for success in an SFA implementation. There is an enormous amount of time used by salespeople in coordination of their efforts, continuous, repetitive data entry, and often unsuccessful attempts to extract and interpret data without the tools to do so. Studies have been done that show that sales time to fulfill administrative functions is almost half of a salesperson's activity. By reducing the time engaged in these administrative or other non–sales-related efforts, the cost of sales is reduced.

Customer Retention Due to Company, Not Product or Service

If your customers are happy, they stay with you, even if they are paying a bit more. Myer Emco, a very successful customer home theater and consumer electronics equipment installer, puts a large amount of time into making sure their customers get excellent service. They probably are 10 to 15 percent more expensive than comparable retail equipment dealers in the Washington, D.C., metro area. However, they have a loyal clientele willing to pay the extra cost, simply because the level of personal service is so effective. It's not about the money, it's about the relationship with the company and, often, the relationship with particular salespeople within the company.

Sales Force Increasing Mobility

The Web is transforming as it creates the New Economy. Perhaps the best example is the increasing use of personal digital assistants (PDAs), such as the Palm or Blackberry's RIM for Internet access. Wireless applications companies are proliferating. Aether Technologies grew from 70 employees to more than 800 in a year, went public, started an acquisition binge and then, after all this, in late 2000, announced proudly that they had their first customer! Wireless Web applications and Web/phone convergence are creating an unprecedented buzz in an IT world that is known for its loud buzzing. Just recently, Handspring, the creator of the Visor PDA, announced that the Visor would have an add-in module that would plug into the back of its unique PDA that would allow Visor to operate as a cellphone. The sales force is out of the office more often than ever—meeting customers, moving through airports, prospecting for leads on Broadway with their PDAs. This is making mobility a competitive issue, requiring effective competitive mobile tools, such as the

Internet and the handhelds. Most CRM companies are moving quickly to establish wireless components for sales, such as SalesLogix for Web phones and handhelds, Siebel Wireless, or the wireless access to the various SFA.com portals.

Easily Available Customer Information with Single View

There are multiple departments that have an interest in viewing the status of a customer account or opportunity. For example, the sales department wants to see the status of opportunities. The accounting department wants to see the state of invoicing and billing for the same accounts. The marketing department wants to see reports on varying degrees of success or failure of their campaigns with individual accounts.

Within each department are individuals with different roles who each have their own agendas for what passes through their crosshairs. The vice president of sales wants to see all the activity of all salespeople in his department, including their contact lists and opportunities. He also wants to get a sales pipeline report to refine his sales forecasts for the coming quarter. The account manager doesn't need that much. He wants a national view of all of the sales activity around the accounts he owns (for example, all the sales meetings and reports related to IBM or 3COM or whoever the customer happens to be at any given moment). The sales manager wants to see opportunity progress, but not all the contact lists of each salesperson. Each salesperson wants to manage the customer accounts he owns. Each of them has the individual view that allows them to see all the data they need to—that is, have the permissions to see—but at the same time, there is a universal view of all the data available to all departments at all times.

The Biggest Barrier to Successful SFA

Salespeople must use it, not merely acquiesce to it or grumble about the learning curve.

Michael Simpson, chief marketing officer for Interact Commerce Corporation, sees it this way:

> Salespeople have to see it as a tool to help them, not as a tool for "big brother" to make them accountable. If they don't enter the customer contact information and properly track their sales through the predetermined corporate sales process, as Solution

Selling, Miller Heiman, and the like suggest, the data that management is using will be inaccurate and essentially useless. Therefore, usability and a short learning curve should be paramount to the software selection process. It is also critical to roll out quickly to show a return on investment as fast as possible. Salespeople are skeptics and individualists. Because they will always look for excuses to not use any corporate-mandated solution, they must feel part of the process.

Sales force automation emerged to allow individuals to not only manage their contacts, but also to allow businesses to manage their accounts. The difference is that in a business, the relationship is owned by the company, not the individual. The larger the organization, and the larger the customer account, the more people are required to be involved with each sale. Sales force automation originated for three primary beneficiaries: the individual salesperson, his or her sales team, and their management. Of course, the customer ultimately benefited because of better service during and after the initial sales process, but just like the bottom line is for most business decisions, the initial purpose of SFA was somewhat self-serving for the company implementing it. One of those purposes was raw efficiency, by enabling sales teams to work better together. If more than one person is involved in an account, such as telesales helping the major account representative to generate business in remote offices after you get a corporate contract, it is critical that everyone understands the history and future plans for the account.

In an ideal world, businesses would be able to continue a successful relationship with a customer regardless of who is on the account. Of course, that's impractical, but it becomes more likely if there is a shared knowledge of the past interactions with that customer. A shoebox or file folder with a bunch of business cards and notes is like crashing, clearing the wreckage, and starting over from scratch. But an online, shared history of an account that includes not only all contacts, but also all promises, conversations, negotiations and meetings is more like refueling in midair.

The business transaction history is as important as the human relationship, so for larger organizations, contact management software doesn't go far enough—especially where there is management accountability or team selling involved.

Sales Force Automation: Functionality

At its roots, SFA has the same fundamental features, regardless of vendor. The differences between vendors are normally small, though there are some differences that are worth looking at. The treatment of the core features tends to vary only in the depth provided and the look and feel of the interface. Accessing feature A from feature B might differ from application to application, but feature A and feature B are both extant on all SFA applications. Some of the additional features or modules added to some of the vendor's suites are a bit of a stretch, others are interesting functional additions, and a few are genuinely useful and unique. But, at the core, the features provided are lead management, contact management, account management, opportunity management, sales pipeline management, sales forecast tools, quotations and orders, a toolkit for customizing the application, and an engine for data synchronization.

Contact Management

As you saw in Chapter 3, contact management is a basic sales tool; it has entire applications devoted to it. ACT! has had millions of devotees over the years. Contact management as a module takes on an added degree of complexity when it is integrated into an SFA package, primarily because it has to be linked to all the other modules incorporated. So, for example, when you see Paul Greenberg's name and the company Live Wire, Inc., depending on the specific application you are using, you are hyperlinked to the account management module by clicking on the name Live Wire, Inc. Or click the specific one-line Paul Greenberg activity description and be transported to the activity section where you can get details of his specific activity with your sales team.

Otherwise, contact management covers the basics: name, address, phone numbers, company, title, personal and business information; activity related to the individual; attachments related to the individual; and level of the decision maker. Some applications, such as Siebel Sales, are able to take this contact information and create organization charts for salespeople so they can see whom they have to deal with at what level of the customer's hierarchy—a useful feature, indeed. The most sophisticated versions will include contact behavior characteristics so that each behavior can be associated with templated next steps—valuable for rookie salespeople.

Account Management

This standard feature allows the salesperson or sales manager to handle individual corporate accounts. (See Figure 4-1.) Each account has multiple links to other information, beyond the corporate name or address, including the contacts by corporation and the proposed opportunities by corporation. Fundamentally, it is another view of the customer and potential data that is designed to work with sales departments that have account managers or that want corporate information. It can include either general or highly detailed views of an enterprise.

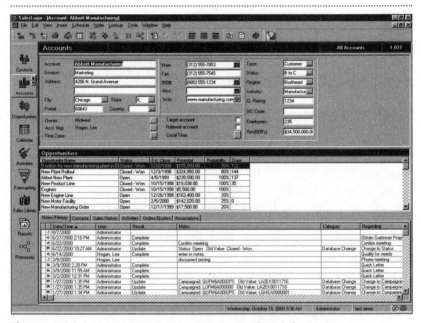

Figure 4-1: SalesLogix2000 Accounts management screen. Typical of account management functionality (Copyright 2000, Interact Commerce Corporation. All rights reserved.)

Opportunity Management

This is often seen as the most essential of the SFA modules. With no drama intended, it is here that deals can be won or lost. The facets that opportunity management covers include the specific opportunity, the company it belongs to, the salesperson or team that is working it, the assignment of revenue credits if there is a sales team, the potential for the closing of this particular opportunity, the final results of this opportunity, the stage of the sales process this opportunity is in, and the potential closing date (sadly, a dynamic function) for the opportunity. (See Figure 4-2.) Additionally, competitive information is included here: who is specifically competing for the opportunity against your company and how big a threat they represent. Even more interesting, in the better SFA packages, a competitive product matrix can be brought up to see how well your product stacks up against the competition's product equivalent. This can give the salesperson a valuable selling point.

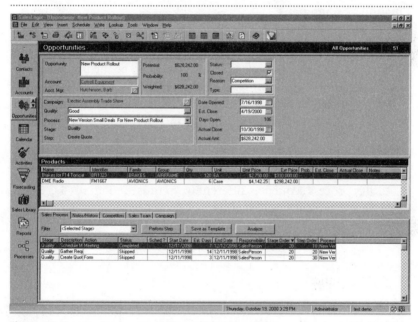

Figure 4-2: Opportunity management is probably the most important function in SFA (Copyright 2000, Interact Commerce Corporation. All rights reserved.)

If the product is really sophisticated, it can provide information on what the weights of different things are to the customer, for instance, how much does price/cost weigh in against functionality, ease of use, availability, maintenance services, or whatever other criteria you want to compare? This provides a decided sales edge. If the salesperson knows that price is less important than availability and rapid delivery, he or she can make the immediate delivery of the goods more important than the price in discussions with the client, since price isn't the primary issue.

Lead Management

If your company buys leads and qualifies them, there has to be some way to weigh prospective value. Lead management functionality can be seen as a subset of opportunity management, though I'm sure there are those who don't see it that way. A qualified lead becomes an opportunity. With SFA packages that have strong lead management features, the salesperson can import leads from multiple sources and, using criteria established through the sales process, weigh the potential of these leads to become opportunities.

Pipeline Management

The "sales pipeline" is a peculiar term for the execution of the established sales process. Each company has its criteria for what constitutes its sales process, but opening and closing tend to be the process bookends. For example, one company could set up salesperson objectives that are weighed by the steps of the sales process. One typical sales process sequence could be the one outlined in Figure 4-3, which shows the SalesLogix2000 visual process generator. The pipeline process reflected in the largest SFA packages may be similar to that in Figure 4-4, a PeopleSoft/Vantive CRM 8.0 pipeline.

A sales process sequence different from those in Figures 4-3 and 4-4, but also typical, could be this:

1. Prospecting

2. Potential lead

3. Qualification

4. Opportunity

5. Building vision

6. Short list

7. Negotiation

8. Closed: won or lost

In other words, every company has its own sales process. The variations may not be infinite, but they are extensive. If you can successfully embed your sales process into the SFA application, you can use the application as it was meant to be used.

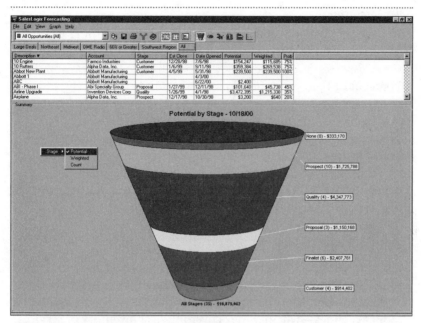

Figure 4-3: Pipeline management à la SalesLogix2000 (Copyright 2000, Interact Commerce Corporation. All rights reserved.)

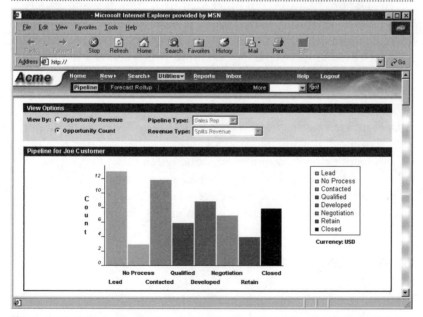

Figure 4-4: For larger implementations, PeopleSoft CRM eSales 8.0 (Copyright 2000 PeopleSoft, Inc. All rights reserved.)

Sales Forecasting

Part of pipeline management is getting the forecasts from sales and then managing the sales activities to those forecasts. Let's face it: if your salesperson is expected to do $2.5 million in business and does 40 percent of that, you (and he) have a serious problem. If that is due to poor forecasting tools that add to the problem, the SFA also has a problem. However, most SFA programs have adequate sales forecasting tools—fairly sophisticated spreadsheet-like tools for forecast fundamentals. But most sales forecasts are still nothing more than good guesses, regardless of how many algorithms you stuff in a program. The value of the tools lies in the management of the guesses in near-real time.

Quotations and Orders

Most good SFA packages have automated generation of quotations and orders. However, what goes into customizing the system to be able to automate that order/quote generation is not a small matter. Product catalogs—whether they cover physical inventory or services offered—have to be created. All the services, products, and combinations of services and/or products have to be entered into a catalog, given an appropriate SKU or other identifying number, and associated with a base price. Then a pricing schedule that allows for special discounts, volume discounts, timed discounts, and such has to be created based on some criteria. For example, your salesperson might be selling 10,000 units of tubing to a valuable customer that you know is being courted by another tubing company. The normal pricing schedule, the North American one, sets a discount of 5 percent for 10,000 units or more of SKU#122222, 1-inch copper tubing. To prepare a quote that would be good for this customer, another pricing schedule for valued customers can be added to this quote, offering an additional 2 percent discount so that a 7 percent total discount is offered. Imagine what goes into creating all that. This is what a good quotation and order generation system in SFA can do.

Sales Force Automation: The Technology

What makes SFA powerful is not just the functionality, but also the combination of the functionality and the flexibility of the technology. The two make SFA useful to both the professional on the road and the manager back at headquarters. It allows them to each ana-lyze data, stay on top of opportunities, embed best practices for future salespeople, and do it with a desktop or a PDA.

One of the most significant technologies is data synchronization. I'm going to give you a flavor of its power so you can understand a bit about what's under the SFA's hood.

Data Synchronization

Data synchronization is the process of updating information among unconnected computers—laptop, mobile, or desktop. Each synchro-nized system gets data that conforms with the data on any other dis-parate system. Salespeople in the field can maintain a subset of the master database and update their local data while others are working with the same data simultaneously. Synchronization also allows cor-porate managers and sales teams to share information created by field salespeople, such as meeting notes, schedules, and forecasts.

Important recent sales trends related to mobility and wireless data make synchronization even more important:

▶ Salespeople are spending more time out of the office with cus-tomers and prospects. Many salespeople are telecommuting—working out of their homes rather than in corporate branch offices.

▶ Salespeople operate as members of sales teams as products become more complex and technical, so the need to share information grows.

▶ Entire sales and marketing organizations are using computer-based customer, sales, and project information to sell more effectively. Field salespeople can leverage this information to close sales faster, and managers can access information input in the field.

This means that for SFA, data synchronization becomes a most essential piece of technology.

The Data Synchronization Process

Data synchronization takes up a fair amount of network infrastruc-ture bandwidth. It actively involves a lot of what comprises the cor-porate information system. To take a look at the technical steps in data synchronization from a lay standpoint, we are going to examine SalesLogix2000 data synchronization, which is one of the most sophisticated CRM data synchronization processes on the millennial market.

How Does It Work?

Field salespeople with laptop computers need to download a pertinent subset of data, manipulate and update the data, and reconcile their changes with the new information from the host database. The typical process of synchronizing data between remote and host systems requires several basic steps, as illustrated in Figure 4-5.

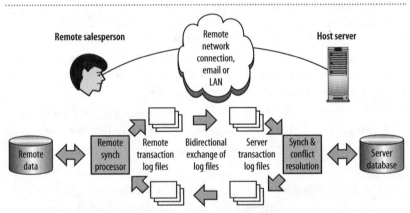

Figure 4-5: SalesLogix2000 data synchronization requires a bidirectional exchange of data between host systems and remote users. The server system should support multiple remote connections at the same time (Copyright 1999, Interact Commerce Corporation. All rights reserved. Reprinted with permission of Interact Commerce Corporation.)

Remote databases are created for mobile salespeople and branch offices. Each database is a relevant *subset* of the corporate database. For example, the information on a field salesperson's laptop need only pertain to his particular accounts.

The synchronization system tracks changes pertinent to the particular salesperson to both the remote databases and the host database. Remote salespeople can connect to the home office using low bandwidth modems or wide area network (WAN) connections. Salespeople or managers who are at a desk can connect via their local area network (LAN). During the connection, log files are exchanged that contain new information to be updated in the respective databases. After the connection is completed, new data is applied to each database so that each database has up-to-date information. It is estimated by the Gartner Group that by using the localized version of data synchronization, where, in effect, only updates are being done, 50 percent of the communications costs will be saved.

Flexibility and Performance

A synchronization system should be capable of supporting large-scale field implementations with potentially hundreds of users, even if your remote sales force is currently small. Some synchronization systems perform fine in small test environments but become impractical in real-world situations, especially for large groups. Besides using the most efficient means to distribute and post data, as discussed above, flexible support for modern client/server databases is critical to meet the demands of data synchronization.

High-performance synchronization requires powerful database capabilities and performance only currently available in databases such as Microsoft SQL Server or Oracle. The synchronization system should take advantage of standard SQL database technology and should support the database standards of your company. Nonetheless, the synchronization engine must be database independent to allow different database systems to reside on remote and host systems. For example, the remote system may use Borland InterBase, but the host system might be Oracle.

Synchronization in Contact Managers

Many companies are using popular contact managers as inexpensive and informal sales automation "solutions" for their field salespeople. While shrink-wrapped contact managers provide easy tools for salespeople to maintain their contact lists, companies using these quickly discover their limitations in synchronizing data. Synchronization features found in these products are inflexible, difficult to administer, and often do not work at all. The result is "islands of data"—critical sales information that isn't shared with others and is often lost when a salesperson leaves the company.

Contact managers use simple flat-file database technology that doesn't support the robust requirements of data synchronization, especially for larger sales forces. Unlike true sales automation software, crude synchronization features found in contact managers were added on as an afterthought, rather than being a core part of the initial system design.

Reporting Tools

The importance of reporting is often underestimated. However, lack of or poor reporting can lead to bad strategic or tactical decisions, redundant work efforts, and missed opportunities. As large companies open more offices and as small companies allow more telecommuting, the need for tight communication becomes paramount. Good reporting tools as part of the technology of SFA (and CRM) are essential.

Many of the reporting tools embedded in SFA applications are third-party tools. The most popular is Seagate's Crystal Reports, which has 160 original equipment manufacturer (OEM) deals. These deals embed the software into other software that is marketed with Crystal Reports as its reporting tools.

Reporting is the creation of customized onscreen or printed views that provide the viewer/reader with information specifically in the form they want and with the content they want. Crystal Reports has a strong report-processing engine that is newly Web optimized. The essential technical factor is the use of dynamic data sources to generate reports by passing the report as it is generating to the client's browser page by page, not report by report. Even more interesting in Crystal Reports 8.0 is the use of Dynamic HTML (DHTML) so that the reports can be seen on your screen in real time. Additionally, there is an option that allows the report to be generated in Java, if you are a Java-centric company. For those applications that need an embedded report viewer in Java, there is a Java Bean option to do that. The report engine supports all the major relational and flat-file databases.

What makes this so valuable is that the engine pulls information from multiple sources, including your financial applications, your customer data repository, and your SFA application, and can put together reports on an ad hoc basis that can be dynamically altered. For example, you can view the sales figures for the year, quarter, or month, by customer, salesperson, or profitability—all by simple drag-and-drop operations. It saves money, makes analysis easier, and can be critical for decision making.

So there is significant functionality and significant technology embedded in SFA applications. Who are the market leaders in SFA? What differs them from one another? Well, that leads me to…

Who's On First?

There are a lot of SFA providers out there, since this is the father of all CRM applications. I'm just going to expose the top five to you because, frankly, there isn't the room to do anything else and because these five represent the best in the business—both large enterprise/ Fortune 500 and mid-market. Each of them is far more than just an SFA company. They are all CRM companies. In Chapter 10, I'm going to do more extensive profiles of the major CRM companies, but here, I'll concentrate on those aspects related to the category near and dear to your enterprise-sized hearts: sales.

Siebel Systems

Siebel and Oracle are inextricably tied. Tom Siebel, founder of Siebel Systems, is an ex-Oracle-employeed protégé of Oracle chairman Larry Ellison and is now apparently at odds with him. Remarkably similar in personality, the two are in constant competition for a dominant CRM market position in the Fortune 1000 domains. For now, Siebel is dominant, owning between 15 and 18 percent of the CRM market and 22 percent of the SFA space—primarily due to their exceptional products and their incredible market reach.

Siebel's rise comes for a good reason: excellent products that are almost infinitely scaleable and entirely interconnected. Siebel's strategy has been to acquire companies to gain both functionality and market dominance. For example, to add online, interactive functionality for its partner management, customer services, and sales and marketing, Siebel acquired Onlink Technologies for $609 million. In an attempt to improve their position in CRM financial services, Siebel acquired Janna Systems, Inc., for $975 million in stock. Janna's product, Enterprise Suite 2001, is aimed at investment banking, institutional sales, and research customers and held a controlling position in the financial services market at the time of acquisition (late 2000).

In addition to its acquisitions, Siebel aligns itself with major enterprises that can benefit its e-business strategy. IBM and Siebel have a completely integrated alliance, with IBM Global Services training thousands of its consultants in Siebel implementations, and IBM making Siebel its standard CRM product sale. A similar alliance, though less closely knit, has been developed with EDS. Siebel has a partnership with supply chain giant *i*2 to provide a complete suite of customer management and fulfillment tools. It is partnered with Cisco so that Cisco's ICM software provides computer telephony interface (CTI) services to Siebel applications. *Ad infinitum.*

Siebel's enterprise product suite is both broad and deep. Since this chapter is on SFA, I'm going to concentrate on the SFA applications. Even there, besides Sales.com, which I will address later in this chapter, Siebel has two SFA products: Siebel Sales, the classic large enterprise version, and Siebel Sales Midmarket Edition, a feature-reduced, less scalable version of Siebel Sales.

The functionality of the enterprise suite borders on the remarkable, creating a product that is feature-rich and learning-curve steep. Typical features are opportunity management, account management, contact management, activity tracking, message broadcasting, Siebel Search, quotas, and incentives functionality; not all that unusual for the base characteristics. Once the implementation is complete, though, the value is immense. A bit of a warning: Siebel implementations can take up to a year or more in a large enterprise, and even the smaller implementations are months long, not weeks. The larger implementations cost tens of millions of dollars. The midmarket implementations can also be expensive if the various, seemingly necessary modules such as eChannel are added.

I'm going to sample the depth so you can see what complexity an SFA application could have. Please take the time to look it over carefully because these are the functions you have to consider when you are planning an implementation of CRM or SFA. It could be overkill or it could be less than you need, though I doubt the latter. Regardless, these are what you are going to be looking at in your feature search.

In the Opportunity Management section of Siebel Sales, you see the following subcategories:

My Opportunities A screen defining the sales representative's current sales opportunities.

My Team's Opportunities If the sales representative is part of a sales team, this shows what all members of the sales team are working on individually. It can be drilled down by opportunity to show the revenue crediting for each sales representative on the team.

All Opportunities Depending on the roles of the individual and the security levels of each, this can show enterprise-wide sales opportunities, regardless of team or individual.

Activities This screen shows the current opportunity-based activities, such as meeting with client *x*.

Attachments This could be a contract, a customer's request for proposal, or a product brochure. It gives the sales team access to various opportunities-related documentation.

Campaign Leads Tied into the Siebel eMarketing application (which was acquired with the purchase of Paragon Software in January 2000), this is the leads list generated through marketing campaigns.

Competition This is detailed information on competitors for this opportunity and the level of threat they represent, plus a competitive product matrix.

Contacts Here are contact lists for anyone who would be appropriately engaged to close the opportunity.

Manager's Explorer The sales manager can look at a total sales department view of all or any of these screens.

Notes If there are notes taken by a salesperson attached to the opportunity, they reside here.

Organizational Analysis This is the decision maker's organization chart—the chain of command drilled down with details on the activity of any of the decision makers.

Products This is a preconfigured, customized product list that has pricing, SKU numbers, and any other detail desired so that quotes can be easily configured and integrated with the back end. It is a catalog of those products that are specifically associated with the opportunity.

Profile This is a profile of the opportunity, including a customer profile, an opportunity profile, and what is called a compelling event description—the motivating factor that makes the potential customer interested in the deal.

Quotes This is a very detailed section that provides automatically generated quotes, with discounts for the deal, volume discounts, or line item discounts, if that's what is demanded. It also can autogenerate an order if the deal is closed.

User-Defined Fields If this isn't enough, you can customize your own fields to show enterprise-appropriate information and methodology.

Charts This makes it all graphic, with the most significant chart being the sales pipeline chart, which identifies the success of the individual salesperson according to sales methodology and the management by objectives (MBOs) attached to each phase of the sales methodology.

This is just one area of detail for Siebel, which also provides contact management, sales pipeline forecasting, quotations, and lead management, among its many features. Currently, Siebel is the undisputed large enterprise market SFA industry leader.

Clarify

Clarify is no longer independent; Nortel now owns it. Clarify has a decent sales component, but is known for its call center capabilities, which is the likely main attraction for Nortel. The call center will be covered in Chapter 9, but a brief look at the Clarify Sales Solution is in order. Clarify Sales Solution is part of the Clarify EFrontOffice 9.0 suite.

There are four products associated with it, though at least one of them is not really functionally a part of the solution unless you buy into the "call centers are profit and opportunity centers" scenario that I mention in Chapter 9. Clarify's ClearSales product does the traditional SFA things: contact management, opportunity management, quotations, lead management, pipeline management, and the like; nothing outstanding or different here. The two products that do stand out a bit are the ClearSales Configurator and the ClearSales Commissions application. The Configurator is a sales order process configuration tool that works on predeveloped business rules and pricing schedules so that orders and quotes can easily be done through drag and drop. The extreme flexibility of the tool is its great benefit. The Commissions tool is almost an application unto itself. It is designed to develop sales compensation programs for salespeople, value-added resellers (VARs), distributors, and partners. It's done so that the interface is simple—a spreadsheet. It not only can develop complex compensation plans, but it can maintain and administer them too. It's a front-office tool with some back-office functionality.

The fourth tool is the Clarify Call Center, which is an overall name for a number of call center–related components. This is their flagship application. While you can always make something of a case for including a call center (now a customer interaction center) in an SFA suite, it is a stretch to include what is essentially a huge customer service application in the suite. However, it is a good product that stands on its own.

PeopleSoft/Vantive CRM

When PeopleSoft purchased Vantive and its second-place 6 percent CRM market share in 1999, there were a number of pundits who questioned the purchase, wondering what PeopleSoft thought they were doing entering the CRM world. With the release of PeopleSoft CRM 8.0 in mid-2000, it's now apparent they knew exactly what they were doing. Vantive's CRM Fortune 1000–level functionality is fully integrated into the PeopleSoft 8.0 product suite, which has been rearchitected from the ground up. The integration of Vantive and PeopleSoft in the pure CRM world is even more complete. In fact, PeopleSoft CRM is called "PeopleSoft CRM, powered by Vantive Enterprise." According to PeopleSoft, the CRM suite now makes up the bulk of their sales. This seems to be the case, as the rise of PeopleSoft CRM has placed PeopleSoft on a par with Siebel according to an October 2000 *Computerworld* article that calls PeopleSoft one of the largest CRM vendors—a successful reinvention of the former ERP company.

There are a number of distinguishing features in the PeopleSoft CRM product suite that separate it from the general CRM pack. The use of knowledge management tools, integration of the front and back offices, integration of the analytic tools that are part of PeopleSoft, strong Web integration, and the tools that Vantive itself brings to the table all provide a large enterprise CRM with a difference. (For more details on the suite as a whole, see Chapter 10.)

This unique feature set carries to the 2001 edition of Vantive eSales. There's a cornucopia of singular features in Vantive's offering that are designed to expand or enhance the more standard management tools that are general to all SFA products. The features reflected in the CRM corporate Web page shown in Figure 4-6 give you an idea of its strength.

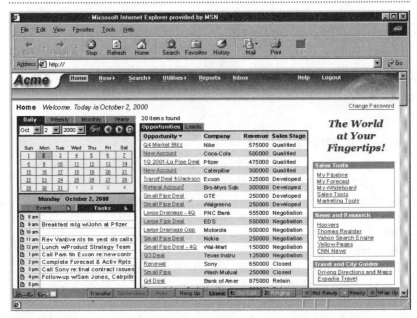

Figure 4-6: The powerful PeopleSoft/Vantive 8.0 CRM home page view (Copyright 2000, PeopleSoft, Inc. All rights reserved.)

The power of integrating the back and front office cannot be underestimated. Integration of any disparate software is difficult enough. Having to integrate a multimillion-dollar ERP implementation and a multimillion-dollar CRM implementation is often nearly impossible and has brought many a company and its system integrator to their knees, begging for mercy. To have integration from the get-go is a timesaver and a money saver. Connectors exist, not only for PeopleSoft, but also for other back-office applications like SAP. In the works is an integration framework product that will make integration with any package easy. This increases the already immense relief of being able to develop compensation plans that are immediately part of your accounting system.

In fact, unlike most SFA packages, PeopleSoft/Vantive eSales adds functions such as enrollment and (literature, not life) fulfillment. You can sign your customer up for a training class and enter them into the rolls of the company—another tie to the back office that, while looking like PeopleSoft's Student Administration functionality, actually comes from the Vantive side.

Equally impressive are the knowledge management tools built into Vantive eSales. Probably the most eye-popping is the Marketing Encyclopedia. The Marketing Encyclopedia provides a repository in the form of a single database that stores product literature, competitive analyses, industry news, sales case histories, and pretty much any sales-related intelligence. What makes this even more fun is that push technologies built into the system can notify sales representatives—by pager or email—when new information that is useful to the particular salesperson is available, such as an updated analyst report on a competitor. So, you can get hot news immediately as it emerges on the website.

Knowledge management doesn't stop there. There is a Capture Insight Tool that will collect critical information and, using the native workflow built into the package, route it appropriately through the sales organization. This workflow engine is powerful, even automating the distribution of leads to partners based on pre-designed criteria for those leads. It can also take prequalified leads that come from marketing campaigns and route them to the appropriate field or inside salespeople or teams. This is what workflow is for. Very few SFA products have this strength. In fact, these workflow properties rival the royal workflow engine of Lotus Notes, the workflow head of state.

A customer data warehouse, something that is not endemic to sales or CRM applications, is a native part of PeopleSoft/Vantive eSales. Through the List Import Wizard, you can import sales contacts and leads, including purchased leads or leads in other external formats to the system.

With the knowledge management and workflow components being so strong, the tools that are designed to use the knowledge effectively are equally powerful. There is actually a best-practices selling tool that prompts the salesperson to ask the right questions and complete the right tasks at each stage of the sales process. This is a rules-based tool that has the characteristics of the best parts of PeopleSoft's enterprise resource planning.

To increase the muscle of this already powerful solution, there is one optional part worth mentioning: PeopleSoft workbenches (now called Insight). The PeopleSoft workbenches were always a major addition to PeopleSoft, providing analytics to the PeopleSoft installation through what is called enterprise performance management (EPM). The analytic workbenches for eSales are personalized and Internet based. They are specific to individual roles, functions, and vertical industries. For eSales, there is a Sales Effectiveness workbench, which can measure individual sales efforts and their impact. Most importantly, there is a Customer Profitability workbench, which can identify what weight to give to which customers—a leg up on the calculation of customer lifetime value (see Appendix B). These are heavy-duty tools. And imagine—browser based, too.

Oracle

Oracle Sales seems to be driven by Oraclesalesonline.com as 2000 comes to a close. Oraclesalesonline.com, a uniquely long URL, is discussed below. Besides that and some retail sales applications, Oracle has two specialized modules for their Oracle Sales Suite. The first is Oracle Incentive Compensation, which integrates back-office financial-compensation processes and front-office sales-oriented functions within the enterprise. The other module is unique to the largest vendors. It is called Oracle Telesales—a call center-enabled application designed for inside-sales representatives, distributors, resellers, and sales executives. It allows sharing of opportunities and forecasts across multiple sales channels. This is a good horizontal module, now being refocused to the online market.

Interact Commerce Corporation

This company is a marvel. Founded in 1996 as SalesLogix Corporation by Pat Sullivan, Interact Commerce Corporation (IACT) jumped to the head of the midmarket pack because of their excellent application suite, the most recent incarnation being SalesLogix2000. Not one to rest on their laurels, Interact reacquired ACT!, a Pat Sullivan co-creation. Staying one step ahead of the technology curve, they developed a highly sophisticated data synchronization engine that both overcame the slowness of MAPI data synchronization (not worth elaborating on) and at the same time set the stage for wireless data synchronization at a transfer rate that was useful, not irritating. From both a functionality and technological standpoint, this product is the real deal.

My company chose to use the SalesLogix2000 SFA suite after an extremely careful and arduous selection process. The selection process criteria and how SalesLogix2000 passed the test are presented here because it will hopefully show what you should be thinking about if you're a midmarket company considering an SFA or CRM implementation. (Of course, there is always the caveat that your company is different from my company.) It also will highlight some of the stronger features of SalesLogix2000. Here they are

Pedigree Pat Sullivan, named one of the top ten influential people in the history of CRM by *CRM* magazine, founded Interact Commerce Corporation. He also was the co-creator of ACT!, the number-one contact manager in the world. The proven track record of ACT! indicated one thing clearly: Pat Sullivan, when he developed SalesLogix2000, knew the needs of salespeople and had a complete understanding of the technology that would meet these requirements.

Vertical market expertise I was able to identify roughly 45 specific vertical markets that SalesLogix2000 had penetrated, including the very difficult legal profession. This means the product is adaptable and customizable.

Toolkit It has the most flexible toolkit on the market. One of the most impressive and useful tools is the visual SalesLogix Architect tool (see Figure 4-7), which allows you to graphically develop sales processes. It can take an existing process and create the flowcharts for that process. You can modify the process directly on the screen. It actually resembles a CASE tool for the masses. It is a truly powerful addition to a great toolbox.

Web-enabled SalesLogix2000 uses a Web client to allow individual access to the complete functionality of the client/server product via the Internet without losing a beat.

Wireless capabilities SalesLogix is enabled for both PDA and Web phone. SalesLogix for Web phones and SalesLogix Wireless for Palm-powered handhelds are their current wireless applications.

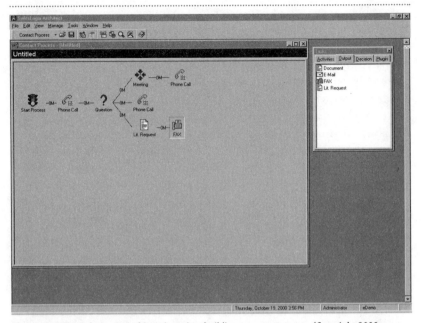

Figure 4-7: The SalesLogix Architect in action, building a contact process (Copyright 2000, Interact Commerce Corporation. All rights reserved.)

Corporate culture Interact Commerce Corporation has an intensely relaxed corporate culture. I went straight to their headquarters and, unlike a number of the other vendors, found them accessible to the top, so that I was able to meet with their corporate chieftains such as Pat Sullivan, CEO and founder, and Mike Muhney, executive vice president in charge of business development. The staff made it clear that partners were a welcome addition to the IACT family.

Functionality SalesLogix2000 is a full-featured application that has lead, account, contact, opportunity, and pipeline management, and quotations, charts, and multiple reporting capabilities. Reporting has recently been enriched with a partnership with Seagate Software. Crystal Reports 8.0 is being included in SalesLogix2000 for increased reporting capabilities. Sales-Logix2000 is structured to scale to the midmarket.

Technology They have the most advanced data synchronization capacity in the industry. The databases it uses are commonplace, including Oracle, Microsoft SQL Server 7.0, and Borland's Interbase engine. The interface is easy to handle. The only difficulties we had were somewhat quirky relations with Windows NT 4.0 Service Pack 6. Otherwise, it was an utterly clean installation/implementation.

Pricing The pricing is actually reasonable. I won't specify this here, since pricing in the eCRM and CRM worlds is very volatile. The unit cost to us was well within the scope of our budget. It had the lowest price of all of the vendors we examined.

Implementation/configuration time The implementation time for a typical SalesLogix implementation is at the outside around three months, far shorter than the much larger and longer Siebel implementation. This represents major increases in potential productivity and cost savings. Ours was shorter than most.

Knowledge of the midmarket IACT has unparalleled knowledge of the midmarket, with more than 3,000 customer implementations in three years. They are the undisputed market leaders in this domain—most likely because they are the only company exclusively focused on this space.

Channel The IACT channel strategy is superlative, leading to around 80 percent of all SalesLogix2000 sales being conducted by IACT partner/resellers. This is comforting to me because it shows the faith the channel puts into the product. There are dozens of technology partners; including Live Wire, which has led to a very large community of producers of additional functionality. That way, I don't have to build the back-office connectivity for SalesLogix2000. I can buy it from Scribe, a company that produces the connectivity, or from any of their many OEMs, such as Sage, Macola, or Made2Manage. I don't need to produce a PRM module. That's done by Elantix, a SalesLogix partner. It made me rest easy to know I can get what I want at a reasonable price and don't have to build it.

SalesLogix2000 is a flexible, successful application that works. What more can I say?

SFA.com

Despite the low entry cost of some of the SFA products, small companies that have no venture capital or angel funding or significant revenue streams still might have a hard time affording SFA. Enter the SFA.com world. SFA.coms are Web "service centers" that provide interactive professional sales tools and services to companies that are too ill-financed to afford the full-figured SFA applications and to small companies that are geographically scattered with a highly mobile workforce that lives on the Net. These dot-coms provide a range of services from free to inexpensive. Their reasonable expectation is that your use of their services will grow with your company. For a small price, they will cover:

- ▶ Calendaring and scheduling
- ▶ Contact management
- ▶ Lead generation (for example, free leads with premium memberships)
- ▶ Task management
- ▶ Pipeline management (some)
- ▶ Forecasting tools (very limited)
- ▶ Reporting tools (small number of customized templates)
- ▶ Customization based on corporate business processes
- ▶ Integration of legacy system data
- ▶ Data synchronization with your favorite PDA (for example, Palm or wireless Web phones)
- ▶ Company briefings (for example, data on private and public companies)
- ▶ Competitor briefings
- ▶ Free consultations with technical support
- ▶ Online education (for example, articles by leading sales experts)
- ▶ Moderated discussion forums with experts for your company or multiple companies
- ▶ International weather, airport reports, and news feeds
- ▶ Collaborative private Web meeting rooms

In other words, these are fully functional online SFA applications for pennies per month. There is an upside to working with these SFA.coms: the service level is solid. Your MIS department has no worries except perhaps some customization and legacy data woes. The downside is your security concerns, which are more often just concerns rather than real risks. The jury is still out regarding scalability, since few of the SFA.coms have a large amount of users yet. The few that do have issues over their high operating costs. Oddly, the most significant weakness of these sites is that the sites are purely SFA. They do not integrate well or at all with marketing applications, customer service applications, and the like. They cannot, at least at this time, provide a full-service eCRM solution. Despite occasional marketing pretensions, they are not realistically an intranet; they are hosted Web solutions.

There are four significant online sales presences, each with a unique model and a separate purpose. While they have a good deal of value to small businesses, they have a tenuous hold, as a dot-com market that isn't profitable is looked upon as happily as an invasion of locusts. In fact, by the end of 2000, Siebel had repurchased Sales.com and brought it into their e-business suite. Interact.com had changed its model from a Web-based services model to a Web-integrated part of SalesLogix and ACT!, purchased as part of the licensing agreement for the applications.

IBM/Salesforce.com

Salesforce.com is the only one of the four major SFA.coms to be independent of a proprietary CRM product. However, that said, it is not entirely independent, having hooked up with IBM in the latter part of 2000. The arrangement with IBM is comprehensive, creating a new website, http://ibm.salesforce.com/. This partnership adds a variety of services through IBM's WebConnections service package. Shared Internet access and business-class email for up to 100 employees, secure remote access, firewall security, website blocking, 24/7 technical support, and an Internet connection via analog, ISDN, or DSL, are all new additions. It remains focused on the small business sales community through the Salesforce.com pedigree.

The Salesforce.com engine functions significantly more like a Web-integrated, client/server version of Siebel or SalesLogix than its pure-Web portal siblings.

This website focuses on providing small businesses with a fairly powerful SFA application. Like the others, it doesn't link directly to any other modules than SFA. It has no interest in propagating anything but itself.

SFA fundamentals are available in rudimentary form: contact, account, opportunity management, calendaring, some not-too-strong sales pipeline analysis, and some forecasting tools.

Sales.com

This is Siebel's stepchild, cast into the world initially as a separate not-Siebel-owned entity, but at the end of 2000 was brought back into the warm Siebel bosom. The portal, http://www.sales.com/, is even built along the lines of Siebel applications including its blue striped color scheme. Not only does it provide the basic sales tools, such as contact, account, and opportunity management, but, with a premium membership, you can generate leads from the Dun & Bradstreet database, get competitive and account intelligence, set up watch lists and monitor competitors or client companies, and, of course, on your personalized desktop, handle your calendar.

This is a one-stop shop for small business SFA on the Web. It is not designed to replace Siebel eBusiness 2000. The likely thinking at Siebel, given the features of the board and the look and feel, is that small companies will grow to the point where they get Siebel Sales, feature-rich and module-happy, with which the small company will already have some familiarity.

Interact.com

Branded by SalesLogix, Interact.com is unique. It is entirely Web-based eCRM and is fully integrated into SalesLogix and ACT! through a hosted service. It all comes together here. It is ultimately aimed at all 42 million sales professionals in the United States. What is particularly fascinating about this site is that it is a transition to a fully SalesLogix- and ACT!-integrated set of services that will eliminate the separate Interact.com Web presence, as rich as it is.

I'm going to spend a bit of time going through this because I think that its model represents a bit of a departure from the typical SFA.com. It combines features of a portal and uses a hosted model (an application service provider (ASP)). It is able to use both CRM and contact management software that can reside on local desktops, laptops, and eventually PDAs, be 100 percent integrated to the application, and provide a level of Web functionality that will make those 42 million sales professionals drool, which will make for a very messy country.

The initial Interact.com core is what they call "Internet Activators," enablers that will integrate specified applications—initially SalesLogix2000 and ACT! 2000, of course—to a raft of other applications, professional and community services, and content. What makes it so interesting is how complete the integration is between the applications and the Web portal. ACT! 2000 and SalesLogix2000 starts out as an extension of the Interact.com portal and eventually, the portal becomes an integrated part of the application. SalesLogix calls it "hot wiring." They use the information that the SFA application or contact manager uses to lock in key data that is secured from the Web. The eventual objective is to evolve and release the successful services through ACT! and SalesLogix directly, including hosted data for Web browser access, Web phone access, and wireless PDA services.

These could also include the ability to

▶ Plan travel, entertainment, and meetings—all from within a personal calendar.

▶ Set up marketing campaigns to qualify leads and make appointments.

▶ Purchase business data from various Internet-based services— that can mean leads, company data, and financial data and news from within contact or account records.

▶ Access automated expense management and reporting.

▶ Participate in online demonstrations, "webinars," and Internet presentations through the community features.

▶ Execute direct marketing campaigns from the application.

▶ Get national digital service.

Not bad for small business, is it? This allows small businesses to be armed with the same tools as considerably larger businesses for considerably less. However, since it is becoming strictly an extension of SalesLogix or ACT! licenses, it may be a little pricier than other options, but still not expensive.

Oraclesalesonline.com

There is a lot to this SFA.com. It is the Web version of a nearly completely featured sales force automation application. That's not surprising, given the marketing strategy behind it. Oracle is offering all the basic SFA modules free online. The idea is that delighted customers will purchase the other Oracle CRM applications, which plug directly into this "webified" SFA. Additionally, there will be some fee-based services that are attached to the site so that Oracle derives some revenue directly from the site. Some of the fee-based services include:

- ▶ Incentive and compensation management

- ▶ Travel and expense management

- ▶ Time and expense reporting

Other SFA modules, such as sales force compensation, are not free and can be add-ins to Oraclesalesonline.com. Among the online application's most advanced features are basic sales forecasting and some pipeline analysis tools. Additionally, unlike the other SFA.coms, it has the facility, though limited, to do partner/salesperson revenue splitting and revenue crediting, to highlight its substantial feature set.

Started in August 2000, by October 2000 it had 6,000 companies using it, and quite a few of them were not small companies at all. For example, companies such as Knight Ridder Publications, India's billion-dollar enterprise Tata Technologies, Rational Software, Oregon Steel Mills, and VTEL Communications were all using the free service—not the market it seemed to be aimed at, but certainly a market that it hit.

Deals with Hoover's Online were completed at the same time to provide services for corporate information and competitive intelligence. Oracle plans to be online with all its CRM by mid-2001. The website is at http://www.oraclesalesonline.com/.

The Verticalization of SFA?

I've said it before and I'll say it again: salespeople are not generalists anymore. They have specific territories, which can be demographic, geographic, or account level. They are industry-specific sales experts—read: vertical marketers. They can be someone in the industry (such as a chemicals salesperson) or someone who is focused on selling into the industry (for example, a salesperson for a procurement software solution that specializes in the chemicals industry). One unique area that is creating a thriving, but still small area of SFA verticalization is in the public sector.

The needs of those salespeople selling into the public sector—federal, state, and local government, and, in a different sense, the education market—are significantly different than others. Rules and regulations, often called "laws" in the case of the public sector, are far more stringent and much more enforced because of the public posture of neutrality that governments are required to have. However, governments are made up of people, and standard networking principles apply there too. It's who you know. The biggest problem is that there are literally millions of government workers and thousands of proposals issued by the federal, state, and local governments in any given month. The public sector market is currently one of the largest market verticals, with total annual contracting activity exceeding $580 billion. The federal government portion of this market alone annually exceeds $230 billion.

Salespeople have a hard time tracking government-issued requests for proposals (RFPs) and the government organizational charts. The standard SFA applications can handle org charts, just not usually with the complexity of a federal agency with assistant- and under-secretaries who are different from executive assistants and secretaries. They also cannot even contemplate the proposal tracking, much less do it. To fill this gap, there is a growing segment of the SFA market dedicated to the special needs of government contractors. One interesting company in this space is epipeline, a product-focused dot-com who actually has a strong SFA/CRM add-on product.

In mid-2000, epipeline launched a Web-based product specifically for contractors competing in the federal procurement market. The core of epipeline's offering is the ability of users to create a focused workspace targeting the identification and management of federal contracting initiatives. What makes this a very powerful SFA add-on is the application toolset. These tools complement the more traditional sales force automation tools found in the other applications mentioned here. The tools are focused more directly on the relationship between opportunity identification and the requisite research contractors need to perform. The product is delivered via a secure

ASP model. Let's do a brief review of the tools, so that the idea of a "vertical" SFA sinks in.

Vertical-specific opportunity delivery Each user or company can construct profiles to provide them with the specific opportunities they are looking for. Thus, the product can deliver business opportunities within the federal contracting vertical to individual users or entire corporate departments. A user can target business development in a wide or narrow geographic boundary, within certain financial ranges, and in very targeted industries. Once a user has identified a relevant opportunity, he or she begins tracking the opportunity with filtered market news items and relevant information from epipeline's research and resource centers. In addition to the proactive opportunity delivery, the epipeline application allows contractors to enter their own opportunities into the shared pipeline.

Vertical opportunity management Shared profiles promote collaboration by allowing users to access identical account views. A sales manager could set up identical profiles for every member on her team to enhance the speed and efficiency at which the team acts on the opportunity and moves into proposal development mode. Each salesperson on the team can set up individual profiles and give the sales manager exclusive access or give the whole team access. Users can attach relevant news and notes to the opportunities they are tracking in a special section of the application entitled, simply enough, Tracked Opportunities.

Research tools Users have the ability to search through 15 years of detailed historical contract information. In addition to past contracting information, users have access to the entire Federal Acquisition Regulation library, a body of regulations governing the activities of procurement officials and vendors during the procurement and fulfillment process, as well as epipeline's proprietary summary information concerning the relevance of regulations and standards.

Contact management This is not really SFA contact management, but rather, it is more focused on content and intelligence. Users can access epipeline's contact directories containing the names and contact information for procurement officers, government contracting audit officials, and congressional staffers, among others, and attach relevant contacts and related notes to tracked opportunities. These are kept up to date by epipeline. In addition, the user can store and reference contacts within his or her company as well as partner companies. Another source of contact information are the Federal Agency Profiles that provide intelligence about the organization, budgets, and acquisition patterns of major agencies within the federal government and the large contractors.

Teaming solutions Teaming in the public sector refers to the collaboration of companies in response to contract opportunities. More often than not, in the federal marketplace, companies join together because of governmental participation mandates requiring the lead contractor to include small businesses in the performance of the contract. Attempting to facilitate partner relationship management (PRM) is at the core of epipeline's teaming and collaborative CRM services. epipeline's teaming network allows contractors to locate potential partners and conduct past-performance analysis in the same virtual workspace. The prime contractor can collaborate with the subcontractor via epipeline's inter-company collaboration tools. Through epipeline's technology partnership with WebEx, teaming companies in different locations can participate in online meetings. epipeline provides a prepopulated database of potential teaming partners to its users. Subcontractors can profile themselves in epipeline's teaming database and build relevant contract history. This almost automatically increases the level of collaboration between you and your partner. These are *strong* PRM features.

The vertical add-ons to SFA can add content and regulatory expertise to the more general SFA applications. While not yet a big market, they play in a big market space. Depending on your corporate focus, they may be worth looking at.

The SFA Return on Investment (ROI)

There is a pre-ROI benchmark that gains a faddish kind of following when a hot stock market becomes shaky. It is called "path to profitability." The prevailing wisdom of the concept works like this: ROI doesn't matter now because you are currently investing what you have to in getting to a point where you become profitable. *Then* you will be looking at ROI, but until then, the investment is in building the road, not traversing it. Most analysts say this is hooey, but you can get away with it for a while. At no time, though, can you turn your back on ROI.

Sales organizations work with fairly straightforward benchmarks for ROI. How many sales ultimately occurred due to the investment in SFA? That is the ROI's bottom line. But it is not the interim lines of ROI. There are a large number of factors in SFA ROI at P-L-A-Y. Some depend on what sales processes you set up. For example, if you are a company devoted to telesales, an increase in the number of successful calls per day per salesperson would be more important than an account manager who is looking more for successes with a longer sales cycle and higher revenue per success. Another metric could be the success of the sales forecast—the closer to 100 percent accuracy, the better. Other metrics could be lowering administrative time, decreasing cost, increasing the win rate, or decreasing the time from process step 1 to process step final. The measurement of ROI is a matter of corporate "taste." Chapter 12 covers CRM ROI in depth.

SFA on the Move: The New Economy's Mobile Sales Force

It's all so cool. You're a salesperson, you're on the road with your cellphone, your PDA, and your wireless modem, and you're young and hip and wow! Good life. How productive is all this really cool stuff, though? What can it do that will at least emulate some of the features of the desktop system or the SFA application? How can it work on your phone?

Most of the SFA applications, such as SalesLogix for Web phones, Siebel Wireless, or PeopleSoft/Vantive's wireless capabilities, do the same basic things. They provide calendar, contact, and account information on the phone or PDA. The types of services you'll be able to get on your Web-enabled cellphone are essentially directory services—names and phone numbers, street and email addresses. Then you make a call or send an email from the phone. This will become part of a viewable history by contact or account. To-do reminders and all those other features you have come to expect in a comprehensive calendar on your desktop will be available on the phone. Actually, what makes this very attractive, if not sexy, is not the features, which are the standard features you can get in SFA applications when it comes to the phone. What *is* sexy is that you don't have to download this information from anywhere or carry out the functions, such as email, elsewhere. It's all on your handheld PocketPC or Palm or in your cellphone; it's self-contained. Synchronization is not necessary. You can be cool, young, and mobile and not tied down to anything but the four winds and your customers— with information at your disposal that only the desk jockeys had access to previously. Plus, if you need to be on the west wind and are floating on the north wind, you can get GPS directions on the phone too!

The under-the-hood features are very strong. Installation is a point and click administrative task. The wireless SFA phone features are registered through a Web URL, the phone is enabled, the data is downloaded to the phone along with the appropriate applications, and you are ready to rock.

Security is also quite good. For example, SalesLogix for Web phones deploys a three-stage security model, similar to the other wireless SFA services, though not identical:

1. Transmission and identification of unique phone ID.

2. Secure data transmission using industry-proven protocols.

3. SalesLogix2000 server data access password protected and security profile driven.

What we have here is a revolution in SFA that has moved from a traditional sales management functionality, to a client/server-based CRM philosophy/architecture/technology and now a wireless, Web-based mobile eSFA. Not bad for something that is both old as eons and new as muons.

Chapter 5

Marketing Automation Isn't Automatic

Companies market. That is, they sell themselves. That is a simple fact of business life. In small companies, the level of marketing that goes on can be as simple as a printed brochure and a website. Even the smallest companies are creating static websites that operate as online brochures for their wares. As companies move up the size scale and the marketing budget scale, campaigns use direct mail, email, promotions, interactive voice response, newsletters, contests, events, and other customer "touch points." Indirect marketing campaigns, such as advertising in the print media or on TV and radio, reach traditional mass markets. Then there is "branding": working with agencies to establish name recognition through public relations, media, and advertising.

The estimated total spending on advertising in the United States is about $187 billion a year, including television, radio, newspapers, magazines, outdoor billboards, telephone directories, direct mail, and the new frontier of Web advertising. That figure is growing at about 7 percent per year. However, traditional methods of advertising (such as media ads) are getting more expensive and more competitive, but yielding less return. Historically, the return has been minimal with the conventional service bureaus only able to engage in limited campaigns and produce subjective metrics that may or may not be accurate. The data collection is sketchy, the turnaround is slow, and much of the analysis and the follow-on marketing campaign modifications are ad hoc. Enterprise marketing automation (EMA), a CRM subset still in its infancy, starts to change all that.

Marketing in the New Economy is neither traditional nor is it "new." It is transitional. It still involves the identification and capture of potential long-term and profitable customers that are appropriate to your business. It is still about the competitive seizure of mindshare and market share within targeted socio-economic segments. It is still promotions and advertising and snail-mail pieces and other direct and indirect means of reaching prospects and customers. It is still a high-ticket item that may, at times, leave a questionable return on investment. It is still a bit of a crapshoot. What *is* new about marketing in the New Economy is enterprise marketing automation—also known as e-marketing—using Web-based applications and the Internet to improve the effectiveness of traditional marketing and to create new methods of Web-focused marketing and campaign management.

Unfortunately, certain marketing truths seem to never change. How many times have you wanted to carry out bodily harm over the phone with telemarketers bombarding you during business hours, dinner hours, and recreation time? I received four phone calls in one day from a bank I happen to have a credit card with. How often have you gotten frustrated at the pop-up window that is advertising something you have no need or desire for? How often have you been swamped by spam—that particularly grating, unsolicited email that seems to be as endless as the viruses produced by 15-year-old hackers? It gets worse when the spammers use programs that change the source subject line each time they send the spam, thus defeating many of the filters on the market.

There actually is a name for this kind of marketing—one that seems obvious. It is called *interruption marketing*. Interruption marketing worked well in the television era when you had four or five major channels with more than 200 million people watching shows, and commercials timed to be pretty much roughly the same time and the same breaks during each network's programming. "Now for a commercial message" was not considered a problem, and the ads held your attention. If you are over 40, it's easy to finish the jingle, "Winston tastes good…" even though the Winston commercials haven't aired for more than 30 years. Even now, on a bad night, a popular TV show like "Friends" will capture 17 or 18 million viewers, and a bad show like… well, a bad show can be considered a flop and still capture 5 million viewers. But this is the era of the Internet and there are more than 2 million commercial websites and 55 million Internet users, which means that the average for each website would be around 27 or 28 visitors. It's a whole new ballgame. The choices per user are endless, and the competitive level between like sites is fierce.

The Core Belief: Embedded Permission Marketing

Seth Godin, Yahoo!'s vice president of direct marketing, claims that the average consumer sees 1 million marketing messages a year—which is roughly 2,800 per day. Think about that. An assault on your senses for items that you most likely ignore or minimally respond to with great irritation. The irritation comes from the lack of control you have over this visceral mugging by muggers who want to not only steal your money but also bury you under junk after the theft. At least, that's how it feels.

How would you respond if you were wooed by someone who meant something to you and with something that could be of value—and it was your decision whether the wooing started and whether it became a courtship? This is *permission* marketing as defined by Mr. Godin in his book *Permission Marketing*. Permission marketing asks for your permission to "speak" with you about its product and, at the same time, provides consideration for your acquiescence every step of the way. Mr. Godin identifies it as "dating your customers" and defines it as a five-step process:

1. Offer the prospect an incentive to volunteer to receive your email or other marketing media.

2. Using the attention offered by the prospect, offer a curriculum over time, teaching the consumer about your product or service.

3. Reinforce the incentive to guarantee that the prospect maintains the permission.

4. Offer additional incentives to get even more permission from the consumer.

5. Over time, leverage the permission to change consumer behavior toward profits.

This is a courtship, pure and simple. By the end of the initial cycle, the prospective customer, having been through the five steps, will know your product, your company, and you. He or she will be amenable to becoming an actual customer who will remain loyal because you didn't try to go "all the way" within the first five minutes of the first "date."

EMA enhances the courtship through an intoxicating aphrodisiac mixture of email, e-fax, the Web, the telephone, and other technology tools. It intensifies the experience for the prospective customer when personalized or segmented customer preferences are determined by use of analytical tools. These tools define customer segments that are appropriate to your business and can help evaluate the successes and failures of e-marketing campaigns in near real time so that significant adjustments to the incentives and direction can be made quickly. All the trials and tribulations of the courtship are monitored and adjusted continuously.

Enterprise Marketing Automation (EMA): The Market

EMA is one of the more youthful components of eCRM. It first showed its unwrinkled brow in 1998 with about $100 million in sales and has since grown to what is expected to be a $2 billion market by 2002 according to the META Group. The analyst community is divided about EMA's maturity and even its ability to stand on its own. The Aberdeen Group and Forrester Research think that EMA and sales force automation (SFA) must converge. The conjoint offering must then be integrated into customer support and call centers to succeed. In other words, a fully integrated, complete CRM or eCRM packaged offering is EMA's real chance for success. The META

Group also estimates that 60 percent of the Global 2000 will use the Internet-based EMA rather than the client/server structured database marketing by the year 2002. The Gartner Group sees this progression also, but at a slower pace.

Why the significant upsurge by 2002? In an article in *CRM* magazine, Tom Gormley, a senior analyst at Forrester Research, states that while business-to-business (B2B) e-commerce is currently the rage and is expected to carry transactions worth $5.7 trillion by 2003, it is in the business-to-consumer (B2C) market that the need for e-marketing arises. EMA has the analytic engines that are necessary to identify and personalize campaigns with millions of stored customer data records to slice and dice.

One extant problem with EMA is its high cost. The typical cost of a full-blown EMA implementation is in the vicinity of $600,000 to $1 million, which is a lot for such a small part of the enterprise. Additionally, as of 2000, there are still a number of problems with EMA due to the primitive state of most of the software applications on the market. Few were around prior to 1998 and most have fewer than a dozen customers as of 2000. No vendor really has an entire end-to-end suite, though a few claim to. To pay that kind of money for such a primitive, singular application is a dicey proposition, but the results can be spectacular.

Components of Enterprise Marketing Automation

Why is there any advantage to automating processes that are by nature attempting intimacy with an audience? How personal can you get with the results of millions of customer records? Oddly enough, with the aid and comfort of the software and the Web, you can get very personal. The key here is not what the software can do for you, but what you can do to the software. It provides simple, user-friendly customization that says, "We can give you what you want with a few simple commands. You merely have to spend the few minutes clicking and checking several options." For example, using MicroStrategy 7, you can track stocks, download sports scores, or contact key players at your company—and soon, you'll be able to do it wirelessly. (See Chapter 6 for details.)

EMA is the technology of end-to-end marketing. Its core component is campaign management—the end-to-end organization and execution of a marketing thrust. The "e" component of campaign management is the provision of a single view of the customer to the entire enterprise and those with responsibility for that customer, which are all available with a browser. Most e-marketing toolsets, like those of Siebel or Annuncio, are focused on a suite of products that provide the following:

- ▶ Customer intelligence

- ▶ Extraction and analysis of the intelligence

- ▶ Campaign definition and planning based on that data analysis

- ▶ Campaign launch

- ▶ Campaign monitoring tools that handle lead generation

- ▶ Response management

- ▶ Workflow so that there is a uniform customer view across the enterprise

When used in the near real-time environment of EMA and response management, refinements are related to the individual customer, rather than the ad hoc response analysis of service bureaus. In more sophisticated systems, such as those of RightPoint, data mining and analysis are done from multiple sources.

Marketing Campaigns

What kind of marketing campaigns can the e-marketing applications run? Surprisingly, though they don't often function as smoothly as you might want them, they can cover a lot of ground. Embedded in most of the e-marketing software from many of the major players such as Siebel, Annuncio, Kana, and Broadbase is the process identified by the permission marketing mantra, "opt-in, opt-out."

Opt-In, Opt-Out

How many times have you gone to a website and entered a contest, downloaded a free book or white paper, or played a game? When you fill out an online form at this website with your vital statistics, often at the bottom of the form there are checkboxes that ask you if you would like to receive further information or an email update on the product. This is opting-in. There is also an opt-out variation—the checkbox is already checked and you have to uncheck it to opt out of the newsletter update or further information. When you get email from this company, you feel that it was fine to receive this mail because you allowed it to arrive at your desktop. It was solicited and accepted. That's what "opt-in, opt-out" is. *La Forza del Destino*—control over your destiny, minus the grandeur of Verdi's opera, of course.

To put it another way, opting in means that for some consideration (for example, the contest, the white paper, the discount), you allowed the company you are interacting with to send a solicitation that they expect you to take interest in. Rather than just another email address, you've become a potential customer with a real existence.

Opt-in e-marketing has two functions: intelligence and engagement. The first stage, even prior to clicking your mouse on the checkbox, is the forms you fill out with information about yourself. This information is stored along with your website activity, which is monitored as you meander your way through the site. After the form is filled out, at the point that you've clicked or unclicked on the checkboxes, you are engaged. Congratulations!

Opt-in is often contrasted to opt-out email as the more favorable choice. Let's look at a simple example. Which are you likely to be more responsive to, an unsolicited email that says, "If you do not want to receive any more mailings from us, please type remove in the subject line and reply to this email" (opt-out) or a registration form on a site that asks you to accept emails in return for entry into a sweepstakes for $15,000 (opt-in)? The results are a clear mandate for opt-in. Traditional banner ad click-through rates are 0.5 percent, and traditional interruption mail is 1 percent to perhaps 2 percent at most. Click-through rates for opt-in email are 5 to 15 percent. Tower Records reports a 10 percent success rate for opt-in campaigns, according to *eMarketer*. While for the immediate future opt-out still constitutes the bulk of email, with opt-in email being only around 10 percent of total email volume as of 1999, the total revenues for opt-in email are expected to jump from 1999's $97 million to roughly $952 million in 2002, according to the Forrester Group.

Opting In to Web-integrated E-marketing

Using dramatic carpet-bombing techniques with the hope that survivors will purchase your products is not EMA's métier. That is akin to the idea of creating a commercial so bad that you will be remembered for it.

Using available EMA technologies, opt-in campaigns—or, for that matter, any marketing campaigns—are honed, sharpened, and thrust into a segmented marketplace so that the level of success is potentially much greater. EMA provides the templates and tools for planning, executing, and analyzing these campaigns in real time.

Campaign Planning and Management

E-marketing's great strength is campaign management—the creation of personalized marketing efforts that not only engage the customer or prospect, but also engage the entire enterprise in the effort and provide a single view of the activity to any department or segment of the company. The campaign management features of the technology are end-to-end. They plan and monitor all activity, including:

- ▶ Identification of the prospect

- ▶ Generation of the lead

- ▶ Prospect and customer information capture

- ▶ Lead qualification

- ▶ Distribution of leads to appropriate segments

- ▶ Campaign planning

- ▶ Campaign execution (such as promotions, events planning)

- ▶ Response management

- ▶ Refinement

- ▶ Channel management (for example, joint marketing campaigns)

The diagram in Figure 5-1 identifies a typical e-marketing campaign. This is a Web-based offering that gives maximum flexibility to the marketing team.

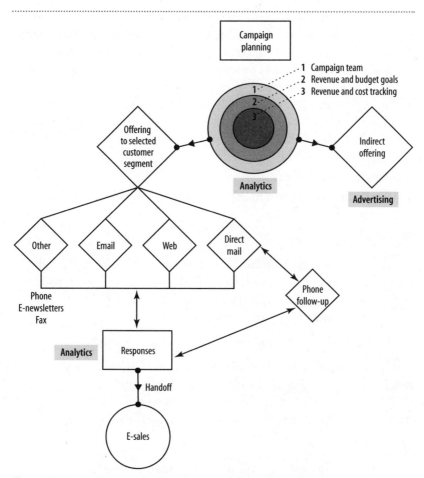

Figure 5-1: A campaign created with enterprise marketing automation tools

Superficially, EMA campaign methods don't seem very different from traditional marketing's methods. The difference, as with CRM and eCRM, is the Internet. EMA uses the Internet to capture, extract, and analyze information about each customer and each market segment. It then gives you the design tools to plan, execute, monitor, and refine your marketing campaigns to the level of the individual within the market segment. EMA tools also provide a consistent, continuous representation of a value proposition across multiple channels. The field, the call center, the Web, and internal departments all see a single view of the customer due to the tight integration between the front office—the customer-facing part of the enterprise—and the back office—which controls functions such as human resources and finances. Enterprise marketing automation workflow allows all parties to see exactly what they are permitted to see in all marketing campaigns as they evolve. No one is left out of the loop, and no department is slighted in the process. Thus, mistakes can be minimized, a great advantage in a large corporation. Let's look at a brief example of how it might work.

Case Study: United Airlines

United Airlines sent me a mailer recently that began with the following:

> Dear Mr. Greenberg,
>
> During the past year, you purchased and flew our expanded United service departing from Dulles airport and we appreciate your business. To thank you, we would like to give you an opportunity to earn free travel and save on United.
>
> Earn double miles and save 15 percent on United.

This seemed short and simple. Not too much information. Not much until you realize that United Airlines has millions of customers and there was information that was specific to me based on my flying habits. To send me this, they had to determine the following:

- ▶ That I was a customer
- ▶ That I had flown on United Airlines within the last year
- ▶ That I was a Mileage Plus member
- ▶ That I flew frequently enough to merit the letter
- ▶ That I flew frequently from Washington, D.C.'s Dulles airport

This was sorted and extracted from tens of thousands of customers flying from multiple airports in the United States daily. Once that information was determined, they:

1. Identified me with a particular promotion that they thought would appeal to me.

2. Decided on the engagement media that United thought would capture my attention.

3. Using opt-in methods, they then stated "To receive additional offers, join the Mileage Plus email list by going to http://email.mileageplus.com." This was asking my permission in the United Airlines–Paul Greenberg courtship to go from direct mail first base to email list second base in exchange for some consideration, such as 15 percent off and double miles.

My mailing was made even more complex by the disparate systems that United, like most companies, has. In a perfect world, a customer data repository exists, the analytic tools have one place to go to extract the information, and the information has reporting tools that provide clearly readable reports with the thoroughly dissected data. Reality is otherwise. Often there are several systems in place—perhaps an enterprise resource planning (ERP) system, a data warehouse or several data marts, Web-based customer surveys and registration materials, email information, faxes, direct mail responses, and input data from the SFA application. The analytic tools have to capture all this information from sources, deposit it, extract the critical pieces, segment it, analyze it based on either templates or customized criteria, and finally, present it in a reportable and useable format. From this, an e-marketing campaign is born.

Business Analytic Tools

E-marketing is distinguished from traditional marketing by the ability to capture, extract, and analyze customer information from multiple and often platform-independent sources and realize the results through the Web. That can mean emails, the Web, direct mailing, voice mail, faxes, and a myriad of other sources that may be indirect (such as magazine articles). EMA applications often cost a baseline of $250,000 and up. However, this becomes a reasonable price if you realize that the cost of acquiring a new customer can be five times the cost of maintaining an existing one. Good analytic software can not only reduce the cost of customer acquisition via targeted and segmented results, but can also identify those customers who are potentially going to take their business to your competitors. These tools have to be scalable, since the tools often sift through millions of customer transactions of varying sorts. They have to be rich so they can provide measurements and customization of the metrics to get the measurements. They have to be clear and distinct with reporting tools that provide you with the information you need to utilize the data it creates in a readable, understandable format. They also have to be fast, since they are dealing with millions of transactions from multiple sources in the course of Internet time. The tools interpret in-depth profiles of customers who are accessing websites, responding to emails, answering direct mail campaigns, and accessing what is called "customer touch points" in any way.

Touch points are either active or interactive nodes of customer communication. They are areas of customer interaction that are considered central to the success of any marketing effort. For example, Siebel eMarketing provides extensive prebuilt market, customer, product, and geographical analyses. The EMA analysis provides in-depth profiling information on customer preferences, buying behavior, revenue, profitability, and purchasing frequency. Successful analytical tools give organizations the view of data that lets them interpret, identify, and capitalize on emerging trends in key markets and focus their marketing and sales efforts on the high yielding market segments. The ultimate result of all of this is personalized customer information.

The market leader in analytics, especially with its acquisition of real-time analytics champ RightPoint, is E.piphany. Let's look at what E.piphany's E.5 analytics applications do:

▶ Analyze bookings, billings, and backlog information. This means revenue can be segmented by customized sets of criteria, which could be geographical or by industry segment.

▶ Leverage data from other CRM and SFA applications to improve sales forecasts, measure sales process metrics, and identify areas of sales focus.

▶ Evaluate e-commerce purchasing patterns and website effectiveness. This will allow the user to identify how successful their e-commerce initiative is.

▶ Monitor the effectiveness of your customer service agents and systems, such as the average cost and time to service requests and the profitability and effectiveness of individual call center representatives.

▶ Analyze your customer base for a clear understanding of customer preferences, buying behavior, loyalty, and profitability.

▶ Develop customer segments based on profitability and lifetime customer value, and link these to international, national, and regional marketing programs.

▶ Measure the effectiveness of indirect channel partners and programs, including distribution of sales, inventory trends, distributors' profit margins, distributors' sales by product line, and channel backlog trends.

As in any analytic application, this data has to be extracted from somewhere. The development of a data warehouse, such as SAP's Business Information Warehouse (BW), and the creation of data marts as customer repositories are becoming commonplace in the larger eCRM implementations. Interestingly, companies like RightPoint, E.piphany's adopted child, developed the technology to extract the data from multiple sources regardless of platform in near real time, allowing for extraordinarily fine-tuned marketing analysis and segmentation.

So far, you've analyzed the data and sliced off your market segment. Using eCRM for e-marketing campaign planning and development comes next. Much of this process is like traditional marketing, but the use of new media such as email and the Web makes it interesting. Interactivity, instant gratification (rather than waiting 6 to 12 weeks for a rebate, for example), and little work on the part of the consumer all become part of the equation.

EMA Components

In this section, we'll take a look at the components of the EMA engine and how this transitional mix of traditional marketing processes and contemporary delivery media is composed and how it is leading to new processes.

Promotions

Web or not, opt-in or opt-out, much of what marketing does is the same. Web-integrated marketing provides the same marketing goodies that consumers have always been interested in: promotions, sweepstakes, contests, giveaways, cross-selling of products, up-selling of products, and discount coupons. Loss leaders are still a lure. Buy.com has a model that calls for selling products for 5 percent *under* cost to lure a customer base. Their calculation is that they will gain long-term customer value through repeat customers over time and that the loyal customer base due to *other* things (such as excellent service and constant promotions) will stay loyal despite price increases later on. They are also advocates of permission marketing and marketing e-tools to monitor their sales deals.

Events

Various vendors have developed robust EMA event-management tools for capturing customer information through event registration and online interaction. The Web is the preferred e-marketing delivery mechanism. Registration for seminars, exhibitions, and so on is possible via the Internet. However, even more interesting is what Annuncio, a leading EMA vendor, calls "webinars"—seminars that are actually conducted over the Web. I highly recommend a newsletter called *On the Frontlines*, by Robert Thompson, the high priest of partner relationship management (more on PRM in Chapter 7). The newsletter is sent in plain text format each week to your email address after you have given permission to do so by signing up on his website, http://www.crmguru.com/. Within the newsletter are embedded URLs for locations on the Web where you can register for a webcast on some future date. A Web-based registration form is filled out, and an email reminder is sent some time before the webcast. Make sure you have the proper tools—either a streaming video plug-in such as Real Player or Windows Media Player or a proprietary player that you download and install at the webcast site—and you're ready to watch either the live or prerecorded webinar. In the meantime, the sponsoring company has captured a qualified prospect—you! The registration page that you filled out on the corporate webcast sponsor's page is part of the e-marketing campaign management toolset, as is the newsletter you received from Mr. Thompson. One other valuable feature that is built into these e-marketing programs is the ability to unsubscribe (opt-out) from the newsletter if you choose to.

Other registration and lead management features provided by most of the EMA vendors include:

- Registration page with opt-in
- Unsubscribe capabilities
- User-controlled profile management
- Lead follow-up from tradeshows and similar venues

- ▶ Campaigns on tradeshow floor
- ▶ User group registration and follow-up

It doesn't seem like all that much, but the ability to opt-in and opt-out makes for a far more satisfied and amenable customer and provides the marginal edge a marketing professional needs to both acquire and retain this customer.

Loyalty and Retention Programs

Frederick Newell, in his book *loyalty.com*, states:

> …we have seen firsthand the confusion that exists between trying to buy customer loyalty with points and discounts versus earning customer loyalty by providing value in ways that are meaningful to the individual customer in her or his terms. We have learned that you can't *buy* customer loyalty.

Very good point. A lot of EMA vendors try.

After all, customer loyalty is much more difficult to retain when all it takes is a different URL and a click or two to switch brands. Customers are constantly bombarded by the next great deal, and access to that deal no longer involves even a phone call or protracted arguments as to the wisdom of staying with the known quantity. Baby boomers and their children are used to easy acquisition of cheap thrills and expensive goods, with sensate gratification easily obtained in a booming economy. The Eighties were the era of free-spending Yuppies, and while they may not spend so freely any more, they have little sense of commitment to anything that's on the market. Even if the product is good, there is going to be a better new generation, something less expensive of the same caliber, or simply something cooler very soon. "Here today, gone tomorrow" looks like the business mantra for the new millennium, unfortunately.

EMA applications build in those small, personalized touches that engender loyalty and retain customers (at least until the customer finds the next great deal). For example, Annuncio Live, the flagship product of e-marketing vendor Annuncio, has templates for the following:

- ▶ Birthday greetings
- ▶ Holiday and special occasion reminders
- ▶ Delivery of gift ideas

- ▶ Welcome programs

- ▶ Points-based programs

- ▶ Win-back programs for inactive customers

Partner and Channel Management

Partner relationship management (PRM) is covered in detail in Chapter 7. Simplified versions of PRM are embedded into many EMA applications. These include features that incorporate targeted, joint marketing programs to promote both your business and your partner's. Some features are

- ▶ Cross-sell of a company's complementary products

- ▶ Promotion of new versions or upgrades of a company's products

- ▶ Joint promotions with partners or affiliates

Needless to say, it is important that the partners have the same software.

Response Management

The campaign is in progress. You've had thousands of responses from the targeted markets to different offerings, and many leads have been handed off to sales. Additionally, you've put a series of surveys online so you can truly fine-tune your marketing during the course of this activity. There is a lot of data to look at. How does your e-marketing suite handle response management so you can analyze the data? More complete response management features include: banner ads, direct mail, print ads, email, website links, surveys, event registration results, Internet registration, and online survey results.

Traditional response management is tedious, even with the use of computers. The time it takes for response gathering, analysis and refinement is lengthy and costly, and often not successful. As Figure 5-2 shows, you have to gather the responses from multiple sources manually and enter it into databases. Alternatively, you must store it somewhere and then do the analysis. After the analysis, you need to work through plans to revamp the next campaign, since the response gathering was often completed after the campaign was completed. This is where EMA shines. Using the Internet as a tool that works in real time, what is now called "closed-loop feedback" has been integrated into the e-marketing toolbox.

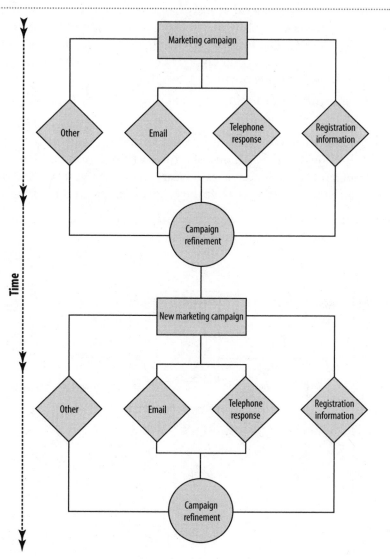

Figure 5-2: Traditional response management

Closed-loop feedback is the nucleus of Internet-based response management. At its best, it is response management in real time. It is the use of the Internet and the tools to compile, extract, and analyze information while the campaigns are in progress. It is the augmentation of those campaigns in midstream and the continuous repetition of that development. In other words, information is generating new activity, which is generating new information...*ad infinitum,* as Figure 5-3 illustrates. The time to gather and analyze information and respond to campaigns is notably shorter. The return on investment here is almost painfully obvious:

▶ Information gathering, extraction, and analysis time is dramatically reduced.

▶ Refinements to the campaign can be done in midstream, improving the possibility of return within the existing campaign. It is no longer a lesson learned for next time, but instead a chance for success while the original campaign is in progress.

▶ Automated tasks free up labor time for other marketing tasks that are not tedious or laborious.

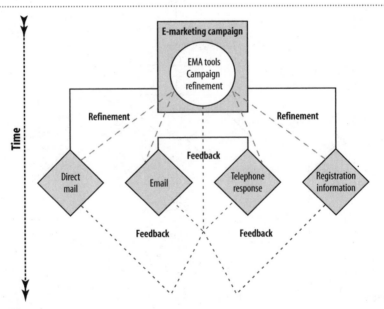

Figure 5-3: E-marketing and closed-loop feedback

Process Flow: EMA Campaign Implementation

You've now seen what the components of this powerful utilization of eCRM are. Now we'll run through a sample generic EMA implementation and look at the strengths and some of the potential pitfalls. We'll use a fictional e-marketing campaign implementation, greatly simplified, using the Siebel eMarketing component of their eBusiness 2000 suite and a couple of the best-of-breed software products for particular tasks.

Case Study: AV Electronics

AV Electronics (a fictional company) realized they had to increase their market share, which was rapidly being taken over by Mitsubishi, Toshiba, Pioneer, and other consumer electronics giants. Jobs were at stake. Despite their introduction of an HDTV-ready line of televisions and one of the first progressive scan DVD players, their business had been flagging for months. The one jewel in the AV Electronics marketing crown was their very active business-to-consumer website, which had full-blown retail sales capacity. They had done about 15 percent of their total consumer electronics sales through this state-of-the-art site and managed their opportunities through the use of the Enterprise version of Siebel Sales.

They recently purchased and implemented several new e-marketing tools, including a new Siebel 2000 module, Siebel eMarketing, because it promised them the capacity to do multistep, multifaceted marketing campaigns that could be managed through the Internet and provide a single view of the customer to the entire company so that everyone was on the same (Web) page. All well and good, but they were by no means a sophisticated company when it came to information technology. A consultant who had been involved in several Siebel implementations began to guide them through the steps to successfully use the e-marketing module. AV Electronics had already implemented the sales module of Siebel months before.

Taking the First Steps

AV Electronics' first step was to form an e-marketing campaign team, consisting of the vice president of marketing, two of his staff, and one person from the sales team. While this didn't constitute all the departments that would have to get involved, it included those who would identify what would best work with existing customers and with new prospects.

The campaign team was given customer data that had been gathered from multiple sources, such as website registration, trade shows, various AV Electronics–sponsored events, and customer purchase information. The information was analyzed by market segment through the use of Veridiem's MPI (Market Performance Indicator) tool so that market segments could be identified by profitability and potential return on investment and through other user-created criteria. This data had been extracted from a data mart that was provided by the core Siebel eMarketing product. After examining their data mart information, the campaign team came up with a proposal to experiment with various types of direct marketing campaigns. For the time being, they decided to scratch any indirect (advertising) offering to the general public. Their campaigns would have a decidedly experimental bent. They weren't sure which of the campaigns would be best for existing customers. They knew they had to get the state-of-the-art techno-junkies, who needed the latest and the greatest as it came out regardless of cost, as well as the customers who needed to improve the equipment they hadn't changed for five years. Additionally, they wanted to bring in the 21 to 27–year-olds who were just becoming moneyed, but were not quite affluent yet. Since the prices of DVD players and multichanger CD players had dropped through the floor in recent years, AV Electronics realized they could now engage this age group, who could now afford AVE's equipment. And Toshiba's. And Sony's. And Yamaha's. And Bose's Life System 3000, which looked really cool and played pretty well, too. Competition was vicious; AVE had to act. Using the eMarketing tools, the campaign team set the criteria for defining the characteristics of these groups. If the group names changed from department to department, the analytic tools would still automatically recognize the criteria, thus preserving the purity of the data and the results.

AVE modeled the campaigns they were going to use and set the models into the applications. There were two campaigns using two separate approaches. First, since the 21 to 27 age group was also pretty Web savvy, it would be easier to get them involved in Web-based promotions and purchases. A major Web giveaway was promoted, with five winners each getting the top-of-the-line AV Electronics complete home theater system. Registration pages were set up through the templates provided by Siebel eMarketing, with a checkbox that asked permission of the registrant to send further information on products. The checkbox had to be checked for this to occur (opting in). AVE had considered having the checkbox already checked so that unchecking would have to occur to *not* receive the information (opting out). The team decided that this was marginally intrusive for 21 to 27–year-olds feeling freedom for the first time.

There were also a number of customized features on the registration pages that were easily created through modifications to the Siebel eMarketing templates, using Microsoft's Web development tool, FrontPage. When the registrant completed the registration pages and clicked the Submit button, the data was parsed and stored by Siebel eMarketing in the data mart. When the data was stored, the registrant was then taken to a separate Web page where there were promotional 20 percent discounted pricing on DVD players and CD multichangers *and* three free DVDs or CDs of your choice from the various Columbia House video and music catalogs.

The second confirmed campaign was a targeted email campaign to existing customers who had purchased equipment in the last three years: 25 percent off on "upgrades" to the A/V equipment the customer owned and a trade-in of $100 or more on the original item, sight unseen. This was to be run through Kana Connect, which could target the audience based on demographic profiles, recency, frequency, monetary value of past purchases, responses to previous campaigns, or any other information of value. Kana Connect would send various targeted trial messages to different audiences. It would monitor the response rates and refine the personalized offers. What the AVE team particularly liked was that Kana Connect could track the level of detail for each recipient down to whether they open messages, click links, make purchases, or use HTML or text as a format. AVE could proactively determine campaign-in-progress refinements. The control samples for these campaigns were randomly chosen by Siebel eMarketing.

The vice president of marketing, as campaign team chief, then worked with the staff to decide on the revenue goals and budget and enter them into Siebel eMarketing. Once this was done, Siebel eMarketing would allow them to track the cost and revenues derived as the campaigns evolved.

Unfortunately, like every commercial institution, AVE had a chain of command and custody that had to be addressed when money is spent and personnel time is depleted. But, once again, the power of the Web prevailed over bureaucracy (to a point). Siebel eMarketing took the campaign budget and sent it to the finance staff associated with marketing budgets and got their "signature" approval with a date/time stamp. The promotions and contest efforts along with the appropriately attached marketing literature were then sent to the AVE legal department for approval, and within a month, the date/time stamp of approval appeared.

As soon as the legal date/time stamp appeared, the vice president of marketing checked the Create Activity box in the Siebel eMarketing application. This launched the campaign and triggered a series of enterprise-wide permissions that allow anyone with the campaign-team-determined permissions to see the progress of the campaign (such as the email list and responses to the email via the Web or phone). It also allowed monitoring and tracking of the campaign, including status updates such as active, hold, or closed. It locked in the start and proposed end dates to see the timeliness of the offerings.

AVE didn't want to pass up any possible sales opportunities, so they set triggers at points of handoff to sales through the modularly connected Siebel eSales offering. For example, a former purchaser decides to upgrade his speakers because of the email offering. He goes to the website with the discount offer number and begins the purchase. Another screen pops up and offers him some further bargains. He takes one of them. This is a trigger point that will automatically gather his customer information and send it to a designated salesperson via Siebel eSales.

Getting Something Back for the Investment

But what kind of return on investment (ROI) does EMA give you? After all, these are not cheap implementations, in part or as a whole. A simple, nearly plain vanilla EMA implementation in a large company is likely to cost between $600,000 and $1 million for software and implementation partner services. The costs of e-marketing activities are likely to go up. For example, a recent study done by Forrester Research estimated that average email spending for companies engaged in email marketing campaigns was $240,000 in 1999 and would be $720,000 in 2004. Roughly 36 percent of those dollars were budgeted for customer acquisition and the rest for customer retention. The click-through rate was roughly averaged to 5.5 percent (with wide variances in the type of email sent), and the average cost per sale ranged from $2 for in-house lists to $465 per sale for sponsored email. This cost is in addition to software costs—product costs often exceed $100,000 and can be as high as seven figures—and ASP costs, which range from a low of $5,000 per month to a high of $40,000 per month. That's just for an email campaign! But the click-through rate, which is more or less equated with a direct mail response rate, is approximately 10 to 50 times the typical response rate for a mailer. Worth it? You have to decide that one.

The difficulty is that there are continuous debates on what constitutes ROI for *any* major information technology investment. One of the reasons for the 1999 ERP shakeout was the inability to define the ROI for that large capital expenditure. For example, SAP costs were as high as $100 million, and yet, no one had benchmarks for measuring the return. How would you feel if you were the VP who authorized the $100 million and then couldn't figure out how to measure your benefits?

Similar problems exist with EMA ROI. Marketing has always been a difficult parameter to measure. Its results tend to be measured with market share and mindshare, which are long term and not necessarily attributable to any one functional area. However, there are certain identifiable metrics. While we'll examine general eCRM ROI elsewhere in the book, let's look at some of the specific measures of EMA effectiveness.

> **Customer lifetime value (CLV)** According to Greg Gretch, the vice president of e-marketing at Kana Corporation, CLV is a measurement of the expected cash flow, gross revenue, and margin contribution to revenue over the lifetime of an individual customer. Several available EMA tools build this measurement tool into their suite (for example, Kana Connect). (See Appendix B.)

> **Baseline marketing operations** This measures the time and materials cost of customer acquisition. How does EMA reduce this expensive cost? Increase in the efficiencies of the marketing process, reduction in time of the marketing cycle, and reduction in cost per prospect-capture usually determine this.

Implementation costs When does EMA return the cost of an implementation that can be millions of dollars just for the e-marketing modules of more full-blooded eCRM applications? This is usually ascertained by looking at the revenue upside—determining a better return per interaction or campaign.

Labor effectiveness Tedious jobs are automated, freeing the staff to do more important work. This means more use value for the dollars spent on salaries/compensation. The trivial work that is often part of the ordinary life of even highly paid employees is automated out of the cost of those dollars.

Unfortunately, EMA is far too new a segment of eCRM to be considered an unqualified (or qualified) success. The efficiencies of Internet use are reasonably apparent, but there is no final answer yet.

The Players and the Products

As with all software offerings, particularly those associated with the Internet, there are too many e-marketing vendors to mention in this chapter. This section contains a representative sampling so you can get a feel for the marketplace scope and, if you're considering an EMA implementation, which merchant you might look to.

Annuncio

Annuncio is considered a market leader in, as they call it, customer interaction software. Its flagship product Annuncio Live is a permission-based application/service offering that provides a wide range of campaign management functions. Founded in 1998 and funded by Norwest Venture Capital, Annuncio has rapidly gained a significant foothold in the marketing automation world, with a good-sized chunk of EMA mindshare. In mid-2000, they followed what might seem to be a logical step and announced that they had developed a service offering for independent marketing and advertising agencies, marketing consultants, and interactive integrators to provide not only their Web-integrated software, but also marketing strategy services to give these agencies end-to-end coverage. The likelihood of success for this aggressive offering is still indeterminate because this type of service is ordinarily beyond the expertise of a software company—even an EMA one.

Their website: http://www.annuncio.com/.

Broadbase Software, Inc.

Broadbase is aimed at customer analysis. Their EBusiness Performance Management (EPM) suite is divided into several pieces:

Marketing personalization (EPM/E-Personalization) Uses the data gathered from other parts of the application suite to design campaigns for the individual customer.

Purchasing behavior analysis (EPM/E-Commerce) Can track customer buying patterns in near real time.

Sales analysis (EPM/Sales) Measures effectiveness of sales pipeline.

Sales opportunity recommendations (EPM/E-Marketing) Provides marketing campaign management and ROI.

Service cost analysis (EPM/Customer Service) Identifies the cost of a customer activity.

Broadbase's mindshare in the analytic CRM market has been improving consistently due to its high-caliber product set.

Their website: http://www.broadbase.com/.

Kana Corporation

Kana focuses on its Kana Connect solution, a comprehensive permission-based electronic direct marketing application. Kana Connect enables e-businesses to engage customers in relevant conversations, delivers individually targeted messages, and drives customers to e-business websites. Its strength is with companies that use direct marketing frequently. While it may have some value for other types of marketing campaigns, that value is less apparent. It has a unique wizard interface that makes campaign planning and definition fairly easy when compared to other products, though Siebel's eMarketing application has a large set of preconfigured templates.

Kana Connect lets users target an audience based on any information available anywhere in the enterprise, such as demographic profiles, recency, frequency and monetary value of past purchases, or responses to previous campaigns. It sends different trial messages to different audiences, allowing you to compare response rates and refine your offers. It sends messages in different formats, such as HTML and plain text, and keeps track of which users can receive which formats. The analytic tools that Kana Connect uses track all campaign information for every recipient (see the AV Electronics case study in this chapter). If customers have questions arising directly from Kana Connect campaigns, Kana has another product called Kana Response that directly handles such questions.

Their website: http://www.kana.com/.

E.piphany, Inc.

E.piphany is the prime mover among the movers and the first shaker among the shakers in the EMA world. In 1999–2000, they were on an acquisition binge, purchasing Octane and RightPoint to address a market that is sometimes called Internet relationship management (IRM). Analysts say that with their acquisitions and their strategic alliances with partners like PricewaterhouseCoopers, E.piphany is poised to become a true market powerhouse. In mid-2000, KPMG committed to 300 consultants trained in E.piphany.

E.piphany's core applications suite is E.5—an integrated, closed-loop suite of analytic CRM software solutions. E.piphany's E.5 system allows companies to identify their customers by extracting and aggregating customer data from all existing enterprise systems. Companies can then use the E.5 system to differentiate their customers using data-mining technologies designed to profile and segment customers. With the purchase of RightPoint, they also purchased RightPoint's proprietary technology, which does data mining from within customer touch points such as call centers, Web registration forms, email, interactive voice response (IVR), and other existing data sources. The RightPoint mining algorithms are sophisticated and can get data from these multiple sources regardless of platform and then create predictive models on prospect and customer behavior. E.5 leverages these active customer profiles and helps companies plan how to best interact with their customers by designing and executing one-to-one marketing campaigns. As companies gain a comprehensive understanding of each customer, they can then use the real-time, fact-based predictive models and personalize every customer interaction.

The purchase of Octane gave E.piphany an operational CRM solution (see Chapter 1 for the definition of operational CRM). Now E.piphany can provide a single Internet-architected application for managing all interactions with customers, suppliers, and partners across all touch points, including the Web, telephone, email, online chat, and fax, through a single universal workflow. Customers receive a consistent experience regardless of their chosen point of interaction. Moreover, employees using Octane 2000 to interact with a customer have access to the entire thread of past interactions with that particular customer across all touch points. Because of the architecture, E.piphany has a drag-and-drop customization toolset as part of its suite.

Their website: http://www.epiphany.com/.

Siebel Systems, Inc.

Siebel is mentioned in almost every chapter of this book and in fact, is the giant of the CRM world. The company is the CRM market leader, with more than $1 billion in revenue in 1999. Siebel CRM implementations are in the high seven-figure dollar range. Siebel dominates a large part of the Fortune 1000 market with only PeopleSoft/Vantive and Nortel/Clarify as true comptetitors. Siebel eMarketing is an internally developed module that is integrated with the marketing encyclopedia of Paragren, a company purchased by Siebel in early 2000, and is well integrated with the other multiple Siebel modules. How well they do in the EMA space is yet to be determined.

Siebel eMarketing software delivers personalized promotions and communications with customers through email and the Web, as well as tools for developing and delivering marketing information and analyzing interaction with customers and marketing campaigns. It is not as sophisticated as many of its competitors, though it certainly is adequate. If you have a Siebel CRM implementation, the integration alone makes it the EMA application of choice for you. Otherwise, there are multiple players that can provide more for either less or the same cost.

Their website: http://www.siebel.com/.

Oracle Corporation

Oracle is putting a lot of effort into its CRM offering and in mid-2000 released Oracle Marketing 11i. It is tightly integrated with the Call Center, Sales, E-Commerce, and Services modules of Oracle CRM. It can provide lead generation links to order management, for example. The feature set includes:

▶ Message handling and creation for campaigns

- ▶ Sales leads list generation and distribution

- ▶ Event planning

- ▶ Promotion execution via the Web

- ▶ Sales processing for front and back office

- ▶ Analytic tools and data mining

This product is different from the other EMA applications for two important reasons. First, there is a strong emphasis on front-office integration with the sales automation applications provided by either Oracle CRM or other vendors. Secondly, it integrates entirely with Oracle 8.*x* and Oracle 8*i*, thus providing a seamless addition to the already huge Oracle 8 customer base.

Oracle plays hard. With the incredibly large installed base of Oracle 8*i* and the growing interest in Oracle 11*i* products, there is no doubt that Oracle will remain a major player in the eCRM and e-marketing domain.

Their website: http://www.oracle.com/.

Chapter 6

Going Global Gets Personal: Personalization and CRM

One thing about customers, no matter how you define them: they like being treated like kings and queens. What this means in the age of CRM is personalization—the art and science of creating a unique experience for every individual customer. For example, if I enter a portal for higher education, my class schedule, my financial records, my campus programs, eligibility for awards, and access to my particular counselor, and other appropriate information sits on the desktop for me to access. If I were a different student, different options of the same sort might appear. If I were an administrator, entirely different categories relating to appropriate functions would appear, and so on. This is personalization. There are a substantial number of software applications out there that specialize in the CRM version of this. This chapter defines personalization, identifies what does it, and tells you (personally!) why it is important to you and your customers as part of your CRM implementation.

E-tail, Retail: What's the Difference?

Many of you have shopped online, maybe to buy this book. Many of you have been to a retail store, maybe to buy this book. To my knowledge, these are the only ways to buy this book. You either went the e-tailer route, which meant you went online, did a bit of research, used the search engine, found the book, gave them your credit card in a secure environment, and waited breathlessly for its delivery. Or you took the retail route, which meant you went to a bookstore, searched the shelves, found one of the copies left (of which there were very few left, of course), gave a human cashier your credit card or cash while you chatted with them, went home, and then breathlessly read the book. Different buying patterns and different purchase model. Very different. Take a look at Table 6-1; it highlights the differences between e-tailers and retailers. The experience is not the same, though that's what the e-tailer is both aiming at and, simultaneously, hoping for. The e-tailer wants to provide the same comfort, ease, and personal attention, but also wants to provide the richness and availability of the tools and information on the purchase for you—all at a better price.

Table 6-1: A Brief Comparison of E-tailers and Brick-and-Mortar Stores

	amazon.com	barnesandnoble.com	Brick and Mortar
Upside	Cheaper price	Cheaper price (even cheaper than their own stores)	Instant gratification with book purchase
	Convenient ordering (never have to leave home)	Convenient ordering (never have to leave home)	Bookstore ambiance and programs
	Huge virtual inventory (ordinary orders have short delivery time)	National inventory (ordinary orders have short delivery time)	Human attention
	Greater privacy	Greater privacy	
Downside	No personal attention unless problem and then difficult	No personal attention unless problem and then difficult	Higher price
	Subject to blind schemes such as dynamic pricing without knowledge	Subject to blind schemes such as dynamic pricing without knowledge	In-store-only stock means more likely out of stock
	Less privacy	Less privacy	Considerably less variety

What this simple table says is that while there are differences between brick-and-mortar stores and e-tailers, there really are no significant differences between e-tailers selling the same things. So what makes the amazon.com "experience" better, in many people's opinion, than the barnesandnoble.com "experience?" Looking closely at it, not much. Perception is part of it—how you perceive the value of the site itself. Personalization is a big part of it. That means how much attention you think you are getting from this cold-hearted Web automaton as compared to Joe who is also surfing the site.

Think about it. As often as you've used amazon.com, how many human beings have you actually spoken to who are employed by Amazon? How many have you even had a personal email interaction with? The likely answer is none. Yet you've shopped onsite dozens of times and gone back for more and more. Convenience, you say? Good prices, you say? Wide selection, you say? Then why not barnesandnoble.com or Borders.com or any one of a dozen interchangeable websites that sell books, CDs, DVDs, and such? "Amazon and I, well, we go way back. They know me better." *They* do? Who's "*they?*"

That's the point. *They* know you better because *they* have a data warehouse filled with information about you, based on your personal profile and your past shopping experiences. You are an individual to them as far as the data that is available about you.

Personalization Is...

In a perfect techno-functional world, personalization identifies the needs and requirements of individual customers *en masse*. It also means that the engagement of named, faced customers has to be ongoing and intimate to the point that the customer hardly realizes that he is not dealing with a person or that he's not actually getting a peer-to-peer response. It must appear to be peer to peer so realistically that the customer wants to stay with you. The benefits are longstanding, happy customers and reduced customer service, marketing, and sales costs.

Wait—engaging individual customers *en masse*? How can that be done? Isn't that a contradiction, both in literal terms and in fact?

According to Mark LaRow, vice president of applications development for software vendor MicroStrategy:

> True personalization of the channel is described as how people want to be communicated to. The idea is to personalize the message or the offer. Generally, it can be described as, what group of people ought to be presented with what offer? The amount of data that needs to be analyzed to make this accurate and interesting to the customer is complex and high volume. If I were to give it a more formal definition, personalization is the process of customizing any interaction with a customer based on his or her explicit interests and preferences, or interests and preferences that are derived from other data about the customer. The personalization of the interaction can take on any or all of the following forms: personalized offer, personalized message into which the offer is carried, personalized preference for communication channel.

Mr. LaRow further identified the perfectly personalized techno-functional world, a world in which personalization does not conflict with anyone's concern about his or her personal privacy:

> The Holy Grail of personalization would be a world in which all individual customer information is known, but is simultaneously anonymous. While this may sound contradictory, it actually could be done through a personalization service that could guarantee and maintain anonymity between the company and the customer. In other words, every company would see you as user XYZ, but no one could connect XYZ to your true name, email, etc. You still reap all the benefits of a personalized experience, with all the relevant product and service offerings made to user XYZ, without any company knowing who you really are.

Hypothetically, this would mean that all your customer data could be used by L.L Bean to determine that a cashmere sweater would be the appropriate sale item for you and for people with your data points. An ad for the cashmere sweater in your size and a picture of that exact sweater could be sent to you without L.L Bean knowing your name until you bought the sweater from their online store. Totally customized, yet anonymous.

Even though, as any Monty Python lover will tell you, the search for the Holy Grail continues, the current personalization technology is sufficiently advanced to get nearly miraculous results—when it works well.

Personalization: The Technology Rules!

When you surf to amazon.com or some other personalized site and see "Welcome back, Paul Greenberg, here are some book, DVD, VHS, CD recommendations for you," you may either get annoyed or marvel at the accuracy of the choices they are suggesting. When done optimally, the choices are going to be uniformly meaningful and you are going to buy something.

Log-ins to portal sites have unique user names and unique passwords that are attached to a profile of the portal user. Each time users log in, they find a specific view with specific information that is related to them on that site. For example, if I log into Oraclesalesonline.com, it provides me with information that I need, such as the meetings I have scheduled, the plane flights I have to catch, the database of my customers and the recent interactions with those customers, and customized news and services designed to make my Oraclesalesonline.com experience useful and personal.

The technology that sits behind the personalization of the information is sophisticated. The amount of data analyzed for this and the number of ways that it is analyzed is extensive, often in multiple terabytes. In the optimal system, a customer data warehouse will gather information on individuals from all customer touch points. These touch points could include:

- ▶ Website information gathered through forms

- ▶ Point of sale (POS) information

- ▶ Information from ERP data warehouses such as SAP's Business Intelligence Warehouse (BW)

- ▶ Call center data

- ▶ Sales force automation customer information

- ▶ Information gathered in varying marketing venues:

  - ▶ Data from marketing automation applications

  - ▶ Responses to direct mail campaigns

  - ▶ Email marketing feedback

- ▶ Demographic data feeds from departments such as marketing and sales that might be directly inputted

- ▶ Any other customer data source

For this customer data to be useful, more than a giant storage bin is necessary. Analytic algorithms applied to this data are the next layer of the personalization architecture. For example, MicroStrategy eCRM 7, perhaps the most highly developed personalization package, uses an evolving, growing library of 350 different analytics. These analytics can help you discover who your customers are, why they may or may not be buying certain items, and how to cross-sell or up-sell new products to them. Each of these can provide a unique way of looking at the customer data, and combining these, can provide unparalleled power in terms of making you an individual in the eyes of the company's customer data warehouse (CDW). Figure 6-1 gives you an example of personalization architecture, MicroStrategy style.

However, it doesn't stop there. For the dissected and configured data to be useful, there has to be some action taken to give it some value. That action could be campaign management, email, direct mail management, further information capture, message creation, or a myriad of other actions.

While many of the personalization applications stop here, some have extended the application's capacity to include:

Narrowcasting This is used in the Marketing Automation module of MicroStrategy eCRM 7. I cover this extensively in Chapter 16, so feel free to skip ahead and take a peek.

Real-time Web personalization This is an interesting category and is a specialty of Net Perceptions. It is the process of dynamically selecting content to be portrayed on specific website real estate based on personalization criteria mentioned above. The keyword is "dynamic." Comparing a given customer to buying patterns or interests of other similar customer profiles drives most real-time Web personalization. Increasingly, real-time Web personalization will be based on explicit interests and executed with rules that are established by both the customer (through opt-in choices) or marketing personnel. The customer could get online via a call center, a website, email, or even a help line. The key is to use existing data that goes beyond the information being captured online as the operation is being executed. How do you match the online activity to the individual information as the online activity is increased?

Export This is the ability to connect to other systems that the personalization application customer might already have in place, such as Siebel, Onyx, or SalesLogix.

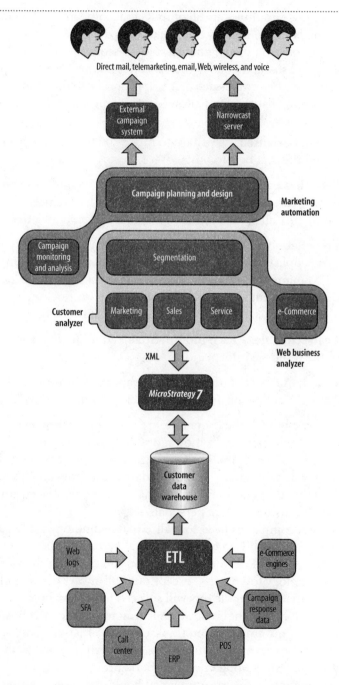

Figure 6-1: MicroStrategy eCRM 7 architecture (Copyright 2000, MicroStrategy, Inc. All rights reserved. Reprinted with permission of MicroStrategy, Inc.)

The previous examples are all outputs that come from a marketing automation layer, or "offer engine," that turns the personal information into action. An offer engine is a rules-based series of algorithms, templates, and so on, that takes the data after it is analyzed and applies it to create the offer or message that is appropriate to the individual customer's information. Mr. LaRow identifies several components of the offer engine:

It is goal oriented. "We have to move 200 televisions this week, so find the best bets to buy."

It watches purchase history. "John Smith bought a saw from us two years ago and bought several dozen tools since. The saw should be dull by now, so send this tool-buyer a saw offer."

It is collaborative. "Our analytic algorithms tell us that typically people who buy documentary DVDs on boxing champions like Muhammed Ali would be interested in a 'Fight Club' DVD. Joe Smith (John's brother) bought four boxing documentary DVDs in the past year. Send him a 'Fight Club' notification."

It can schedule. "Each month, run an ad in the *Post* and gather up the response information."

It can handle event offers. "If it is raining, why don't you rent 'The Perfect Storm,' since you're stuck indoors anyway?"

The offer engine is the (hopefully) revenue-generating machine that makes all the personalization more than just a gesture of attempted B2C friendship. The key to the offer engine is that rules keep getting added as more and more data is captured and interpreted, so that the actions are increasingly accurate at the customer level—in other words, more personal.

That said, companies need to realize that technology alone can only go so far. I would expect that 10 to 20 percent of these offers would make no sense to the recipient. You can't run the risk of relying on technology too much—exceptions will always occur, and companies that can handle this will succeed handsomely.

One example that shows how results can fall outside the business rules is one of my amazon.com transactions. I ordered a book on cruises once, when my wife and I were considering a trip. As a result of that single order, though no other book order I ever had is related in any way to travel, the recommended books that keep coming up onscreen for me are always cruise- or travel-related, even though my buying habits (not necessarily the same as my reading habits) are inclined toward technology, business, fiction, and sports. While I understand why the cruise books show up, this falls into that sense-less 10 to 20 percent category. However, the other 90 percent of suggestions related to my habits and tastes in music and movies are very accurate, so the pinpointed personalization is generally working well. Unfortunately, I fall prey to that part of human behavior that tends to remember the miscue, rather than the successes. In general, this makes personalization a very tricky road to travel. But companies such as MicroStrategy are following it well, with sophisticated products in the marketplace that are truly closer than the other CRM segments to attaining that part of the CRM Holy Grail they own.

Taking It Deeper: Data Mining and Personalization

Data mining is the automatic or partially automated analysis of large quantities of stored data to uncover significant rules or patterns. The analytic algorithms that are applied to the data provide information that can get as complex as the most valuable customers, using dozens of criteria, or as simple as the customers in Virginia over 50 years old who buy Jell-O. This is automation of the traditional functions often carried out by marketing research and advertising firms, which is why these same agencies are acquiring companies that do data mining. The data mining tools are dependent on development of predictive models. These models are evolved from the core business questions of individual companies: What kind of customers do we have? What kind do we want? How are we going to keep them? What can we do to capture new markets?

The results of data mining demand more than just simple automatic responses, however. Human intelligence and campaign design are vital to making something of the results of the data mining activity. Ultimately, it follows the time-honored principle that says the more useful information you have, the more successful you can be in meeting your objectives.

Personalization and Privacy

With all the individual data captured and store, privacy remains an issue. Privacy is an ongoing battle being fought on the Internet as a whole. How much information captured and what information stored constitutes a violation of privacy? Cookies—those little files that are generated by the website that feed data back to the site when you return—are the subject of the general battle. So much so that recent incarnations of Internet Explorer and Netscape Communicator have cookie managers as standard parts of their browsers.

Personalization is a much more comprehensive data-gathering process, and far more information about you, the individual, is ensnared over a long time from many sources. Do you want the info-kidnapping site to know that you download shareware constantly that is related to wills and estates? Do you want all your credit cards on file after you have used them? Do you want www.dot.com to know that you are an elder in your church—information gathered from your downloading a white paper on the nature of the Trinity? Even more, do you want to be besieged with offers for estate-related legal services or religious articles? How much information about your family do you want stored in someone else's database?

Net Perceptions, a real-time personalization specialist, has developed an exceptional privacy standard for customers. Two excerpts will highlight the privacy issue:

> Net Perceptions supports the individual's right to protect their online privacy, thus we collect minimal information. As part of Net Perceptions' commitment to privacy, we actively support or are founding members of several privacy standards. These include:
>
> ▶ Active membership in the Online Privacy Alliance
>
> ▶ Licensee in good standing of TRUSTe program
>
> ▶ Authoring membership of the ICE (Information Content Exchange) standard
>
> ▶ Full compliance with OPS (Open Profiling Standard)
>
> ▶ DMA member compliance with the DMA Privacy Promise

Net Perceptions, like others in the business of personalization, takes privacy seriously. Each of the organizations and standards mentioned is a medium for the protection of the right to privacy of all citizens. By no means should this be treated lightly.

The Online Privacy Alliance (OPA) is an organization that crisscrosses the entire private sector, not just the information technology world. It not only includes companies like 3M and Bank of America, but major associations as diverse as the Information Technology Association of America, the Motion Picture Association of America, and the American Institute of Certified Public Accounts.

As an institution, OPA is creating a privacy standard for its hundred-plus global corporate members to adhere to, which provides powerful protections to privacy. OPA distinguishes the singular components that should be part of any security or privacy package the corporate executive is considering purchasing or using, as well as personalization tools to be aware of. There are five rules for an organization:

▶ Publicly adopt and implement a privacy policy.

▶ Give notice and disclosure of the privacy policy (such as Net Perceptions' easy-to-find disclosure).

▶ Give individuals the choice on how their personal information is going to be used online, especially if the use is unrelated to the purpose for which it was collected (opt-in). Minimally, allow the individuals the ability to have it not used (opt-out). Consent to use for third parties should also be an opt-in or opt-out choice.

▶ Secure data that is gathered and develop standards to guarantee the reliability and accuracy of the data. If the information is to be transferred to third parties, it should be in adherence to this data security standard or procedure. The third party should protect the integrity of the data transfer.

▶ Take steps to assure that the data is accurate, complete, and timely. Mechanisms for correction of problems and for protection against unauthorized alterations should be established.

The TRUSTe program is a highly visible, trusted source in which many e-commerce Web publishers are enrolled. It is directed solely at the online community. Commonly identified by websites that carry its privacy seal, the "trustmark," TRUSTe has developed stringent standards that not only define protections for consumers, but also provide strong proof of regulatory compliance to government officers. This is a profit-making, nonpartisan venture that has been generally accepted in the online community. Members of the TRUSTe program are actually subject to oversight procedures. Reviews are conducted initially and periodically to see that adherence to TRUSTe compliance is occurring. Seeding, the process of creating a dummy consumer with traceable personal information (sometimes called a "red dye test"), is part of the oversight, so that TRUSTe can see first-hand that the site is complying. Finally, they depend on online users to report violations, and they've created a watchdog form to make that process easier.

To further ensure customer privacy as more and more personal information is publicly harvested, there are standards groups, such as Information Content Exchange (ICE) and the Open Profiling Standard (OPS). ICE, run by the same folks who are heading up the CPExchange CRM standard, is a standard for management and delivery of data and content between networked partners and the "syndicator" (creator of the information) and "subscriber" (receiver of the information). The OPS is a model championed by Netscape that provides a foundation for the creation of "personal profiles" on the Web and at the same time protects customers from egregious use of those profiles, through permissions and opt-in/opt-out behaviors.

Now the second excerpt:

> Privacy Standards for Net Perceptions Customers:
>
> Net Perceptions develops and sells a variety of tools designed to help companies offer personalized suggestions of products or content to individuals. Net Perceptions' products do not require the collection of profiling information such as name or contact information to serve personalized recommendations. Net Perceptions encourages all of its customers to adopt privacy standards of their own and make those standards freely accessible.

(Both excerpts reprinted from the Net Perceptions website http://www.netperceptions.com.)

What makes this second section comforting is that Net Perceptions has, to some extent, developed a piece of the Holy Grail: anonymous data collection for accurate personalization. Looking at it from the perspective of privacy commitment, they are creating the paradigm.

Personalization in the Small: We're Going Wireless

The epitome of personalization in the early part of the century is doing it on the small screen. As we break into the twenty-first century, the small screen is no longer the TV, but is now the PDA or cellphone. The mobile salesperson is already being attended to by Interact Commerce Corporation or Siebel or other such companies through wireless versions of their sales force automation applications, but what about the mobile customer? What if I realized I had forgotten my anniversary and had to order flowers, but I was in the car out of town? What if I logged on to my Palm VIIx (after I'd pulled the car over and parked) and saw a message that said there was a special on roses for customers who had used the flower site before? Click. Click. Click. Roses are ordered and sent instantly. The stored personal information pushed the appropriate offer to me on my PDA, and the stored personal information was used to reply to the offer with an order. This is a likely scenario for the very near future and is being enacted in a small way now.

Web shopping is growing to a major segment of the retail industry. In fact, this is such a potentially lucrative venture that the software for personalized Web shopping is expected to grow to $10.39 billion (pretty specific) by 2005, according to a study done in late 2000 by Ovum, an international research and consulting firm. Additionally, the handheld market is one of the faster-growing hardware markets. Despite the tight supply issues, International Data Corporation expects the market for PDAs to grow 55.9 percent in 2000 (up from 26.6 percent growth in 1999) with an expected annual growth rate of 27.8 percent for 2000 to 2004. The combination of increased web shopping with the explosive growth of handheld sales is deadly for the purse strings of American consumers and has lip-smacking potential for merchants. No longer is stationary or enclosed the prerequisite for shopping. Now, purchasing can happen on the go, anytime, anywhere. All the prominent PDAs—the Palm, Visor, and Blackberry—have wireless capabilities, either native to the device or attachable through snap-on modems from companies such as OmniSky.

Personalization is ideally a wireless application, able to communicate with any wireless device, from your PDA to your cellphone to your pager. As it stands as 2000 closes, this is a long way off. Dozens of companies have formed, such as mailmycell.com, to deliver some sort of personalized news content—sports, technology news, business, world events—to your wireless device. But these tend to be 12-character news bites that more often than not are uninteresting. While the concept is valid and at times useful, there is no real killer application for this yet. There are some significant portals opened or opening that have this potential though. Palm, Inc., the creator of the Palm and the wireless Internet-receptive version, the Palm VIIx, built a portal scheduled to go live at the end of 2000. Oracle has Oracle Mobile, a wireless portal that delivers content to your PDA.

There are a number of personalization companies going wireless. MicroStrategy is perhaps the best example and the most advanced on this new horizon with its portal http://www.strategy.com/.

What makes the wireless world exciting for personalization is that there is nothing more personal than the cellphone you carry or the PDA that sits in your pocket or in your purse. Unlike a desktop computer, which is a fixed, immobile instrument unless you throw it out a window, the cellphone is ubiquitous and the PDA is yours and rests on your person somewhere. Both travel with the user constantly. Same with pagers. By creating the small footprint software to broadcast information to you, the service you are getting seems so, well, personal. It's on your cellphone that rings on your belt or sings out that Beethoven tune when the personal information is delivered. That is not only useful, it's cool. Don't think that the personalization companies of the world don't know that. Useful and cool sell.

In fact, that's why analysts are bullish on MicroStrategy. In late 2000, Robert Tholemeier, a technology analyst at First Security Van Casper, stated in *Washington Techways* magazine "...Strategy.com is a category killer in the wireless information business." Not bad, since the Yankee Group is predicting one billion mobile Internet devices by 2003. That's one helluva category.

Let's look at the utility of wireless personalization. I'm going to show you a series of screen captures (Figure 6-2) from Strategy.com that will give you an idea how the process works. This is how using the personalized information input on Strategy.com by you, the customer, and preferences captured by Strategy.com and other sources through your online presence combine. Follow the airlines information that is being exhibited through Strategy.com on your cellphone.

You can then book the appropriate alternative flight "on phone" and solve your problem before it becomes a problem.

This is the ultimate sexy personalization venue. Each individual has a device that is customized to provide information and actions for that person alone.

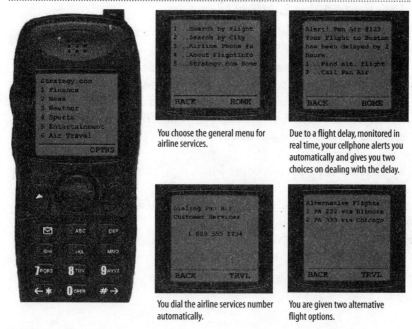

You choose the general menu for airline services.

Due to a flight delay, monitored in real time, your cellphone alerts you automatically and gives you two choices on dealing with the delay.

You dial the airline services number automatically.

You are given two alternative flight options.

Figure 6-2: The general Strategy.com services menu for your cellphone (Copyright 2000, Strategy.com Incorporated. All rights reserved.)

Other Companies Do These Things, Too

MicroStrategy certainly doesn't stand alone in the personalization market, but there is no question of their dominance. In late 2000, Annuncio, an enterprise marketing automation vendor (see Chapter 5) announced the release of Annuncio Bright, a personalization tool acquired in the purchase of Brightinfo.com in early 2000. It is a product that lets individual customers tailor a website to their specific content and taste. As the Aberdeen Group calls it in analyst-speak, it is "an additional execution channel for managing multitouch marketing campaigns." Annuncio Bright's ease of use is its best feature. Personalization plans can be created without much Web development design. There are analytic tools to measure the benchmarks of effective personalization included in the software.

In a sense, I suppose, turnabout is fair play. In MicroStrategy's eCRM 7, there is a EMA module included in the package.

How Personal Is Business?

"Well," you say, "how does this benefit my business? I know how it benefits amazon.com." In this configuration, you're forgetting one thing. amazon.com is a business, too, whether its appeal is to consumers or to other businesses. It is a wannabe profit-making entity, pure and simple. Keeping customers (you) is central to their business model, and I assume, yours. Personalization provides you with a marketing tool to give you an extra sword in the battle for customer market share.

There are millions of people who shop online and in stores who will soon be shopping via cellphones and PDAs. Personalization tools make it cool, make it easy, and make it an individual experience. They work.

Chapter 7

Partner Relationship Management

As the Internet economy begins to evolve to greater complexity, and as it increasingly penetrates the so-called Old Economy, the need for managing partnerships becomes increasingly important.

IDC, a leading analyst group, estimated that over 60 percent of all IT business in 1999 was done through indirect channels. That's $120 *billion* of a total of $200 billion. And that's just information technology. That's a bit of a trick statement since IT is most likely to be involved in partnerships and channels because of the complexity of the solutions and the inability for all but the largest companies to be all things to all people. For example, Siebel is nearly all things to all people in the CRM world, and it has perhaps the largest partner program of all the CRM companies. It depends on partners in different niches and vertical markets.

Interact Commerce Corporation (formerly SalesLogix), a leading midmarket sales force automation product, built a 2,200-customer list on $35 million in revenue over a two-year period from 1997 to 1999, and the channel was responsible for almost 80 percent of all their sales. They had, as of June 2000, more than 300 partners who operated as resellers of their software, Web offerings, and services.

With the growth of a ubiquitous Internet, the channel also becomes part of the corporate ecosystem, an independent segment integral to and dependent on the overall ecosystem built around any given company. The channel needs your products/service offerings to sell to their customers; you need the channel to sell your products/ service offerings to their customers, who indirectly become your customers. Symbiotic? Yes. Very hard to manage? Yes.

How many broken partnerships have you been involved in? How many different levels of partnership does the company you're interested in partnering with have? Take a quick look at Siebel's partnership program and levels:

- ▶ Siebel Consulting Partners

- ▶ Siebel Platform Partners

- ▶ Siebel Technical Partners

- ▶ Siebel Content Partners

- ▶ Siebel Software Partners

Within each of those are three levels of programs:

- ▶ Technical

- ▶ Marketing

- ▶ Sales

Within each of the five categories there are also varying levels:

- ▶ Strategic

- ▶ Premier

- ▶ Base

Each of these has individual rules and regulations. Within each category, there is a commitment—financial, manpower, or other— required to keep the partnership. In other words, if not managed properly, a mess ensues. Thus the new, growing offspring of CRM and eCRM: partner relationship management (PRM).

PRM was not unlike CRM in its conception. Robert Thompson, the founder and president of Front Line Solutions, Inc., a consulting and research firm specializing in PRM, says:

> PRM is a business strategy to select and manage partners to optimize their long-term value to an enterprise. In effect, it means picking the right partners, working with them to help them be successful in dealing with your mutual customers, and ensuring that partners and the ultimate end customers are satisfied and successful.

Mr. Thompson is considered the master of PRM in the industry and in fact is the creator of the very successful CRMGuru website (http://www.crmguru.com/), devoted to PRM and eCRM.

Sometimes you will see e-partnering used interchangeably with or alongside PRM. PRM and e-partnering are not identical. E-partnering represents the all-encompassing system—the combination of strategy, processes, e-tools, and methodology. PRM is the strategy and tools in the equation.

PRM is one of those smaller segments of the eCRM world that has superb potential. In the year 2000, it was expected to be a $500 million business, which should double to $1 billion by 2002. That is a reflection of the growing interdependency of companies in the New Economy. There is not a single company currently existing— Old Economy or New Economy—that hasn't realized they depend on their supply chain. This has always been the case, but with the increasing need to get to market quickly, the corporate ecosystem becomes more intertwined than ever thought possible by even foresighted supply chain specialists like I2. The supply chain is now superseded by the corporate ecosystem.

There are some major benefits to partnering, some apparent and some not. IDC identified three in a 1999 report on PRM sponsored by Allegis Corporation, the leading PRM vendor as of the millennium. They cite the following:

- ▶ Expanding market coverage

- ▶ Offerings of specialized products and services

- ▶ Broadened range of offerings and a more complete solution

I would add to that:

- ▶ Your possible competitors become your allies.

- ▶ Your company can concentrate on its core capabilities and still have full service coverage.

- ▶ The "my staff is your staff" principle governs your relationships, so you can call upon your partners to work with you to cover your gaps with your customers.

Managing Your Partners

The problems in managing partners are far different and far more complex than those of sales management. Each partner has a business interest of their own, a set of business processes that are endemic to their company, a group of their own partners and paying customers that may or may not overlap with yours, a business model that is most likely not identical to yours, and a group of personalities that vary as widely as the different corporate cultures. Thus, the way they allocate their time and the intensity of their partnering effort will vary from partner to partner. The contractual obligation of each partner will vary to some degree. However, each partner is essential to the infrastructure of your ecosystem and vital to the offerings to your customers.

An additional degree of complexity is added when you have to figure which partners are appropriate to which customers. The number of partner programs will vary depending on the category. Is your partner a value-added reseller (VAR) selling your product and adding services? Is your partner an independent software vendor (ISV), developing a software solution that is founded on your product? Is the partner a training partner? Is the partner a joint business partner who is providing a software solution that you don't have from a third-party vendor? These are functional and cultural concerns. What about technical issues? Is the IT architecture that your partner uses able to integrate with your architecture? With you at the hub, this becomes a mission-critical question for each partner, usually each using a different configuration due to their corporate needs and each trying to juggle architectures with their partners from their hub.

Look at a company like IBM. They have thousands of partners with multiple roles and programs and purposes. For example, IBM Global Services has so many subcontracting partners that they have established a program outsourced to 22 subcontractors to subcontract

other subcontractors to either do or administer all of IBM Global Services subcontracting assignments—unless there is a niche need such
as ERP so that an "other than the 22" subcontractor can work with
IBM Global Services directly. Even those arrangements are impacted
by the nature of the alliances IBM has with companies such as Siebel,
which has its own service organization, which doesn't stop IBM from
working with SalesLogix, and on and on.

Complicated? Yes, it is, and that is precisely the purpose of Internet-
integrated PRM applications: to manage what can be a plethora of
complex partner relations that are often conflicting. Mr. Thompson
again:

> A channel strategy is a prerequisite to effective PRM. Internet-
> based technology is often (but not always) a part of PRM
> because it's the only practical way to manage hundreds to tens
> of thousands of partners in large complex channels.

PRM Is Not Just Sales Force Automation and a Partner

There are some similarities to sales force automation applications,
but not enough to delete the subfolder. In order to understand the
differences between SFA and PRM, let's begin with another comment from Mr. Thompson on the necessity of integrating SFA with
PRM to develop a complete ePRM:

> Not unless there is true team selling when direct and indirect reps
> are collaborating on deals and need to communicate what's going
> on with a specific opportunity. Then it makes sense to connect
> SFA with PRM applications, or find one application that will
> serve both parties well. Another example is distributing leads that
> may come out of a CRM/SFA application and need to be for-
> warded to a PRM application. So, yes, there can be connection
> points, but not in every case.

In a nutshell, SFA with partners is not PRM.

PRM Means Partner Network

PRM applications handle considerably more than simple channel
management. Channel management ordinarily covers the simple partner relations that characterize the days gone by. Robert Thompson calls
the channel a "static, linear distribution process." In fact, the channel

has been most closely identified with value-added resellers, more than any other type of partners. Recently, *Smart Reseller* magazine, recognizing the tides of indirect channels were shifting, renamed themselves *Smart Partner* magazine.

The new definition of the channel is probably characterized by the transliterated Yiddish term, "*schadchen*," which, in English, roughly translates to "matchmaker." The demands of the corporate ecosystem call for a network of partners spawned or redefined by the Internet, chosen by the corporate network members, that can deliver a true solution sale or end-to-end service offering for the customers of any one member of the network. However, with the advent of the Internet version of PRM, the role of the indirect partner increases even more. Mr. Thompson:

> One thing that I do feel is often overlooked is the role of "influencer" channel partners—those who don't purchase products for resale, and may not earn an agent fee, but nevertheless are an important channel for companies to support. Integrators, consultants, and industry analysts are good examples. Customers buy based on recommendations of these influencers, but since the purchase is made direct, the role of the influencer is hidden.

What is the authority of these influencers? As the economy becomes more customer-intimate, the authority of the indirect partner—the influencer—becomes increasingly important. Industry analysts such as the Gartner Group, IDC, and Aberdeen do reports on who the players are, and the new mindshare champion is crowned in that market. For example, Allegis paid for the PRM report I quoted earlier from IDC, and there is a significant segment on Allegis Sales Partner as a market frontrunner for PRM. The "Paid for by Allegis" stamp tends to dilute IDC's conclusion a bit, but there are unmistakable PRM truths being stated by IDC and they carry credibility. A consultant who has established himself in the IT world in a particular discipline carries a lot of weight in the recommendations he proposes. Just as much as an additional category—friends. How frequently do you as an IT manager seek the counsel of knowledgeable friends and pay close attention to their recommendations? This is the value of the *schadchen*.

Assessing PRM

PRM functionality is multifarious. Because of its intricacy, there are a significant number of different attributes that any company assessing a PRM system must consider. What are the processes that should be embedded in the application? Let's look at the partnership cycle.

Partner Program Development

Siebel's aforementioned partner program deserves a more intense scrutiny to grasp the level of partner management that these kinds of programs involve. The basic requirements for a typical Siebel partnership type, Consulting Partner, illustrate these issues.

Services provided include business process redesign (using Siebel, of course), end-user training, project management, systems integration, systems administration, and training. Other characteristics are geographical focus and vertical market expertise to fill Siebel gaps. Dedicated Siebel-certified resources ranging from 1 (Base Partner) to 50 (Premier Partner) to 300 (Strategic Partner) are also required. The fees are significant—from $7,500 to $50,000 annually—and there is a marketing development fund commitment ranging from nothing for the Base Partner to $1 million per year for the Strategic Partner. The benefits are logo usage, varying levels of training appropriate to partnership level, partner posting, getting on the inside with Siebel, joint success stories, partner area access, marketing, demonstration, development licenses (though for the Base Partner there is a fee for this), technical support, attendance at the Siebel annual user conference, and of course, plenty of advertising, especially for the upper levels (they *are* paying for it!).

In the other categories, such as Software Partner, while the requirements and benefits vary from type to type and level to level, there are even more layers of interwoven intricacy—such as the Siebel Validation program that will certify your software product, which is different from the Siebel Certification program that certifies the successful training and completion of the testing of Siebel consultants, which is different from the certification accorded varying partners after customer audits conducted annually, which is different than the certification accorded partners for… you get the picture. This is not an easy process to manage.

Partner Recruitment and Profiling

Partner recruitment has undergone a dramatic shift in the last two years. If you look at major vendor partner recruitment or global services company partner recruitment, there have been drastic changes in time and method for all but a handful of companies. In the pre-1999 era, partnerships were "granted" by the vendor to an elite group of VARS, ISVs, or consulting services companies who gave the vendor something of significance—a place in a vertical market, a significant presence—and who brought business to the vendor as an offering. Typical ERP partnerships took eight months to build unless you were Accenture (formerly Andersen Consulting) or IBM and getting into them was harder than admission to Harvard. But in the last couple of years, that eight months has become one to three months, and though most companies are still selective about who their partners are, they are far more forgiving on the criteria for entry. Now, time to partnership is shortened in many cases and the "rules" of partnership are being eased. These, in combination with a shortage of qualified manpower and a very crowded domain-expert vendor field have led to hundreds, even thousands, of companies trying to become partners or create partner programs to fill the gaping holes. For example, dozens of SFA vendors on the market vie for your company's attention since they don't have the staff to implement their own software nor do they have the sales force to approach the markets you are attacking. You are now a valuable commodity to a vendor, rather than a potentially blackballed member of an elite society.

Partnership Goal Management

Once you have a partner, expectations must be established. What are the objectives for the partner? Do they have sales requirements to maintain the partnership? What kind of marketing development funds (MDF) do they have to commit? How does the application assign goals and objectives? How does the application flag under-performance or trigger responses to over-quota performance?

Sales/Marketing: Lead Generation and Distribution

Let's face it—a lot of partners are in it for the business leads the partnership generates. There's nothing wrong with this as long as they are prepared to bring business as well as take it. However, it's a fairly dicey proposition for the hub partner to distribute appropriate leads to the appropriate partners, since others may feel they are being left out or burnt in the process. Criteria for distribution and management of lead distribution are part of the package as it is presented.

Partner Life Cycle Management

Partner life cycle management is PRM's core functionality. This is where the partner is proven to be a partner, not a leech or a trophy-spouse.

Life cycle management is a buzzword in the IT world now for customers, partners, employees, and any other social or economic category of people that you care to think of. Simply stated, it is the entirety of the engagement with that group or individual, both long and deep—long in the sense that it extends the entire lifespan of the relationship, deep in that it covers all areas of the partnership, including the risks and rewards for that particular arrangement. PRM life cycle management characteristics that should be part of the application include:

Productivity and rewards How the partner is going to produce and benefit by that production. This means that the partner will have specific program-related objectives. Should they hit those objectives, they are rewarded in a particular fashion, for example, a percentage of the sale or a premium partnership status.

Forecasting The projections on how the partner is going to produce and benefit. An important part of life cycle management is what the company thinks it can expect from its individual partner. This addresses how much attention the partner is going to get from the company since all partners are not created equal.

Reporting The description of how the partner is going to produce and benefit, using reporting tools endemic to the functionality of the application (often Seagate's Crystal Reports is integrated with the application). Life cycle management reporting is critical because how you formulate the report is key to the understanding of the report results by the reader of that report. Corporate decisions are made correctly or incorrectly, often based on how well structured the report is.

Contract management How the partner is legally obligated to produce and benefit by the partnership. This is a tracking function to make sure that contractual obligations are met.

Architecture

The Internet's open standards are pretty much the only way for an "e-hyphenated" package to go. That means able to handle HTTPS (secure HTTP), XML, and various Java encodings, plus perhaps Active Server Pages (ASP), and Java server pages (JSP). This plus good old HTML should do the Web-trick.

Integration

Integration, which is covered in Chapter 11, is of paramount importance unless you have never done anything with information systems at your company. Since that is highly unlikely for anyone reading this book, what is more likely is that your company has invested between tens of thousands to tens of millions in information systems. Dennis Ryan, president of Allegis, noted in an interview that most Allegis customers had some CRM or simply an SFA application in place prior to their purchase of the steeply priced Allegis Sales Partner. Additionally, most companies may have ERP up and running, legacy client server best-of-breed applications, mainframe applications if they lean toward the Pleistocene era, and who knows how many other Web applications their sales and marketing forces already employ.

Ease of Deployment, Change, and Use

How important is this one on a scale of one to ten? Ten. Getting the application up and running, customizing it without the consulting firm that implemented it, and then using it without teeth-gnashing is vital to successful implementation of what can be a costly piece of software. For example, Allegis Sales Partner and Channelwave Software are sophisticated PRM applications, but cost an arm and a leg to code so that customized versions are available to the channel management team. On the other hand, Partnerware's extended Enterprise 2000 (XE) automates most of these processes through eXtensible Module Designer templates and design tools, which eliminates most of the coding. That means you don't have to pay for custom coding every time you change your partner programs or business processes. This is important for the return on investment expected. Being able to implement and deploy the application and then simply go to the Web and go to work is essential with the need for speed that governs the world of business-to-business.

Security, Performance, and Reliability

When the system is up and running, it has to stay up and run.

Return on Investment

There are differences of opinion on both the metrics for ROI and the validity of the ROI at this stage of the PRM game. Those analysts and pundits who have made prognostications about the infant PRM field have all agreed that PRM does or will have a tangible benefit, but when seems to be in question. IDC cheerleads for a rapid ROI that they think is not only possible but absolutely necessary in making the determination to purchase PRM. They make statements like these:

> Companies need to be able to see results and recoup their investments. The days of lengthy implementations without accountability are over. They also need to project future investments accurately.

and:

> PRM also allows companies to better measure and improve their return on investment (ROI) in channel programs and activities. (Source: International Data Corp., "Partner Relationship Management: Enabling eBusiness for the Channel.")

Robert Thompson, on the other hand, took a more cautious approach in our interview:

> Potentially [there is a tangible ROI for PRM], but there aren't a lot of case studies yet. However, some companies like Cisco Systems are well known for employing PRM systems in dealing with partners. Although their technology was homegrown, the results have been impressive in terms of sales productivity and reduced support costs. More important, however, is that Cisco has created loyalty relationships. Many of the companies I've interviewed are chasing similar goals, but have little tangible results to show so far.

Research shows that Mr. Thompson is perhaps closer to the tempered mark.

The Technology: Who's Who and What's What in PRM

Despite PRM's relative newness, there are several established names in the field who have fully functional, well-developed, often expensive applications. These are the major titles.

Allegis Sales Partner

Allegis Corporation is among the leading ePRM players in the market-place, providing a fully Web-integrated e-channel management solution. While there are several other players mentioned at the end of this chapter, Allegis is currently holder of the mindshare for this fledgling domain. Hot on their trail, is, of course, the eChannel solution of Siebel Systems, as Siebel continues its drive to be the Microsoft/Oracle/IBM of its genre. Let's look at the Allegis Sales Partner application, the most sophisticated ePartnering application on the millennial market.

Partner management's intricacies are well covered by Sales Part-ner, a sophisticated Web-integrated software that covers the PRM territory completely. Through your browser, you can handle dozens of different aspects of PRM. There are four major components, each of which is broken down into several subsets.

Content and Lead Matching

This is an entirely customizable criteria-based set of applications that provide channel managers with the ability to best fit leads generated by the partner "parent" to the partner. This can be done singly, manually, in bulk, or automatically. Business rules are built into the modules so leads move to the right partner automatically, and partner acceptance is necessary for the completion of the loop. One somewhat iffy part of the Lead Matcher module is the capture of partner win/loss results, which can be deemed intrusive.

Another module in this subset is the Content Matcher, which uses criteria-based business rules to move specific content to specific part-ners. The actual content is designed and delivered through online templates for the nontechnical content providers.

Finally, Partner Finder and Partner Profiles fill out this segment of the application. This is the domain that covers not only detailed partner information, but the roles, approvals, edit/view rights, and other privileges granted to that specific partner, as well as the criteria that identify that partner for lead and content generation. In other words, this is the administrative stuff.

Territory and Channel Readiness

This is a truly mercenary module. It prepares partners to sell ven-dor products. Registration and ramp-up activities are taken care of effectively. Business plans for the partners are generated dynamically; objectives are linked to partner programs that can be customized to each individual partner. When programs are accepted, they are monitored automatically. If there are partner requests, the eRequest submodule automates and answers them.

Program and Funds Management

The partners love this one. It is a toolset that creates customer demand for each partner and manages the co-marketing funds from the vendors. It creates master budgets and automatic reports on the administration of those budgets. It tracks and analyzes partner sales programs for vendor goods. It has a comprehensive Best Practices Library that is used to find the criteria for the most successful programs for each partner.

Ecommerce Management

This is the newest and the most comprehensive module. It is the B2B procurement of products and services from vendor to partner. It handles needs analysis, partner by partner. There is a comprehensive product catalog so the partner knows what is available from the vendor. Quotations can be issued directly via the Web. Broader procurement functions include the vendor's ability to route a sale emanating from the vendor to the best-fit partner automatically or to the channel manager for manual "partner fitting."

This is a premier PRM application, and from strictly the standpoint of functionality, nothing else really comes close. However, you are paying a steep price for this level of functionality. Aside from initial setup and customization costs, the *minimal* cost for Sales Partner as of mid-2000 is $20,000 *per month*!

Their website: http://www.allegis.com/.

Partnerware's eXtended Enterprise

Partnerware's eXtended Enterprise (XE) is the most user friendly of the lot. In the eCRM and CRM worlds, service costs are often between one and three times the software costs. That's why the figure of approximately $1 million is often quoted as the entry price for a basic eCRM implementation. However, that doesn't include what is often the follow-up consulting services costs when modifications have to be made. The bucks are big and the consulting services companies are getting wealthy doing the follow-up. XE's application framework is built around the need for speed and simplicity.

According to Partnerware, it is thin client, browser based. The implementation time is short, often a matter of weeks. Customization is done through templates that are provided with the eXtensible Module Designer (XMD). These templates are easy enough to use for end users to provide forms for partner management.

There are six core modules: pAcquire, pProfile, pLeads, pFunds, pProgram, and pSales. Each of the modules is thoroughly integrated with the others, though the quality and comprehensiveness of functionality varies from module. For example, a review of XE in the June 5, 2000, issue of *InfoWorld* took notice that the pSales module has exceptional reporting functionality, but the reporting functions of many other modules are far more limited and rough hewn.

XE can be hosted via application service providers and thus keep the costs to a minimum.

Their website: http://www.partnerware.com/.

Intelic's ProChannel

Intelic's ProChannel is an interesting PRM application with some direct channel integration. It has 16 modules that are focused on transaction types, a bit of a departure from both Allegis and Partnerware. Some useful examples:

Catalog Interactive online search by part, description, family, or competitor.

Interactive Quoting Catalog pricing (general), quote details, and price targeting (price targeting includes special discounts or some other form of special pricing so the salesperson or partner's salespeople remain competitive or get the victory margin).

Distribution management Price adjustments, debit authorization, point of sale reporting, debit reconciliation, instant feedback. This is all automatic through established business rules.

All of the other modules, such as Commissions, Price Management, and Opportunity and Design Tracking, are also transactional. If your partnerships are focused in these domains, this unusual PRM package (more like PTM—partner transaction management) could be what you need. Otherwise, Partnerware or Allegis will be more appropriate. One reason for this unusual PRM application is Intelic's genesis in the manufacturing world.

Their website: http://www.intelic.com/.

eCRM with Limited PRM Functionality

ECRM and CRM companies are all realizing the benefits of partner management. As a result, several of the eCRM leaders are incorporating some PRM features into their applications. A few examples follow.

Onyx Partner Portal

For a company not engaged strictly in PRM, Onyx takes an intriguing tack with the creation of its Partner Portal. This is a full-time self-service product that uses the Web to deliver partner services. The application focuses on sales, with lead generation, joint sales capacity, and sales pipeline management. There is a library feature that allows the partner to download appropriate partner marketing collateral and send it to their clients. However, like the other eCRM companies that had a start in sales force automation, this is highly concentrated on the selling aspects of the PRM application world.

Their website: http://www.onyx.com/.

Siebel eChannel

eChannel is one of Siebel's newer modules. It covers all the basic needs of partner-oriented institutions, such as lead management, MDF management, service requests, and order/quote online. As you can see from the screen capture grabbed off their website (see Figure 7-1), presentation of the partner management tool is clear. However, this is not where Siebel makes its mark. For a partner program as complicated as theirs, Siebel would be better off using someone else's PRM application. However, Siebel is the leader in this field, so integration with Siebel's other eCRM and CRM applications is without peer. You can bet on many future additions to the robustness of eChannel.

Their website: http://www.siebel.com/.

Pivotal PartnerHub

Pivotal, whose eRelationship 2000 will be discussed in Chapter 10, has a component focused on the channel named PartnerHub, which they claim is part of a system they call eBusiness Relationship Management (eBRM). While not nearly as robust as the applications from the pure PRM vendors (such as Allegis) some of the fundamentals are covered. It is comprised of four modules that are reached and

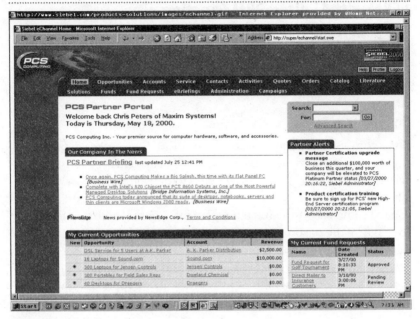

Figure 7-1: Siebel eChannel—a partnership portal

regulated through either of the two major browsers. Their focus is more collaborative and cooperative, which, while certainly adequate, is more a function of direct marketing and sales than indirect channels.

PartnerHub creates a virtual sales team that combines the online capabilities of each of the partners. Collaborative information sharing on competitors, placement of orders for collateral or products from any given partner, co-marketing collaboration, and monitoring of the joint customer orders are done seamlessly, regardless of the partners physical geography. PartnerHub provides reporting tools and a robust customization and development tool, Pivotal eToolkit, that allows for modification or creation of new "eBRM" applications from scratch. This is not a true PRM application, but more a collaborative set of applications for partners.

Their website: http://www.pivotal.com/.

Chapter 8

The CRM Rainbow: Beyond the Traditional CRM

There is no doubt that the definition of eCRM is broad. The only two things that the analysts and pundits can agree on are that eCRM means Web based and customer facing. Otherwise, there is no satisfactory definition, except, I hope, those mentioned in Chapter 1 of this book.

There are several CRM variants, with a few that could stand out in a potentially viable niche market and those that have already successfully broken into the marketplace. Rather than a comprehensive look at all the variants, we'll look at a few that show promise, reveal a unique fresh perspective, or are at the cusp of explosion.

Verticalization: Business to Business

Verticalization is a concept gaining increasing credence as niches that need to be filled define how the Internet is increasingly used. That "vertical-market-as-a-niche" is seen everywhere, with portals for chemical, auto, trucking, and other traditional manufacturing industries springing up. eCRM particularly is a flexible system that allows for vertical customization fairly easily since its foundation is customers and "customized" definitions of customers that can be easily programmed. This is leading to a proliferation of verticals that are founded on the eCRM platform, such as Live Wire, Inc.'s student relationship management (SRM) solution for campuses and the extensive number of vertical industries that both Siebel and SalesLogix have in their customer base because of the easy customization of their products. Some of the more interesting CRM "rainbow" applications of eCRM/CRM will be targeted in this chapter.

One Size Does Not Fit All

"One size fits all" could not be farther from the truth in the CRM space. Every company has its own needs based on the unique characteristics of their customers and markets where they compete. Ask any ten "experts" in the CRM space to describe in detail what features and functions an ideal CRM system should have and you are likely to get ten significantly different answers. At first glance, these systems seem to follow the same basic principles and patterns, but an investigation at any finer resolution will show that one ideal system may be dramatically different than the next. So which one is correct? They all are.

When a company implements a vertical version of eCRM, it must be tuned to account for the unique blend of characteristics found in their customers and the industry in which they compete. These characteristics must be identified at an early stage in the implementation cycle and factored into the solution to avoid project failure and ensure the maximum ROI.

To illustrate, a semiconductor equipment company should have high per-transaction value, low-volume, business-to-business transactions with its customers. It would be relevant to track information such as the type of facility the customer operates and its hours of operation. If they were running a 24/7 300mm facility, it would be important not to attempt to sell them 200mm equipment and to ensure tech support was available during off hours. It would also be important to have a formalized problem escalation process integrated into the CRM, as customers who make multimillion dollar purchases typically require this.

In contrast, a company that sells books and CDs would have low per-transaction value, high-volume, individual consumer customers. It might be important to track the birthday of the individual so a "birthday special" promotion could be sent to him once a year. Or perhaps to provide a Web-based or automated email-based response system that allows the customer to request shipping status on their last order, thus reducing a potentially overwhelming volume of phone calls.

It can quickly be seen that the requirements of eCRM differ substantially from industry to industry. However, most of today's solutions do not target any vertical industry niches primarily. By doing so, they would constrain themselves to selling only to participants of the targeted industries. The result is a square peg product trying to fit a round hole problem. To address this discrepancy, vendors tout product features such as "highly configurable" and "powerful API"—translated, this means lots of expensive custom consulting work.

A Case for Verticalization

In the 1800s, if you had chest pains you would likely visit the same town doctor who pulled your aching tooth last week and delivered your wife's baby last spring. He would probably be the same person to prescribe remedies for any other ailments you may have, from blurry vision to back injuries. Today, you use a general practitioner for a preliminary diagnosis, but any one of a dozen specialists such as cardiologists, dentists, or obstetricians may be engaged to address specific medical issues.

The specialization of medicine is analogous to the verticalization occurring in the eCRM market. The rapid adoption of eCRM technology has sparked an evolution in the sophistication of this space and is now serving a very broad range of business models. While every vendor understands and must deliver the basic components of CRM and to some extent eCRM, similar to a general practitioner, there is a growing need for specialization. For eCRM products, this specialization is the creation of vertical solutions along the lines of industry segmentation such as healthcare, technology, transportation, finance, or communications.

The main advantages to purchasing a verticalized solution are the reduction in tailoring to make it fit your business and the comfort in having a software vendor who truly understands your business. After all, if you were operating a semiconductor business, how comfortable would you feel about a product that was recently installed for an online toy store or an insurance company? The way customer relationships are managed is one of the most critical competencies in your company—could your operations be so generic that this same product will meet your needs? Of course not. That is why you will pay thousands, or even millions, for integration consultants to configure the system until it does meet your needs.

Who Is Going Vertical

Some eCRM vendors who understand the value of industry specialization are already capitalizing on the vertical approach. For instance, Siebel Systems offers several verticals, including eAutomotive, eEnergy, eTechnology, eHealthcare, and even eApparel and Footware. Another CRM leader, Clarify (acquired by Nortel Networks) also markets a dozen vertical solutions. Because the difference between a technology-focused eCRM and an automotive-focused eCRM is probably not much more than data fields, a couple of reports, and some marketing, companies who have any of these products can quickly jump into another vertical industry space.

This has led some analysts to speculate that the underlying software of eCRM will soon become a secondary consideration to the industry expertise of the vendor. This could put the current market gorillas at a significant disadvantage against smaller, highly focused companies. For instance, in a target market of semiconductor companies, how well could Clarify's generic High Technology vertical offering compete with a hypothetical brand like Semiconductor CRM Inc., a company run by recognized semiconductor industry experts who focus exclusively on solutions tailored for this industry?

Semiconductor CRM Inc., in addition to their highly specialized product, might differentiate further by providing value-added, industry-focused services such as content aggregation, competitive equipment databases, a preloaded semiconductor FAB database complete with contacts, reports that adhere to Semitech consortium specifications, a prewired semiconductor focused trading hub, and a turnkey EDI network with all major vendors in the semiconductor industry—just as a start. It is not inconceivable that this type of laser-focused vendor could chip away at the CRM market-share pie one small niche at a time.

Vertical CRM solutions are certainly a special tool for a special job. Only the market will determine the level of specialization that will occur. Companies that play in these small niches will have a much narrower customer base, so it is likely they will have to find other value-added services to augment their revenue lines. But these same value-added services are exactly what will help them differentiate. The value proposition for this type of product remains extremely compelling.

Case Study: The Challenge of eCRM in Higher Education

Today's students stroll into the institution of their choice with expectations that are directly proportional to the size of their tuition bills. The students and their parents demand that they have access to the prevalent technologies of the day. Internet access, wireless networks, online course registration, automated classrooms, and distance education opportunities are not viewed as "nice-to-haves," but as imperatives. After all, these are kids who have had computers since they were toddlers and who view technology and Internet access as necessary as the air they breathe.

In most institutions, the academic and administrative leadership understands the need to be responsive to these demands. But they are faced with a dizzying array of rapidly emerging technologies (or repackaged old technologies) sold by well-oiled marketing machines that make a profitable living by over-promising and under-delivering. These unsuspecting decision-makers, confused by technologies and overwhelmed by costs, are often convinced to commit to product purchases that have significant underlying implications on architecture, standards, and resource requirements.

Institutional CIOs traditionally faced budgetary challenges that prevented them from recruiting the cream of today's crop of technical talent. They now face an even bigger problem. With coffers opened for large scale re-engineering of their application environments, higher education's technology managers find themselves unable to compete for the small number of qualified employees who can implement complex ERP and Web-based applications. How can they compete with the dot-com down the road offering five-figure signing bonuses, six-figure salaries, stock options, and the promise of retiring at the ripe old age of 35? As if that isn't daunting enough, they also have the privilege of communicating the bad news about the total cost of these projects to their superiors—not a fun message to deliver! Rising costs, unrealistic expectations, and a general lack of experience and resources are a recipe for disaster.

Never ones to miss a new and lucrative opportunity, in march the big consulting companies and implementation partners, offering to address the resource and expertise issues. All too often, they turn the noncommercial higher education environment upside down with their structured methodology-driven, mega-project solutions.

The result is confused and dissatisfied leadership, spending more money than ever on architectural upgrades to support ERP and large system implementations that never end. They find they have invested in systems with seven-figure price tags and half the functionality of the tired old legacy systems they replaced. They still haven't effectively re-engineered old processes, addressed the needs of today's student, or exploited the promise of Web-enabled applications. Soon the focus has shifted almost entirely to the systems and technologies—with all of their problems and overwhelming costs—and away from the fundamental focus of their mission. Education is supposed to be "all about the student," not "all about the technology," or "all about the Internet," or "all about the implementation partner," or... well, you get the picture.

The parallels to the pre-CRM commercial market are obvious. In higher education, the focus has begun to shift from technologies, systems, and architectures to a more appropriate focus on the customer—and those technologies and solutions that enable the institution to better understand, better serve, and better retain that customer. Of course, the customer in this market is the student.

eCRM in the Higher Education Environment

To understand how the student compares to the traditional customer, you first have to understand the unique nature of the student. Unlike most customer relationships, higher education relationships go through a series of interesting transformations, solicitations, and forms of pursuit and acceptance. Traditionally, the relationship begins by the applicant saying, "I want to be your customer," and the institution saying, "We accept you as a customer." This unusual relationship involves the student and/or parent paying potentially large amounts of money for the education service. As long as all parties remain satisfied with the value equation, the student graduates to a new form of customer, the alumnus. At this point, the roles are reversed and the institution begins pursuing the former student for donations. Along the way, the customer assumes multiple roles (student, athlete, intern) and the institution engages many different customer service representatives (faculty, tutors, coaches, associations, administrators). To complicate matters, the institution itself is a complex beast, much like a small city. Not only does the institution deliver an education, it also embeds products and services that span industries, such as hotel, restaurant, public safety, sports, theatre, retail, and media. Given the complexity, diversity, and dynamic nature of these relationships, some form of CRM would seem to be mandatory! But how do traditional/commercial forms of CRM apply to higher education?

Student Relationship Management

In today's competitive education realm, the need to view students as customers has never been greater. With the rush to online learning and virtual universities, applicants have more choices than ever. Students (and their parents) are demanding greater access to resources via the Internet. Faculty are increasingly looking for ways to extend the normal boundaries of the classroom. IT departments are so overwhelmed from the rigors of ERP implementations and the frenetic pace of technology changes that applications to support the growing needs of the students, faculty, and administration are appearing very slowly, if at all.

Through student relationship management (SRM), Live Wire, Inc., is leading a group of forward-thinking schools and technology partners who are beginning to apply CRM and eCRM principles to the challenges of today's higher education environment.

It's fair to say that CRM is "all about the customer." The premise is simple: manage your customer relationships more effectively, deliver a product or service with a significant value proposition, and you will attract and retain more customers than your competition. And if you do that, you will be successful. It's also fair to say that higher education is "all about the student." Manage your student relationships more effectively, deliver an educational experience with a significant value proposition, and you will attract and retain more students than your competition. It becomes obvious that the concept of student relationship management is a customized form of CRM designed to meet the demands of higher education.

Product and service vendors have recognized this opportunity, but are struggling to determine how to exploit it for commercial gain. Higher education is a tough market to break into, and has many unique challenges and roadblocks for the outsider to overcome. Live Wire has leveraged its experience with colleges and universities, and built a staff of former senior IT professionals from within the higher education ranks. By doing so, they have engaged a series of customers and technology partners in an effort to build an online learning community around the concepts of SRM and a marketplace to deliver SRM-appropriate products and services.

The Importance of Community

Higher education as a vertical market can be viewed as a tightly knit community of schools, associations, faculty, administrators, alumni, and students. Generally, the traditional "commercial approach" to sales in higher education is viewed as abrasive. To make inroads in this market, establishing a sense of community—built upon expertise, experience, and mutual respect—is very important. SRM, which by itself is not a product or service, is well suited to be established within this large community as a sub-community. Live Wire believes that the best way to further refine SRM expertise is to build an online community that encourages members of the higher education community to participate in the further evolution of SRM, and champion the acceptance, growth, and direction of the products and services that are meant to enable effective SRM. And so was born MySRM.com.

MySRM: Portal, Community, and Marketplace

As the creator and custodian of MySRM.com, Live Wire has taken an innovative approach to evolving SRM community expertise and awareness as a means of further evolving SRM-appropriate technologies, products, and services. These higher education insiders have combined portal technologies from Plumtree (http://www.plumtree.com/), CRM expertise from Interact Commerce Corporation(http://www.saleslogix.com/ or http://www.interactcommerce.com/), and enterprise integration tools from Scribe Software (http://www.scribesoft.com/). They are using these technologies to build community, foster e-learning, create and share expertise, incubate products and services, review/appraise solutions, and share product and service experiences online. By utilizing the tools and technologies they are also selling, MySRM.com represents the type of portal, components, and enterprise integration the institution can expect to realize if it were to purchase these tools.

SRM Lifecycle

A critical piece of this puzzle is the "lifecycle" associated with implementing SRM products, services, and process improvements. SRM emphasizes the concept of "one size fits one." Each institution has a unique set of needs, constraint, requirements, and opportunities. Given the tendency toward risk mitigation, and yet the need to quickly meet rising demands, the most effective methodologies avoid big bang, big mess solutions. Instead, they employ the SRM lifecycle built around scalable, iterative opportunities to buy, build, and leverage custom applications that can be deployed quickly and tightly integrated to the existing enterprise applications (legacy or current-state).

While many vendors claim to have mega-frameworks that will accomplish just that, the MySRM Marketplace promotes the dissemination of scalable, cost-effective components and integration tools that are readily available today. More important, SRM tools can be combined with approved SRM integration services to integrate tightly with backend enterprise systems in a series of small-scale initiatives. This allows schools to add value today, while working toward the ultimate service goals of tomorrow.

Higher education has a penchant for sharing solutions, knowledge, and resources with other institutions—even those that would be considered their direct competitors. In the true spirit of community, the MySRM portal and community provide a vehicle for SRM customers to sell, trade, or give away SRM components they have developed. All members of the community have the opportunity to share SRM success.

Changes on the Horizon for Education

SRM is not only a means of redefining traditional views of the student-institution relationship. It is also an effective means of introducing what could be viewed as competitive—even threatening—advances in distance education and virtual universities. Isolationists in the higher education community view virtual universities as a passing fad that has little or no chance of succeeding long term if pitted directly against prestigious established schools in a competition for the best and the brightest students. But optimists in the commercial sector see great potential here, especially as the cost of education rises and the shortage of qualified graduates in a tight labor market continues. The pursuit of advanced degrees, professional certifications, and continuing education through a virtual university is becoming more generally appealing. It won't be long until the brightest high school kids recognize that they can shortcut the traditional four-year stint at college by taking good paying jobs at resource-starved brick-and-mortar (or click-and-mortar) companies, while simultaneously pursuing degrees online. The most opportunistic employers have already begun underwriting the cost of online education as a means of attracting a new segment of the labor pool. Through effectively embracing SRM and paying attention to the needs of the student, brick-and-mortar schools can begin transforming at least some of their offerings to click-and-mortar models. At the very least, they can begin to partner with virtual universities and join the efforts to reinvent the learning experience. SRM requires its participants to assume that the world will continue to change, and that embracing, exploiting, and even encouraging that change is the ticket to long-term SRM success.

Their website: www.MySRM.com.

eCRM as a Platform: *x*RM

Relationship management is perhaps the most important factor in building any successful business. This factor has been driving the proliferation of *x*RM solutions, where *x* is a variable that represents the role of a target audience, such as a customer or supplier. The more specifically *x* is defined, the more vertical the solution. For example, where *x* equals customer, you find traditional CRM products that are marketed to a very broad audience. Where *x* equals student, you find a student relationship management vertical solution with a niche market of academic institutions. When x equals tenant, you find a vertical solution targeting real estate organizations, and so on.

Essentially, eCRM is evolving into more of a platform for developing focused applications rather than being an end solution itself. Once the basic relationship management components have been developed, it is not difficult to program specific business rules that define the x in xRM. Some basic components of the xRM platform include:

Account management Track and manage people

Case management Capture, trace, and route issues

Knowledge management Mine knowledge from previously closed cases

Interaction management Manage communications with the audience x either via email or Web extranet

There are hundreds of possible flavors of xRM. It is quite possible that by the time this book has gone to press there may even be a software vendor that provides a framework for new ISVs to build their vertical xRMs.

eCRM Lite

As CRM products have evolved, they have become heavy with features and proportionally more complex and expensive. Integration of these products into the enterprise can easily run into the millions and take months or years. In many cases they are never actually fully implemented. In addition to being expensive and time consuming, this integration process also knocks your best people out of commission while they teach the system integrators how your business works. After eCRM has been implemented comes the challenge of recruiting and retaining the technical staff required to keep these products running. This task is not to be underestimated in one of the tightest labor markets in history.

This implementation challenge is obviously surmountable for large companies with deep pockets; however, it is well beyond the reach of smaller businesses. It seems that in the rush to sell, vendors have overlooked more than 1.5 million businesses with 5 to 100 employees. These companies generate more than 3 trillion dollars in annual revenue in the United States alone. This may explain why only 9 percent of the CRM market has been captured even though solutions have been available for a solid ten years.

There are a variety of solutions on the market that can help you accomplish your eCRM objectives. In particular, look for hosted solutions coming from applications service providers (ASPs). An ASP-based eCRM (see Chapter 15) is an ideal model for small businesses since there is zero software, hardware, or network infrastructure to purchase or maintain. These solutions are provided over the Web as a service for a monthly charge—typically between $50 and $200 per user per month with $0 to $10,000 setup fees. There are two types of ASPs: those that host brand name enterprise applications, and "pure plays" who host their own applications designed specifically to be hosted solutions. The first is typically more expensive and still requires significant levels of integration. Vendors in this space include USi, Corio, FutureLink.net, Talisma, and Portera. The "pure play" category is typically a much lower priced solution focusing only on its own brand. Examples of vendors in this space include SalesForce.com, InstantCRM.com, and TenNorth.com.

Mail Management Solutions

In addition to the traditional eCRM solutions, there are a number of mail management products on the market that are also well equipped for managing customer interactions. These products primarily focus on email management by providing programmable rules that allow you to define how inbound emails that target corporate addresses—such as support@mycompany.com—should be dealt with. Vendors in this space include Brightware, eGain, and Quintus.

In addition to routing messages to the appropriate individual in your organization, this type of product can potentially reduce the support burden on your staff by filtering and automatically answering certain questions. The target customer for vendors in this space typically includes companies who deal with a high volume of customer email traffic. While most products in this space are typically implemented as a traditional enterprise deployment, vendors like eGain provide their solutions as a hosted service, reducing implementation costs and headaches.

Hypercoordination

Pipeline Software, Inc., (http://www.pipelinesoftware.com/) takes a radically different approach to eCRM. Their Hypercoordination technology is a hosted B2B interaction management application that re-examines the basic nature of the vendor-customer relationship. Unlike a CRM, which is essentially a vendor's database for tracking and managing its customer interactions, Hypercoordination is an interactive, two-sided, coordinated, relationship management medium.

Any company who obtains an identity on the Pipeline Network (typically their company domain ID) is eligible to participate in hypercoordinated business relationships. For example, the customer (requestor) makes a phone call or sends an email requesting some type of service from a supplier. Assuming that the supplier is CRM enabled, there is a good chance that a case will be opened and tracked for the requestor. And if the supplier is really on the ball, they will provide a customer extranet where the requestor can check on the status of their request. That is typically as far as current CRM models go.

By contrast, if both requestor and supplier were participants in the Pipeline Network, they would be able to hypercoordinate on this interaction. For example, the requestor would make a request not via email but by creating a supplier request object. This object automatically routes itself to the supplier via the Pipeline Network carrying all requestor profile and request detail information. Upon opening the request object, the supplier's system establishes a connection with the requestor's system and opens a "conversation" channel that will persist until the request has been satisfied. This conversation channel will act as a conduit for transfer of email, documents, chat, and other media pertinent to the business case. During the life of a request, all related interactions are recorded and automatically inserted into an audit log for both the requestor and the supplier.

Pipeline believes its model is essentially a paradigm shift where relationship management will become an equally managed, equally participating event for both requestor and supplier.

Other Interesting Products

Another interesting approach is from V2Commerce.com. They provide a very low-cost ASP solution for managing customer interactions. Their product is a remotely configurable email management and form management tool that can be quickly integrated into any corporate website. It allows a company to develop custom data collection forms such as surveys and manage customer responses, all without installing a single piece of software.

Chapter 9

Call Centers Mean Customer Interaction

@#$*(@#*#. Isn't this the first thing that usually occurs to you when you think of customer service? Who hasn't cursed someone at a customer service center or on a service phone call? You who are without this sin may cast the first phone. The cost of this @#$*(@#*# is not cheap either. Studies have estimated that the cost per PC of an internal helpdesk operation that is dysfunctional is between $6,000 and $15,000 per year. The other tangible measure is customers lost due to poor service and deals not closed by telesales reps. Large companies, huge expenses. However, with the technological evolution of the customer service sector, @#*(@#*# may be a thing of the past and ☺☺☺ may be the future.

First, there was the customer service counter—the place where you would (and often still do) return those things that didn't fit to live human representatives. Then came the helpdesk, which you would call to get help on Word because it crashed when you typed the word "lotus." Then there was the call center, which, using the voice technologies of the 1990s, would provide your service representative with enough information so he'd hear you out on why your computer wasn't working again. Now as we move through the Internet Age, we have the customer interaction center (CIC), also known as the customer contact center or the multimedia call center. CIC sophistication lets you call in on your phone (and soon with wireless transmissions, courtesy of your PDA) and walk through a website that will handle the most common problems easily, with online information at the ready. The functionality is deep, the technology is complex, and the results are strong.

Keep in mind that a customer interaction center or a customer contact center doesn't necessarily mean a customer service center. It could apply equally as well to a telesales center or a field service operation.

Many of the really big players started out in the customer service market. Vantive and Clarify in particular were known for their call center strengths and incorporated other functions later as they grew to prominence. Nortel Networks, given its telecommunications history, was an obvious partner for Clarify's call center qualifications. It has been speculated that CRM started here, though as I mentioned in Chapter 4, sales force automation is likely the real grandfather of CRM. The customer service segment could be either the great-uncle or the step-grandfather.

Calling this facet of CRM a customer interaction center or a customer contact center is not something to treat as a marketing pitch. There is a lot implied in the statement. It is recognized that, in the twenty-first century, it is no longer valid for the customer just to be a transmitter or receiver of information. Collaborative activity is one aspect of what makes this a CRM application. The customer directly interacts with the company through a customer service representative and a variety of communications channels, and both use tools that make the interactions valuable. The customer could be interacting with the website through self-service applications. If a human being isn't involved directly as a customer service representative, there are virtual service representatives. Now that all but the most difficult and complex problems can be automated, customer satisfaction has been improving dramatically.

One of the problems in this world of rapidly changing customer expectations is that the evolution of the call center to the CIC or contact center is slow, though its rate of change is accelerating. The Gartner Group expects that only 20 percent of the existing call centers will have integrated live Web contact points or some form of automated email response by 2002. It is expected that by 2005, it will be at 70 percent—a monstrous leap. However, we have to get to 2005 through 2002, meaning that for the most part, call centers, regardless of what they call themselves, will still be call centers with human operators for awhile yet. This is not to say that the changes aren't already underway.

What does this segment look like? What can it actually do? How is it intertwined with the other parts of CRM and when is that not a good thing? Let's take the plunge.

The Functionality

Think about a typical call you might make to a computer company technical service representative.

1. You dial the computer company's number.

2. You press several buttons on the telephone that gets you through menu options, ordinarily guided by a human voice.

3. You wait for a customer service rep while music plays.

4. If you haven't punched in an ID of some sort prior to this on your phone, you are asked for an ID.

5. The representative, reading off a screen that outlines your entire history with the company, including the recent calls or email inquiries you made, the level of difficulty of your problem, and the success or failure of the results, queries you on the nature of the problem, request, or concern.

6. When you have spoken with the rep about it, the rep enters the information, checks several possible results that show up on a screen, and if one of them resolves the problem, marks it off. If none of them resolve the problem, you are sent to a new level to undergo a higher level of customer service (a manager if it is not technical and a level 2 support technician if it is), with all the new information on what didn't work or what problem wasn't resolved.

Whew. That's a lot of potentially frustrating activity. But think about all the functionality involved in this call. There is call routing, assignment management, queue management, call tracking, entitlement processing, workflow, problem resolution, performance measurement, and service management, among other things. There are activities that are going on without the knowledge of the customer, such as logging and monitoring. There is also an audit trail that is keeping track of all the information through a log. For example, if a call is opened, it is tracked and a record is kept of its disposition.

The Technology

The technology for CIC and customer contact centers is complex and involves a mix of telecommunications and other communications channels, such as email, the Internet, or faxes and CRM software. By adding advanced telecommunications and Web-enabled CIC technology, the ante is upped heavily. How can media traffic flow be handled so that there are dynamic interactions with what could often be an emergency or at least urgent situation? The bottom line for *any* CIC technology, classic phone center only or Internet-enabled, is its effectiveness in helping to resolve a customer interaction successfully. This means that the technologies are designed to create a collaborative environment for the customer and the customer contact representative (CCR). That also means self-service.

What are some of the technologies that are involved in this? On the classic telecommunications side, we are looking at the acronyms ACD, IVR, and CTI traditionally, and now, with the ascendance of the Internet, VOIP—all voice related. But what do those acronyms mean?

ACD (automatic call distribution) This is phone call workflow, which is how a call gets routed based on the defining characteristics of the call.

IVR (interactive voice response) You're entirely familiar with this one. This is the one that drives you nuts with the menu-driven voices that are specific to the choices you make by hitting the varying numbers on your telephone pad. Its actual benefit is that it can handle routine transactions without the benefit of a live agent—for example, when you call in to a credit card company and get your balance automatically.

CTI (computer telephony integration) These are the technology applications and interfaces that allow data integration with telephones. For example, CTI-enabled functionality allows both Internet-based information and phone-based information to be gathered and sent to a particular agent or routed to a particular desktop.

Using inbound and outbound call-routing software has been the traditional means of handling call loads effectively. However, the Internet has changed all that. Now, because of the ubiquitous role of the Internet, Web-enablement of the call center is of paramount importance.

Call center Web-enablement is a substantial investment. The first thing that you are dealing with is the overall social change in the perception of acceptability of the customer. What was an acceptable level of frustration on the telephone (x minutes before ballistic missiles went off in the customer's head) is no longer acceptable because of the multiple channels available to the customer. That adds huge complexity to the issue of how agents handle phone calls. There has been a substantial amount of effort put into customer response time. There is actually an algorithm that was developed early in the century and refined in recent years called the Erlang-C equations that exists to find the optimal number of agents required to handle call loads. Its recent incarnations not only take into account historic call reception and agent skill sets, but also busy signals and call abandonment. That might not sound like much, but think about this. If you have 100 agents and only enough calls for 50 for six months and 75 for four months and 25 for the other two months, you are spending a lot of money on agents who aren't needed. Now, make that daily: 50 calls in the hours from 10:00 to 1:00, 150 calls from 1:00 to 6:00 and 85 calls from 6:00 to 8:00. What's the right amount of agents, since you can't shuffle the agents' numbers very easily? Also, if you underestimate the number of agents, including during the call spikes that are expected as part of a given time period, how are you going to handle the overload? You'll have lots of unhappy customers—again, a cost you can't afford.

With the Web now ubiquitous, the complexity increases by manifolds. You have new communications channels that have to be dealt with, such as the Web, email, fax, chats, instant messenger, automated voice, voice over the Internet (à la Net2Phone), and others I'm simply not thinking of. Web-enablement is a priority.

Making It a CIC: Web-Enabling the Call Center

Keep in mind a cardinal principle: CIC means customer *interaction* center. Web-enabling the call center is agreement with the New Economic principle that the customers want control over their decision making. They don't want to be forced into their vendor's rules nor do they want to be railroaded into a decision. Self-service becomes a critical psychological component as well as an effective one.

Self-service has existed for awhile with IVR. The problem with IVR is that it involves the time it takes for a virtual human voice to provide you with something that would be visually understood in a millisecond, so it becomes frustrating. Nested menus on the phone are very irritating, and IVR has created as many problems as it solves. Normally, when someone is on the telephone, unless she is calling in for something absolutely routine and attainable (like the aforementioned credit card balance), she is calling because *she needs to talk to someone real.* She isn't looking for self-service. She is looking for service.

The Internet is another matter. It is a place for solitary interactivity. You don't ordinarily need a voice on the Web—though that is now an option, albeit a very primitive early-stage one. The Web's greatest strength is comfortable self-activity that provides a true measure of control. For service centers, this is vital. Frankly, too, it is easier to sell on the Web (to someone who shops on it) because a cross-sale or up-sale is impersonal. If I'm on the Web and trying to solve a problem by going to a FAQs (frequently asked questions) list on my problem and I see an ad for something I am interested in that is related to it, I might buy it. But if I'm talking to a human being about my problem and the CCR tries to sell me this same object, I would be mad. One is my choice without pressure. The other is an attempt to railroad me, at least according to my perception. With self-service, I'm solving my own problem and am happy with the company that posted this to save me the trouble of dealing with customer service. A buy is more of a possibility. I'm more satisfied. Talking to the CCR, I just want the problem (and the beleaguered CCR) to go away.

Okay. So how do you Web-enable the call center? Start by planning around certain concepts:

> ▶ Though it is a technology being implemented, the customer is the focus. The customer is calling the center to get answers to issues and questions—in other words, resolution is the central

focus of the entire process. Even while the problem resolution is the purpose, the experience has to be pleasant for the customer, which means that the customer needs as much interactive control over the multichanneled process as possible.

▶ The technology chosen to "e-ize" the call center is the one that is most appropriate to the business rules of the company.

▶ Web-enablement is time consuming, not just for functional and technical implementation, but in the retraining of support personnel, the increased intricacy of the job, and the change in the mindset of the personnel necessary for success. This means learning email management, how to understand multiple channel information and use it, and what appropriate response times are, not just based on "traditional" New Economic criteria (service level, customer value), but also on knowledge of New Media response times. Documentation skills become hyper-important because of the email responses.

▶ Use the existing tools if possible. Don't build from the ground up. Integrate the existing tools with your legacy system. For example, why not use PeopleSoft/Vantive since they have years of experience in how customer contact centers work and have the best practices often built into the software? Better that than building your own. There are packages like PeopleSoft/Vantive and Siebel Call Center for the enterprise and there are packages that handle pieces of the puzzle. For example, a package was released in 2000 called Virtual Hold, by—what else—Virtual Hold Technologies. It works like this:

1. Customer listens to recorded message with time to wait for an agent.

2. If he doesn't want to wait, he chooses a phone option that tells the system to make a call as soon as an agent is available or allows the customer, via the phone number pad, to schedule a date and time up to seven days ahead.

3. The phone number is captured and holds a place in the ACD queue for the customer.

4. The Unified Queue Module does the same thing for the Web. If your agents are busy when the customer clicks on

the website, a similar choice is available: telling the system to have an agent callback as soon as available or a calendar pops up to allow the customer to schedule the time and date up to seven days ahead. The two formats (phone and Web) converge in the Universal Queue so there are no conflicts. Takes care of ACD and inbound routing issues and provides the Web-based customer with the maximum experience, even to the point of letting the customer know when the next agent will be available (updated every 15 seconds). Niche covered. Would you want to build that from the ground up?

▶ Plan to give higher priority treatment or some other reward to the self-service Web users. Encouraging that behavior is important because two things have occurred by the use of the Web. First, the user normally isn't interacting with a live agent. Second, the information captured is a lot more effective and there is simply more of it, providing a quicker ability to put the publicly available problem resolutions back up on the Web so that more and more can be solved by self-service.

▶ Don't assume it will take the place of the human being. It won't. It is an alternative that is valuable and useful, but can't be forced. Not everyone uses the Web. Contrary to popular belief, not all Web users want to use it for something like this. Sometimes a human voice is better than a mouse click.

▶ Try to implement software that will capture information well enough to constantly improve your knowledge base. (See Siebel Call Center example below.)

▶ Keep the interface simple. It is important that the customer sees the same interfaces that the CCR sees. That way, customer interaction with the CCR is consistent, either on the Web or on both the Web and the phone. Explanations of what one is seeing are useless.

Assume you've Web-enabled your call center and have a full-featured CIC now. Let's look at the technology behind a phone call that is made by a customer to the CIC (this is Siebel's take on it, so it may be a bit different for other software, but generally it's about the same).

The customer phones into the service center for the first time. He gives the corporate configuration ID, which is matched against a table that shows the customer's company is a Gold Service holder, thus providing the customer with the highest level of service offered by the company running the CIC. Then the individual gives name information and is assigned a unique configuration ID (called a config ID for short) that is attached to the config ID of the company. Once that occurs, it will be used for recording the call, as well as logging and monitoring future calls through what is called the Siebel Audit Trail. The customer service representative (CSR), who for the sake of the New Economy and Greenberg's Political Correctness, I'm going to continue to call the customer contact representative (CCR) for the rest of the chapter, then asks the customer what level of urgency the problem has. The categories are Low, High, and Urgent, which are available to the CCR through a pick list. Each category has business rules and workflow attached to it accordingly. When the choice is made, the workflow and rules automatically kick into gear. For example, if the call is categorized as Urgent, there are three people, including the CCR who answered the call, who are responsible for getting the question resolved within two hours. If it is marked High, there might be six people who get serial routings, depending on where the call has to go, and who have 24 hours to resolve the question. The status field is automatically flagged as open when the call and config ID are logged. It remains open until it is marked as resolved, and the information is then logged and stored in a table that is attached to the customer's corporate and individual config IDs.

The workflow is a very important part of the Siebel, PeopleSoft/Vantive, or Nortel/Clarify call center operation because it handles the automatic routing that is critical for timely resolution of problems. In the example above, if the first assigned engineer fails, the problem is escalated automatically to a specific person called the backline—really the level 2 support—and this goes up the predesignated chain until resolution or final failure to resolve. If it is closed successfully, screens pop up for the ultimate CCR who solved it that ask him questions to be answered, such as what was the problem, how was it resolved, and who resolved it. The name of the person answering these questions auto-populates the Assignee field, under the assumption that the final resolution lay with that person. There is a date and timestamp field that is auto-populated once the "resolved" flag is checked.

Should the same person from the same company call in with the appropriate config IDs later, several things occur. The information that was entered into the system at resolution and along the way will pop up for the use of the CCR now dealing with the newer call. Additionally, there is the capability for a query to find like defects that may have occurred either within the customer's company or from other companies that are being serviced by the same service provider. The fields with this information are attached to a business object, which is attached to a table with the information that answers the query.

Automated Intelligent Call Routing

What is the importance of call routing? It seems simple enough. You call in, you wait a few seconds or minutes, and you may or may not speak to someone or carry out something with a touch pad. You are then directed to a particular person. It sounds pretty easy, but it is one of the functions most prone to failure in the world of volume transactions. Intelligent inbound and outbound traffic direction is a central condition of an effective CIC. Call routing gets difficult when email, chat, VOIP, and Web routing get involved. High volumes make it scarier yet.

Managing this means using call-routing software that can handle increasing volume, geographical dispersion of the CCRs, multiple channels, and workflow. Typically it would identify who is calling and why they are calling (see the Siebel example), use the customer database to identify the history, and then find the appropriate party who is available at the time the caller calls. The software should have integrated IVR so that some of the processes can be routed to automatic responses. It should have CTI to capture information and use the databases effectively. Its distribution should be multichannel, which means an open architecture. It should be easily scalable, since call volumes will vary widely between companies, times of day, year, and month. It should be able to capture real-time data and use it in conjunction with the historical data on the customer that exists in the customer data repository (or customer case repository, as the "case" may be). It should be Web-enabled so that Web-based routing to the appropriate menus can occur and so that the information given is easily captured and centrally stored. It should allow live collaboration on the Web. It should provide remote agent support so that branch offices and small office/home office (SOHO) agents can be utilized in the problem resolution. That means that the home agent and the branch offices can access most of the functionality that is provided to the HQ agent. This eases the weight of the high-volume days without tying up valuable HQ real estate.

The software should have strong scripting capabilities and an open interface. That means the interface can control IVR scripting that is governed by applied business rules.

Finally, it should integrate workforce management tools with its call-routing capacity so that the CIC's agent capacity and scheduling forecasts can be integrated into the use of the call-routing functionality in micro specific ways.

The larger companies outlined build much of this functionality into their CIC software. However, there are vendors who do nothing but this. One award-winning example in an uncrowded field is Telephony@work's CallCenter@nywhere intelligent routing applications. This is unique, cutting-edge software that is recognized for its advanced nature by the industry that spawned it. It won multiple awards in 1999, with the most significant being Product of the Year from both *Computer Telephony* magazine and *CallCenter Solutions* magazine.

What makes it at least a significant step in evolution for the CIC is that it is easy to install. It offers literally all the pieces of the call center puzzle in one preintegrated suite of applications. The platform gets its name from the fact that it can queue and route interactions from anywhere (phone, fax, and Web), it can be installed anywhere (through support for T-1, E-1, ISDN, and analog lines), and it enables call centers to deploy and seamlessly blend agents and supervisors from anywhere (local, branch office, and remote locations). Not bad for a start. But take a look at their "Programmers Not Required" technology. The users can install CallCenter@nywhere's complex routing system! Not just the "you get the call from Joe because Joe is a Gold Level service customer" functions, but also IVR scripts, multimedia queuing, and skills-based call routing. Think about it. You can install it and you aren't even technical.

Workforce Management Software

In a manner of speaking, workforce management (WFM) software is what lies on top of the call-routing software. The two features that are most important are call volume forecasts and agent scheduling.

Remember the Erlang-C equations that I mentioned a few pages ago? They are built into the good workforce management software programs. Equally as important is sophisticated pattern recognition. The foundation for pattern recognition is not recognition of patterns, oddly enough. It is recognition of the pattern anomalies. For example, if, over a year, there are exactly 250 calls per day every Monday but three, it recognizes the anomaly in the three days and tries to figure out how those anomalies come to pass. If those anomalies are explainable, the basis for a different number of agents assigned to those three days is there and thus, the money is saved or the customer is satisfied. Logging and monitoring are also part of workforce management. By capturing and collecting the data day to day, the ability to manage performance and schedule appropriately is increased by multiples. The more depth defined, the better the system.

LOGGING AND MONITORING

Logging and monitoring software provides the granularity needed to do precision scheduling and improve performance management. Besides such obvious things as collecting information that is based on caller IDs of some sort, there are several other features that good logging and monitoring software has the following:

► The means to develop criteria to capture appropriate samples across the entire CIC network

► Extensive and very flexible reporting tools

► Universal connectivity to ACD systems

► Strong interfacing with the WFM applications

► Analytic tools that can score data so that weight can be assigned to captured information

► Easy export to other systems

One company that specializes in the performance management domain is e-talk Corporation. They provide some of the most comprehensive logging and monitoring tools in the business and have four applications. The two that are apt for this usage are

Recorder This is the logging application. It enables customer contact centers to record and evaluate complete customer interactions through multimedia, such as telephone, email, and Web interaction.

Advisor This application enables contact center management teams to evaluate, measure, and manage quality and productivity.

By incorporating logging and monitoring systems with WFM, the effectiveness of the CIC will increase greatly. But then, how do you measure productivity and return?

The Measurements

At the time Robert Kaplan's *The Balanced Scorecard* was published in 1996, the metrics that defined success or failure in business tended to be quantitative. *The Balanced Scorecard* was one of the reasons for the move from purely quantitative analysis for success to combinations of both the tangible quantities and the less tangible quality measurements.

This, a bit more slowly, has affected the CIC world as well. Traditionally, the measurements of success were quantitative:

- ▶ How long is the average handling time?

- ▶ How much of the time spent from the time the customer dials in to the end of the call is idle time?

- ▶ How many of the calls in hang up before the call is completed (abandonment rate)?

- ▶ How much time is the customer in the queue before a representative speaks with him/her?

- ▶ How quickly is an agent available from call to call?

- ▶ Once the caller is engaged, how much time until the call is completed, either successfully or unsuccessfully?

Grab a waiting call that was on a short time and complete the call successfully in under a minute and you did really well. The problem with these measurements, particularly in the customer service world or even the telesales world, was that no metric really defined whether the problem was solved. The measurements were strictly on volume. The assumption was that some percentage of the calls was successful.

These days, the Web, email, and fax play a role in this, so the quantitative measurements have to change. The other part of the equation comes into play too: how do you manage the inquiries regardless of the channel?

What is often proposed is a ratio of customer profitability to number of calls. One step further for measuring the ROI here is to differentiate service levels in conjunction with the number of calls or visits, or the involvement of CIC-employed labor with that customer in relation to the customer's profitability. Perhaps the best example of a successful program in that realm is the frequent flier premier programs that all the major airlines have. Fly with us for 25,000 miles or 30 segments and we will recognize you as someone we want to spend more time with and give more value to because you are sustaining our airline substantially.

The Internet makes these measurements a bit more difficult because what Web pages a customer surfs on the company site and how email responsiveness is handled plays an important role in the measurement of the metrics. Logging and monitoring software (see above) can handle the quantifiable side of these measurements.

Who Handles the Calls?

There are a number of established and newly minted companies that form the bulk of the CIC market. Many of the CRM front-office solutions companies—those that offer end-to-end services—offer a CIC or customer contact center. However, there are some that either have long roots on the software side (such as PeopleSoft/Vantive or Nortel/Clarify) or come from the telecommunications end, like the new Lucent spin-off, Avaya Communications. When it comes to the enterprise-level multimedia call centers that these represent, certain technological standards and metrics prevail:

▶ Response time to each transaction has to be sub-second.

▶ High transaction volume has to be handled easily.

▶ Scalability is critical.

▶ There needs to be a common architecture across all interrelated applications, preferably a single framework.

▶ A common data model should prevail—one dominant model that allows a single view of the customer to each and all agents. This data model should be concurrent across call centers, not just a sole call center.

The marketing approach that all of the companies seem to be taking is interesting. It is something akin to, "Your customer interaction center can become a profit center if you do it our way." How that's the case is pretty uniform, with direct links to sales and marketing and giving the customer service representative the ability to cross-sell and up-sell. From a technological standpoint, this is doable. From a human standpoint, customer service representatives aren't necessarily going to be good salespeople. There is a reason that some people go into sales and others to customer service. But I guess pure good customer service is no longer enough. Sigh.

PeopleSoft/Vantive

Vantive's heritage comes from the call center. Their application meets all the above criteria well. They have some extremely large customers. Some large call center examples include Gateway Computers, running more than 5,000 seats and EDS, running more than 3,000 seats. These are single call centers, where each agent has access to all the customer information. Contrast with other vendors who claim large numbers of licensed "seats" for a single customer that are actually deployed in a number of individual call centers. Agents in this type of deployment cannot easily share information, as they run off of different database schemas.

PeopleSoft/Vantive has a number of modules that are used for service and support. They are Field Service, Support, and HelpDesk. Each of them has an "e" version that provides Internet channels for the problem resolution. What makes PeopleSoft/Vantive particularly interesting is that they incorporate the analytical piece that no one else strongly holds. As part of the CIC products they use the Support Effectiveness Workbench. The features are extremely powerful. It measures things like:

- ▶ CCR handling of customer issues
- ▶ Prevalence of product quality issues
- ▶ Cost of supporting products and customers
- ▶ Performance measurements over segmented time periods
- ▶ Effectiveness of creation of sales opportunities (this can be drilled to types of opportunity)

The slicing and dicing features of the Insight tool are pretty extensive. Time, territory, customer, CCR, product, channel, and contract are all categories that information can be centered around. The classic volume transaction-based measurements can be evaluated, but so can dozens of other attributes.

The products that use this powerful tool, with their "e" versions in mind, are

Support This is the end-to-end call center management tool. It includes pretty much everything mentioned in this chapter as part of its toolset, across multiple channels, with a single customer view. It is all purpose. Beyond those features mentioned, strong branch scripting that is workflow-triggered, graphic views of service-level agreements to see how the agreement stands (what remains accordingly), distributed task management, and filters to dynamically sort information are also part of this extremely powerful tool.

FieldService This is much like the other field service applications, but more complex. It not only handles the SLAs and manages the workflow. That is to be expected. It also handles return material authorizations (RMAs), those numbers and letters that get assigned to you when you want to mail something back. It also tracks product configurations, manages spare parts inventory, and has an "e" based adjunct that lets the field engineers do it all through their browsers and wireless devices. The "e" version adds Dynamic HTML (DHTML) architecture on the client side to keep the pressure off the heavily taxed servers.

HelpDesk Similar to FieldService and Support, HelpDesk additionally includes asset management so that hardware and software configurations can be catalogued. Some of its more prominent features include:

- Automated routine tasks (such as workflow, escalation, and routing)

- Rapid access to diagnostic information, including third-party detail

- Command Center, which provides a single point of access for all closed-loop problem resolution

- Autofill to handle FAQs by the CCR entering a problem code

▶ Advanced problem tracking; multiple tickets on a single event are shown in a single view

▶ Classification to improve notification

▶ Paging

The "e" version does what all PeopleSoft/Vantive "e" versions do: Web access, increased channels, DHTML, and n-tier architecture. There is no client software needed, only a browser.

This is a very big enterprise-level program that can handle thousands of CCRs and thousands of calls.

Nortel/Clarify

There is a reason that Nortel Networks bought Clarify. Call centers fit well with a telecommunications backbone. Since the completion of the acquisition in late 2000, Nortel/Clarify has gone on an e-business offensive. What is interesting is how they approach their call center operation. One of their taglines expresses it best: "Clarify eFront-Office. Turn your call center into a commerce center."

This makes even more sense when you see that they bundle their call center with their sales force automation suite, a stretch by most standards. Conceptually, the idea is that call centers, rather than just customer service locations, are profit centers. To accomplish this weighty feat, eFrontOffice, the Nortel/Clarify flagship product (see Chapter 10) integrates call centers, websites, field sales, and service teams with sales and marketing.

Help Desk The eFrontOffice Help Desk combines a number of Clarify components, including ClearContracts, which helps create personalized service level agreement that is IDed by employee, department, or problem type. Contract costs are automatically calculated. The ClearHelpDesk application then integrates all information with asset management systems down to the bill of materials level. It has ownership and commitment tracking functions that allow CCRs to enlist others to help solve problems, and it provides follow-up responsibility tracking to ensure resolution is accounted for. It uses risk assessment to solve moves, adds, and changes (MACs) issues through routing to the appropriate agent with the proper skills. It provides a complete history of a request. It integrates with the Clarify ClearQuality module, which traces the history of repairs of physical technical products. As all the major front office products have, it has workflow, audit trails, a shared customer data repository, and a good toolset.

Customer Service This is *the* "turn your call center into a profit center through up-selling and cross-selling" application. It, too, has ClearContracts and ClearQuality. Sandwiched in between, though, is ClearSupport, which carries all the major functions for a closed-loop (opening the problem to resolving the problem) system, including integration with telephony systems using advanced features such as screen pop and soft phone control technology; configuration control; problem resolution soup-to-nuts; and as above, ownership and commitment tracking.

Field Service In the marketing literature, Clarify's intent is pretty blatant. "With Clarify, field teams can ensure that customers are charged for additional services not covered through normal contracts." This can't be more obvious than it is. Field Service functions are oriented toward making money. Nothing wrong with that. It just flies in the face of conventional wisdom, though contemporary wisdom is pretty much this. The modules are the same as Customer Service with the addition of a couple. First on the path is ClearLogistics. This particular module can dispatch field technicians, manage spare parts inventory, and enable high-volume repair center transactions. The other difference is the addition of ClearEnterpriseTraveler, definitely an awkward long name for an advanced module. Using the mobile data synchronization we have grown to know and love, field reps can download service calls, histories, and account information to their notebooks. It is a server-side application so that the information warehouse resides for all on that server.

Siebel

Siebel is playing the field, with both enterprise and midmarket editions of their Call Center software. Siebel is following the strategic path of the other enterprise-level players, which is to turn the service center into a profit center, be it enterprise or midmarket. In fact, with the applications—Siebel Call Center and Siebel Service (plus, of course, their "e" variants)—one of the most obvious facets of the applications' screens is that they have views that include all the sales opportunities in the entire enterprise (viewed with proper roles and authorizations), all the marketing campaigns, and all the service tickets outstanding, all from within Siebel Call Center. It even shows some of the SFA attributes such as contact and account management—a bit unusual for a call center application.

Siebel also has push broadcasting to the desktop so that the CCR's manager can send messages that will pop up to the desktop for one reason or another. The interface can narrowcast details specific to a single CCR if so desired.

Siebel Service and Siebel Call Center have powerful response templates that are customized. Let's say an email comes in from me, and I have a history in the database, a config ID, and a particular identified problem. A simple click on Reply preloads my email address, gives the option of greetings, and offers an extensive pull-down list to pick out the answer to the problem identified and a choice of closings. Three clicks and a "Dear Mr. Greenberg, if your problem is xyz, you need to…" and I'm done. The problem resolution list is dynamically added to as more new problems are solved. If the CCR wants a more dynamic proactive process, he can use SmartScript, another slick feature that compiles all the information on Paul Greenberg and his problem, verifies his entitlement to service, identifies the problem, and puts together a suggested list of steps to settle the problem. It also identifies such information as how much time there is to solve this particular issue and how far along in time the issue is. SmartScript also will then check on the current promotions associated with the asset or customer that would be appropriate and even sends the notifications of those up-selling and cross-selling opportunities to the customer. Again, I'm no big fan of this, but it is a sales opportunity. SmartScript can even prepare the quote and tell Paul Greenberg to go ahead and hit AutoOrder—voilá, a sale.

Siebel Call Center can also conduct customer satisfaction surveys and compile the results, charting peaks and valleys in call center activity. It has strong telesales and telemarketing functions that I won't cover in this section.

Avaya

These guys are the year 2000 spin-off formed from Lucent's Enterprise Networks Group. They are not exactly a startup, with thousands of customers and $7.4 billion in revenues from the get-go. CRM Central 2000, their flagship product, came with them from Lucent. They have serious alliances with companies like Siebel in the

CRM world and are actually in a position to be a major force in CRM in a fairly short time. Their name sounds pretty cool and probably means something, but who knows what that is? They are in the CIC market from the telecommunications and networking side.

CRM Central 2000

The best way to describe this product is "framework." It is a framework for a comprehensive engine focused primarily around the CIC. The core of it is their Intelligent Work Management Engine. This is where the corporate business rules and processes are embedded and the workflow is centralized. Some of the features of the engine are sophisticated, setting up automatic inbound call routing based on employee skills, customer value, dynamic event management, and service level objectives. What that means is that each time a customer calls in, his history, service level agreement (SLA), and algorithmically determined "value" to the company are brought up with the call (based on some form of ID). This information is matched through the workflow features to a table of CCRs who are available to speak to the customer, and the call is automatically routed to the appropriate and available CCR.

On the other side of the phone, fax, email, or Web interaction, is the Customer Interaction software provided by CRM Central 2000. This actually is a dynamic preference engine that allows the customer to proactively determine the nature of their interactions with the servicing company. It provides the choice of media mentioned above (among others) and the times and places that each one would (or wouldn't) be used.

All this data needs to be put somewhere. CRM Central 2000 has an interesting variation on the customer data repository called the Customer Case Repository. This captures and stores all individual customer transactions from all media and dynamically allows the CCR to see the entire "caseload" at any point in the service process. It also updates the back and front offices with the contact history and handles attachments with data or documents related to the individual—again, available at any time updated and complete.

Finally, there is the CRM Central Client, which isn't what it sounds like. It is actually the customization toolkit for creating interfaces that can handle automated workflow and are intuitive for CIC agents.

Chapter 10

The Sandbox Playmates

The sandbox is getting to be the size of a beach. A *big* beach. As the second unofficial and first official year of the millennium hits us, the size of the CRM playing field continues to increase to levels that are almost frightening in its numbers. Big vendors, big consulting companies, small vendors, small consulting companies. CRM generalists, CRM niche players, CRM-only companies, e-business companies with CRM practices. The list is endless. There are the vertical-niche[2] CRM companies—niche players in a niche segment of the CRM market—and the companies that have CRM characteristics that are part of their products but are not CRM companies. Then there are imposters and analysts and commentators and independent consulting firms that are package independent—all in the CRM world. How can this confusion be sorted?

Truthfully, it can't fully be sorted. Proliferation is a function of time. The moment you've completed the sorting of the options, since time has passed, there are hundreds of new options. Thus, a bulk sort doesn't work.

When I conceived this chapter, I thought I would do a matrix of what was out there. After reviewing the possibilities and charting it against a bubble chart (just kidding), I decided that this would not be a useful chart at all. There are several matrices I will recommend to you at the end of the chapter. However, what I am going to do in this chapter is to cover my top CRM companies, according to the-wisdom-of-Paul-Greenberg, with encapsulated corporate profiles of each of the sandbox players. These will be a mixture of companies that have made it as successful CRM companies generally or have a market specific niche that they have been successful in. This is not meant to be exhaustive at all. There is no way to push forward the complete list of excellent companies. Those included are the companies that have, over time, stood out in their respective market segment—companies that I would either personally recommend or have personally considered when making my own judgments in CRM-related enterprise matters. These are short profiles to be used for your assessment. For example, rather than cover each of the products in the product section, what can be assumed unless I mention otherwise is that each of the products has the basic functionality that is expected—sales, marketing, and services. If they are specialists in any given one—such as MicroStrategy's specialization in personalization—that will be noted. Each profile provides unique information on the company at hand. I'm sure that if you poll the CRM pundits, several may not agree with my assessments. However, the whole purpose of this chapter is to provide you with a thumbnail sketch of the important CRM companies. Again, it is not the complete and certainly by no means the only list of good companies out there. I am highlighting those I can vouch for as companies with good products, good service, or market leadership.

There is a noticeable trend among a large portion of these companies. They are repositioning themselves as, effectively, "beyond" CRM. They are now "e-business companies." This is a bit frightening. One of the failures in the ERP market was taking the approach that "we are not just ERP, we are all things to all people." That is never a successful strategy. When companies stray far afield from their core competencies, they tend to be in a field of chaff, not wheat. When you choose a company, choose one that fits the needs you have, not the needs everyone has.

That said—let's get on with it!

Simply the Best...

These are the Greenberg Sandbox Players.

PeopleSoft/Vantive

PeopleSoft/Vantive has an interesting history. It is a two-company history—PeopleSoft and Vantive became one in January 2000 with the acquisition of Vantive by PeopleSoft. PeopleSoft was founded in 1987 by David Duffield, a corporate innovator with a big heart (check out his Maggie Fund if you are an animal lover). He created a company that was focused on human resources software, financials software—all for the back office—and a company that was people focused. The enterprise resource planning (ERP) software was a major hit, growing PeopleSoft itself to a $1.4 billion company by 1998. However, with the decline in the ERP market and the stock hit that all ERP companies took with the approach of Y2K, David Duffield brought in Craig Conway, a contributor to this book, to run the company. One of the key moves that he made upon his ascendance was to acquire Vantive Corporation, one of the three leading CRM large enterprise packages on the market.

Vantive Corporation began its life in the early 1990s as a call center application company, but quickly grew beyond that with a highly scalable architecture that emphasized reliability and response time.

When PeopleSoft acquired Vantive, the analysts looked at it with a skeptical eye. But the long revenue-producing histories of the two companies, the execution strategy of Craig Conway, and the natural interconnection between ERP and CRM products led to a very successful marriage.

Their cultures, after an expected rocky honeymoon, integrated really well. I've had direct experience with the PeopleSoft culture. It is perhaps the friendliest, most people-centric culture I've ever seen. In numerous trips to their Pleasanton, California (even their location name...) headquarters, the relaxed nature of their employees and their attention to their customer—be they a consumer, partner, or employee—is truly astounding. In the last year, their internal focus on business execution has improved dramatically, without the loss of the friendliness and attention.

PeopleSoft/Vantive CRM is now the company's best-selling product.

Strategy/Mission

PeopleSoft's philosophy is to provide a best-of-breed solution for any given business process. They believe that business empowerment is based on dynamic collaboration between customers, employees, and suppliers supported by operational and analytic applications. In other words, back- and front-office integration and real-time interactions between all parts of the business food chain.

Products

With the release of PeopleSoft 8.0 and PeopleSoft 8 CRM, PeopleSoft is able to provide a full front-office suite of operational applications and a full back-office suite, including financial management applications, supply chain management applications, human resources management applications, e-commerce applications, and portal products. This is indeed a staggering suite of products that can provide end-to-end solutions for the larger enterprises. Built into the 8.0 products is open integration between the PeopleSoft/Vantive CRM products and other external applications such as SAP. Pure internet application delivery enables access to applications with only a browser. PeopleSoft's expertise with the three-tier architecture in the client/server world bodes well for their use of it for their Web-based applications.

The PeopleSoft 8 CRM Internet architecture powers PeopleSoft 8 CRM enterprise applications. It is an open and scalable architecture, based on HTML, Java, and XML. This allows the user to access the PeopleSoft/Vantive 8 CRM applications with a browser on the desktop, with a Web-enabled phone, or through pagers and PDAs.

The product suite has also incorporated a powerful, transparent personalization portal that gives quick access to customer information. In turn, the information pulled from a centralized customer database allows the user to apply complex analytics, through the PeopleSoft Insight applications. Five of the most significant workbenches in the product suite (which can be integrated with PeopleSoft CRM or stand alone) are

PeopleSoft 8 Customer Scorecard This product leverages the balanced scorecard methodology to measure and monitor performance of your organization's key customer-related processes.

PeopleSoft 8 Profitability Insight This product provides the information needed to better understand the profitability of your organization's customers, products, and channels.

PeopleSoft 8 Marketing Insight This product enables your company to evaluate the effectiveness of your marketing activities, such as email campaigns, direct marketing, advertising efforts, and telemarketing, promotions, and cross-selling and up-selling efforts.

PeopleSoft 8 Sales Activity Insight This product enables your company to determine the effectiveness of sales process based on pipeline status, forecasting accuracy, discount analysis, sales cycle time, and fallout analysis.

PeopleSoft 8 Support Insight This product enables your company to optimize support processes by looking at product quality information, call and caseload trends, agent utilization, and performance-to-service-level agreements.

Future

PeopleSoft is moving toward the logical CRM future. Wireless and mobile device support for PeopleSoft CRM is being added as the need for it is growing. It is being done wisely, adding functionality when user habits warrant the inclusion. The overall market toward Internet applications that are integrated with front- and back-office business processes is helping PeopleSoft gain market share, because of their experience in both venues.

PeopleSoft will be placing increasing effort in analytic CRM because their visionaries recognize that analytics are becoming an integral part of all users' experience, whether it's a consumer or a businessperson who needs to make decisions. As mentioned previously, they are and will be incorporating the PeopleSoft Insight applications, which they have experience with through the PeopleSoft enterprise performance management (EPM) suite that originally sat in their ERP packages.

PeopleSoft will continue to leverage Internet capabilities in areas of portals, e-commerce applications, application delivery via ASPs, and hosting services. The recent creation of their eCenter hosting services is the first step toward this future. Their release in October 2000 of the PeopleSoft's customer, employee, and supplier portals are also the harbinger of this PeopleSoft future, which looks very good.

Websites

http://www.peoplesoft.com/
http://www.vantive.com/

Interact Commerce Corporation

SalesLogix Corporation was founded in January 1996 and shipped its first product in April 1997. Originally devoted to sales force automation for the midmarket, in just three years, the product evolved into a fully integrated customer relationship management suite offering sales, marketing, support, and e-business solutions. The focus of SalesLogix for the midmarket has remained constant.

To broaden their offerings to provide a solution for the individual and small workgroups, SalesLogix Corporation acquired ACT!, the leading contact manager brand, on December 6, 1999, and launched a revolutionary technology that integrates sales-related Internet services right into ACT! and SalesLogix. An interesting note is that Pat Sullivan, the chairman and CEO of Interact Commerce Corporation and its executive vice president, Mike Muhney, were the original cofounders of Contact Software, the makers of ACT!.

To reflect these two strong brands, the company changed its name to Interact Commerce Corporation on April 26, 2000.

The new name reflects the company's desire to reach a broader marketplace with relationship management and selling solutions. As a company grows, it can move from ACT! to SalesLogix. Midmarket businesses and divisions of large companies can implement the sales and marketing module of SalesLogix and easily grow into the support and e-business modules.

Interact Commerce has developed a reputation as one of the most channel-friendly companies in the industry. Because of that friendly behavior, the channel provides them with 80 percent of their sales.

In fact, Interact Commerce's resellers have a comfortable give and take communication with the company that allows them full access to customer and prospect information. In turn, resellers actively report their progress on deals in the pipeline.

Their easy relationship with each other enables Interact Commerce to report a phenomenal 97 percent visibility of deals in its pipeline—more than most companies know about the pipeline of their direct sales team. In addition, resellers can access a variety of support materials they can use to champion the company's products. I can speak directly to this because I've been a SalesLogix partner for over a year, and they have been nothing but supportive throughout that time.

By integrating its front-office software with back-office financial applications and Web business, Interact Commerce gives small and midmarket companies a more complete view of its customer interactions.

Strategy/Mission

The philosophy that drives Interact Commerce has its roots in the history of ACT!: its products are designed with users in mind. What makes this bottom-up philosophy interesting is that it creates a very flexible product. This philosophy runs counter to the current thinking in many software companies today. In fact, many of those companies force users to adopt technology that's either more complicated than their current process or that they perceive to be of little or no value to them. Very often, the users refuse to go along. Not a good thing.

Instead, Interact Commerce maintains an ongoing dialogue with users and resellers to inform them of new products and enhancements. In essence, they force the technology to fit users' needs—leading to high user adoption rates and credible data.

Interact Commerce works hard on their "for the user, by the user" philosophy of software development. They make their features easy to use and build very significant out-of-the-box functionality into the SalesLogix applications using industry standard technologies. They have a highly customizable toolset for incorporating user customizable fields and administrative customizations. The entire interface can be modified without any major difficulty.

To make it even easier for the users, customer data is accessible and modifiable through a remote, standalone computer, a network, the Internet, handheld PCs, or wireless Web phones or handheld devices—almost any means of communication but advanced osmosis.

Products

There are two distinct product "lines" that come from Interact Commerce Corporation. They are the contact manager, ACT!, and the full blown SalesLogix 2000 product.

ACT!

ACT! is the world's best-selling contact manager for individuals, small businesses, and some large corporations whose selling models are built around relatively small sales teams or lots of independent professionals (professional services firms). However, since it is a contact manager, it is not part of the scope of this book. It is significant enough to mention, however because it integrates features that provide Web-efficiency with the desktop.

SALESLOGIX

More than 3,300 companies use SalesLogix, a fully integrated suite of CRM components, with that number growing by about 300 every quarter. SalesLogix has successfully dominated the middle market and even some smaller businesses with sophisticated sales operations.

SalesLogix enables business teams to access customer information collected across the enterprise in a surprisingly cost-effective manner. That information is available to them anytime, anywhere through wireless capabilities that are included with the basic license fee.

SalesLogix consists of four components:

SalesLogix for Sales This provides the basic SFA functions with ACT!—like ease of use. It also provides the power, scalability, reporting, and customization capabilities of high-end sales force management solutions.

SalesLogix for Marketing This product provides analytical tools and marketing campaign management. It automatically tracks marketing campaigns and website visitors, and enables companies to send email, faxes, and literature personalized for specific customers. It also provides powerful data mining tools and lead-tracking reports.

SalesLogix for Support This uses a friendly, Windows-based interface, but one that allows support reps to work with detailed customer histories, including sales data. They can also generate on-the-spot reports and track customer support levels. Additionally, SalesLogix for Support enables companies to link their PCs, network, and telephone switch into one system.

SalesLogix for Quotes and Orders SalesLogix for Quotes and Orders enables companies to use the Web as a seamless extension of their front office. It automates information sharing between these channels and back-office systems, with the aim of fostering a consistent customer experience and maximizing new selling opportunities.

SalesLogix database information is accessible over wireless devices such as Web-enabled phones and handheld computers. And SalesLogix has a Profile tab to provide current information about companies from the Internet.

To extend the capabilities of its products even further, SalesLogix has teamed with back-office financial firms to offer the first fully integrated front- and back-office solutions for the midmarket. These alliances are with major midmarket players such as Macola, Sage, Made2Manage, Foresight, and ACS. They enable customers to take advantage of these companies' expertise with both SalesLogix and the back-office solution. Add in data links between SalesLogix and software from others such as Great Plains, Solomon, J.D. Edwards, and SAP, and you have a real midmarket powerhouse.

Addressing the needs of a wide range of vertical markets, SalesLogix also provides, through its Open CRM Initiative, customized solutions that can be applied to companies involved in financial services, public relations, marketing, car dealerships, staffing, and many more.

Finally, in addition to a direct sales and implementation team that handle mostly larger implementations, SalesLogix also has the biggest distribution channel in the industry with more than 500 certified SalesLogix Business Partners that sell in more than 60 countries. This is considered by many observers (me, among them) to be one of the company's greatest strengths.

Future

Interact is one company that is very aware of its history and how it provides strength in the marketplace. The company will continue its focus on the individual and SOHO market with ACT! and on the midmarket with SalesLogix.

It also will further embrace the notion that its customers should not be penalized by the way in which they choose to access the information so vital to their success and growth. ACT! and SalesLogix are already leaders in wireless access, with the best CRM solutions for handheld computers and Web phones. What makes this interesting in both the present and future is that SalesLogix includes the wireless solutions in the cost of the licenses, which keeps the pricing way down. This also keeps them centrally focused on their "anywhere-anytime" strategy.

Interact Commerce Corporation keeps its strategy in view at all times. It continues to build on the products that made it successful in the past and present by adding the wireless future. That will ensure IACT a very successful future. A good company indeed.

Websites

http://www.saleslogix.com/
http://www.interact.com/

Onyx Corporation

Onyx has a unique take on CRM. By being the most visible portal-based CRM company, it has made CRM something that can be shared. Most CRM is actually for internal employees. One of the things that characterizes eCRM is that customers have personal interaction with their own records and, often, can contact employees of the vendor company through the Internet—the Web in particular. Onyx has developed portals that allow just that for customers, employees, and partners.

Onyx's culture is humane. A member of executive management sending one of his staff to a spa for an entire day because that staff member had done a high-stress job well characterizes it. This certainly wasn't part of the employee's compensation plan, but the executive management team member did it anyway, simply because the employee deserved it. It is a place where the CEO is accessible to the employees and feels accountable to them. It is the kind of culture that is highly professional in its approach to business. It is hardworking, with employees voluntarily working on weekends and past midnight to meet deadlines simply because they care enough to, not because they are asked.

That kind of culture bodes well for a company with good products and the growth of Onyx shows it. Revenues for the first nine months of 2000 were $83,589,000, up from $40,254,000 over the same time in 1999, an increase of 108 percent. This is with more than 600 customers.

Strategy/Mission

Here is a statement straight from Brent Frei, president and CEO of Onyx, on their mission:

> At Onyx, we have one overarching passion: to help our customers win in the Internet economy. We think we do this better than any company in the world. Our success is built on the success of our customers, and according to recent surveys, we have the highest customer satisfaction rating in our industry.
>
> I believe the main reason no competitor can match us in customer satisfaction is this: we aren't merely vending technology, we are forging enduring partnerships with each of our customers—partnerships aimed at making them successful, today and tomorrow. And we do whatever it takes to accomplish this.
>
> We are in an industry where, according to a recent Gartner survey, only 24 percent of the seats sold by a leading competitor were actually ever deployed. So here's a telling fact: 92 percent of Onyx seats sold are up and running. Others may sell software that ends up sitting on the shelf, but our job isn't done until our customer is using Onyx to win new business, build customer loyalty and beat the competition.
>
> Which means our job is never done, because companies' need to stay ahead of the competition never stops.

Their strategy anticipates consolidation, merger, and corporate demise in the CRM market so that only the "big boys" will remain. Onyx sees part of their job as remaining in that big boys mix when the market shakes out.

Products

Onyx's product suite is called Onyx 2000. It is an XML-based system to extend the same functionality that they had in their client/server system to a fully Web-based product. To do that they've centered their new system architecture, introduced in the first quarter of 2001, around what they call logical business objects (LBOs).

Most IT people understand the concept of business objects, as object-oriented programming revolutionized and changed the rules in computer program development, organizing around objects rather than actions, data rather than logic. Object-oriented programming takes the view that what programmers really care about are the objects they want to manipulate rather than the logic required to manipulate them.

A logical business object is then defined as a stream of XML that contains all the definitions and values of properties for a business object. Onyx's LBOs:

- ▶ Provide a flexible foundational framework

- ▶ Allow for real-time, cross-system integration and communication

- ▶ Allow immediate detection of irregularities in the relationship network before customer data is committed to the database as a permanent change

- ▶ Allow for a much thinner client because the changes are happening via the Web

- ▶ Provide the ability to hook customized functions into the core Onyx infrastructure

The Onyx product suite includes three thin-client portal applications built on top of an extensible n-tier, component-based architecture. The suite can be configured easily at all three tiers. Onyx's product suite comprises:

Onyx Employee Portal This product provides individual front-office employees with a highly personalized, consolidated digital workplace for enterprise-wide CRM.

Onyx Customer Portal This product provides prospects and customers with a Web-based window into the business, enabling them to collaborate with employees throughout the customer life cycle.

Onyx Partner Portal This product provides business partners with a Web-based window into the business, allowing collaborative management of prospects and customers throughout the customer life cycle.

Onyx e-Business Engine This product provides server-based, data-driven business logic and data management services.

The portals are thin-client, audience-specific interfaces designed to meet the particular needs of each constituency. All three portals present customer information and customer interaction information from the Onyx Enterprise Database, as well as relevant information from other enterprise systems and the Web.

They have also recently released two mobile products that can be used from a laptop or a PDA that reflect their commitment to a wireless future:

The OEP—Mobile Client This enables every employee, remote or corporate, to utilize the same customer information whether they are connected to the corporate network, on the Internet, or working on an unconnected laptop.

OEP—Outlook This is a portable solution for managing Onyx contacts and incidents. Mobile employees can interact with their Onyx customer information and incidents through Outlook's contact, calendar, and task folders.

Using the two-way synchronization both products provide, mobile employees can keep their offline customer data up to date with the e-Business Data Center. Mobile user data is synchronized when the user connects to the e-Business Engine.

Future

Onyx is methodically moving toward a bright future. They are migrating toward a completely Web-based product suite. By not eliminating client/server products entirely, they are attempting to service that part of the business universe that is still operating partially on the client/server model, even though they are aiming entirely at the Internet in the future. The other component of this is mobility. People now are just starting to embrace wireless capabilities, but such capabilities are not yet considered mission critical.

As of year-end 2000, Onyx has full-service offices in ten countries and hundreds of customers in countries all over the globe, with more than 30 percent of their annual revenue generated by overseas sales. Their future involves a serious commitment to international growth organically through partnerships and through acquisitions. This way they stay among the shaken-out "big-boys."

Website

http://www.onyx.com/

Siebel Systems

This is the company that made CRM what it is today—a multibillion dollar industry. This is also a company that is as much a reflection of its founder, Tom Siebel, as Oracle is of Larry Ellison.

In fact, Siebel is not only the market leader with somewhere between 15 to 18 percent of the overall CRM market and 22 percent of the sales force automation market, but it is also a nearly generic name for CRM.

They are not an ordinary company, but in fact, resemble the giant they came from. They have 4,500 employees who operate in more than 28 countries and 97 offices around the world. They are active, acquisitive, and scarfing down as much of the industry as they can in their hunger to be the number one player in the sandbox at all times. Being number two for even a minute doesn't interest them. Their management team is from the giants—veterans from Oracle, SAP, IBM, and Informix. Only Craig Ramsey, the senior vice president of worldwide operations, is from somewhere even vaguely small—nCube.

Siebel's culture flies in the face of the casual, personal business cultures that were spawned with the IT industry's growth. They are a business-suited, Madison Avenue–dressed culture with smart employees who'd better have their shoes shined. Their primary targets are the Global 2000 and if they don't have all 2,000 as Siebel customers, they aren't happy. The results they claim for this policy are 98 percent customer loyalty.

They have a partnership program that companies are begging to join, yet it is very expensive for those same partners, ranging up to a million dollar commitment from a partner for joint marketing to become a Strategic Partner. There is no dearth of applicants. Yet, they have spent much of 2000 repositioning themselves as an e-business company rather than a CRM company. Rarely, if ever, will you find mention of CRM on their website. Trust me, it is a CRM company.

Strategy/Mission

Siebel's strategy, like everything else they do, is blunt and forceful. If you need to add functionality, acquire a company that has what you need. If you can't get it that way, merge with the company. If you can't get it that way, partner with them. This has been their strategy since they introduced Siebel Service Enterprise at the end of 1996—a customer service application—three years from the founding of the company. Since that time, they have acquired, merged, or signed strategic deals with:

1997: Interactive Workplace, Inc. Intranet-based business intelligence software.

1997: Nomadic Systems, Inc. A pharmaceutical sales application.

1998: Merged with Scopus Technology Customer service, call centers, field service applications.

1998: 20-20 Group An end-user training company.

1999: OnTarget, Inc. Sales and marketing consulting services and training.

1999: IBM Strategic agreement to jointly market and develop CRM software. IBM canned their Corepoint CRM competitive product.

2000: Paragren Leading vendor for marketing automation.

2000: Mohr Development Sales training for financial services, manufacturing, and technology vertical businesses.

2000: OpenSite Technologies The leader in Web-based e-commerce solutions at that time. This was an important acquisition because it was the precursor of Siebel repositioning itself from a CRM company to an e-business company.

2000: Janna Systems Major acquisition of a company that specialized in enterprise relationship management (ERM) for the financial services sector.

2000: OnLink Technologies A catalog-based product selection tool.

2000: EDS Strategic alliance for consulting services.

Amazingly, this is not all that was done in the year 2000 or prior years. This is just a representative sampling of what Siebel has done to date. There are alliances with wireless companies and acquisitions in the future to be carried out. For example, Siebel products lack analytic functionality, so, at the year end 2000, Siebel announced Siebel eBusiness 2000.3, which included Siebel eBusiness analytics. Problem solved.

Products

Siebel products originate in the customer service world. Their product line is called Siebel eBusiness 2000. Note that it is not CRM 2000—it is eBusiness 2000. Their products cover a global range. Their solutions are horizontal, vertical, wired, wireless, big, handheld, expensive to implement, and flexible to customize.

Siebel implementations are perhaps the most expensive in the industry, resembling ERP implementations in length of implementation and cost. There is no doubt that their products work well and are well integrated for the very large enterprise market, but they are spreading their product lines widely. For example, they have the most comprehensive vertical applications covering (with a "Siebel e-" in front of each of these industry-specific monikers) automotive, public sector, communications, consumer goods, apparel and footwear (SAP did this one, too), energy, finance, insurance, healthcare, pharmaceuticals, technology, and retail. What makes each of these special is the knowledge of the business processes of the particular industry. For example, in the eApparel and Footwear application, it covers the standard stuff and takes into account products with complex attributes such as style, color, size, and season.

Siebel covers the other expected market segments, such as sales, service marketing, and the channel. They do service with a bit of flair. Their field service applications include sales, field service, professional services, an "econfigurator and epricer" for complex product configurations and pricing online and through self-service, incentive compensation for the customer service sales force, and finally, in a bow to the wireless world, an application for handheld, voice, and wireless.

They use their somewhat big architecture (migrated from a pro-prietary architecture to an more open standards n-tiered architec-ture, though not fully) to provide some very good tools for the CRM engine you are purchasing. Their architecture is comprehensive, with a personalization engine, remote working tools, and a pretty sophis-ticated workflow. Winner of the Greenberg's Most Interesting Siebel Tools are EAI (that stands for enterprise application integration) which has embedded integration hooks with such heavyweights as IBM's MQSeries and SAP, and a flexible toolset that allows the cus-tomer or the hired guns to build integration hooks to any third-party application. Additionally, Siebel provides a visual development tool that lets a customer create interfaces, embedding their own business rules and data.

In addition to the inclusion of the analytics in Siebel eBusiness 2000.3, they heavily beefed up their eMarketing application with the industry's first "pre-built" customer data warehouse and added interfaces they call "extractors" to PeopleSoft and SAP R/3, thus tying the front and back offices together.

If you are interested in checking out their sales tool, they have a Siebel Sales Personal Edition they are giving away on their website. What you give them in return is a fair amount of information that will potentially qualify you as a lead, and a chance to call you when they are ready to. The product is interesting and worth looking at. It is a dumbed-down version of Siebel Sales 2000, Enterprise Edition.

Future

The wireless world and the midmarket are among those things that have Siebel drooling. Siebel inked deals with Avaya, Sprint, Palm, and Nokia to develop a small footprint capability for wireless—cell-phones, PDAs, and pagers such as the Blackberry. This portends very big things in Siebel's future and rightly so. Mobility and access to Siebel large enterprise applications via your Palm or Compaq IPAQ 3650 is what Siebel is working toward.

Additionally, in mid-2000, Siebel released Siebel eBusiness 2000 Midmarket Edition, a product aimed at the smaller part of the enter-prise market. The reason for this is Siebel's recognition that the mid-market is ripe for CRM and where the high-volume customers seem to be. However, because they are not born in the midmarket, they are not yet comfortable in the midmarket. The Global 2000 has 2,000 possible customers. The midmarket has more, along the lines of several hundred thousand. How Siebel plays here remains an interesting question.

Websites

http://www.siebel.com/
http://www.sales.com/

Nortel/Clarify

Acquired in 1999 by Nortel Networks after many years as a successful call center applications company, Nortel/Clarify branched heavily into other venues in February 2000 with the release of their eFrontOffice 9.0 CRM products suite.

In mid-2000, Nortel/Clarify signed a major deal with SAP, the fourth largest software company in the world, to create a multimedia contact center that would provide unified information for the users of mySAP.com, SAP's very powerful portal, regardless of the customer point of contact—email, fax, telephone, face-to-face-contact, and so on. SAP took all of the functionality of Nortel/Clarify except the sales and marketing functionality, playing to Clarify's strengths.

Strategy/Mission

Nortel/Clarify's mission is to incorporate all customer touchpoints under a single framework. They are focused on providing a bridge between the offline and online worlds. For example, dot-coms moving to customer activity offline and brick-and-mortar institutions moving to the online world can use the Clarify product to handle both ends from the middle. Because they can provide a communications and network backbone to go with this, it can be a powerful incentive to use their solution.

Products

The chief Nortel/Clarify product is eFrontOffice 9.0, which is a feature-rich major league player in the CRM world. It is a huge package with more than 50 identifiable separate products. The product range covers sales, marketing, orders/billing, inventory, online customer service, mobile field service, contracts, field logistics, and of course, development tools. It is aimed at consolidation of the multiple channels available to customers through a single set of interactions.

What is notable about their massive product set is that regardless of category, ultimately the Nortel/Clarify suite is centered on customer support, communications services, and call centers. They apparently lack the large array of analytic CRM tools that products like Vantive have. They also don't have a strong partner management toolset. But there is a mind-boggling array of CIC/call center–related applications that are among the most powerful on the market—which is one of the primary reasons SAP cut the deal with them.

There is one innovative schema that Nortel/Clarify has developed based on what they call "return on relationship." Return on relationship is essentially measuring customer profitability over time. It views relationship-based customer transactions rather than transactions-based activities and uses a bit of "balanced scorecard" thinking by saying the intangible measure of corporate strength is engendering loyalty.

Return on relationship provides metrics for CRM systems to measure the use of its resources to provide differentiated service, particularly for a company's highly valued customers.

Nortel has patented a "loyalty goal" formula that it embedded in their eFrontOffice suite through Global Account Manager. This is where the customer data has a number of the formulas applied to it. Then other reporting packages (normally external) can be used for the slicing and dicing necessary for analysis.

Another place where Nortel/Clarify products are distinguished is with the integration of what is called enterprise incentive management (EIM), a new and growing market segment that some analysts peg at a potential growth of $6.4 billion. This market rests in the space between CRM and ERP. It allows for highly personalized views of front- and back-office functions such as individual salesperson compensation tracking. EIM can involve the sales team and how successfully each individual would meet his or her goals. It then involves the accounting and finance departments to handle the results of that success or failure.

Nortel/Clarify is integrating the EIM technology of incentive systems into its sales offering, especially the incentive system features such as flexible plan maintenance and personalized compensation reporting. This does provide some powerful tools for an enterprise-class application.

Future

Nortel/Clarify is apparently trying to emerge from pure CRM and move to more of a "customer-facing" e-business platform. In that effort, they have released the Clarify Customer Portal, which is linked to Clarify's e-business applications. They have added chat and auto-response to the portal to enhance customer interaction. The idea seems to be to expand the services being offered to include not just CRM, but also product configuration online, receiving, tracking and ordering online—in other words, procurement in a primitive way. Nortel Network's communications services strengths provide a strong backbone to the Clarify product.

Websites

http://www.nortelnetworks.com/
http://www.nortel.com/
http://www.clarify.com/

MicroStrategy

Consistent products are the MicroStrategy hallmark—it has some of the soundest, most innovative, and horizontally specific products in the CRM panorama. The products released by Michael Saylor's company are used to provide highly personalized customer services to millions of customers. They do it in the large (monster customer data repositories) and in the small (PDAs). They do it with a very classy operation that is professionally run. They do it without wasting time, money, or effort. I saw their Virginia operation and what was apparent was space is used, support is there, and competent people are in charge of the products. A hight comfort level.

This culture has created a no-nonsense group of 2,000 highly articulate professionals, which explains their product quality. They have a culture that actually encourages this professionalism, winning them awards such as the 1999 Arthur Andersen Best Practices Award and a 1999 *Fortune* magazine "100 Best Places to Work" slot.

One of their recent "walk the walk and talk the talk" inventions was a full-featured Web store where MicroStrategy's software, education, technical support, consulting services, and documentation can be ordered, regardless of time or place. Additionally, they are giving away evaluation copies of their MicroStrategy eCRM 7 Developers

Kit at the store. They are one of the CRM companies that actually practice what Web B2B philosophy they preach.

This gives them more than 1,000 customers, many of them blue chip. They range from the Ohio Department of Education to Metropolitan Life to Warner Brothers.

Strategy/Mission

Here is their mission statement directly from their Web page:

> MicroStrategy wants everyone in the world to have the right information at the right time, in order to gain insight, security, and to make better decisions.

This represents their philosophy as well as their mission. Providing deep, highly personalized information to all users. This mission statement leads to their strategy to make their personalization software multichannel and omnipresent. Not only does it capture customer information from emails, website visits, phone calls, and any other means that you care to imagine, it sends the information through client/server machines, Web-based architectures, and any wireless device that exists from cellphone to PDA to pager. The right information at the right time.

This mission is also reflected in their Strategy.com strategy. Strategy.com, discussed in Chapter 6, is a site that provides personalized content aggregation for wireless devices.

Products

Again, their approach is not the usual product suite approach. They work from MicroStrategy 7, a business intelligence platform that generates a number of product offerings, and MicroStrategy eCRM 7, a product I cover thoroughly in Chapter 6. The platform is based on an open, server-centric XML-based architecture and has been designed for the Web from the ground up. MicroStrategy 7 focuses on the analytical needs of business intelligence, eCRM, ERP, Web traffic analysis, and in its most interesting incarnation, mobile commerce. It is Unix or Windows NT or 2000–based and supports every major relational database, bar none. It is by far the most adaptable in that vein and is very scalable. It actually comes in three editions:

Personal Edition For the single user.

Workgroups Edition For departmental or small groups of users.

Enterprise Edition For entire companies plus their suppliers and customers. This scales to thousands of users.

MicroStrategy 7 is a huge framework for the most detailed and complex analytic functions on the market. It has several critical components, which I will briefly examine here.

Intelligence Server This is a highly concentrated enterprise server that handles all business intelligence functions. It can be accessed through Web, wireless, and voice.

Agent This works in conjunction with Architect as a business workflow tool that integrates query capabilities.

Web The Web platform leverages an extensive library of more than 150 statistical, financial, and OLAP functions that is entirely accessible and customizable through the Web. You can work with predefined reports or create new reports through flexible prompts.

Architect This is the development environment. What makes it unique is that it can handle terabytes of data so that it is almost infinitely scalable.

Administrator This does what any administration tool does. It configures the system, creates the security and the new users, and maintains the existing users with their administration-assigned security levels.

Transactor This is a very cool product. It collects information from back-end databases, Web servers, and ERP systems, according to predefined criteria. It then takes that information, "translates" it to XML so a desktop Web browser, a personal digital assistant, or a WAP-enabled telephone can receive it.

Telecaster This is a very complex telephone-based product. It is an intelligent voice server that enables narrowcasting (see Chapters 6 and 16) to any telephone, mobile telephone, or voicemail system worldwide. Each telecast is personalized to deliver one-to-one conversations with hundreds of thousands of recipients. It can use recorded sound files and real-time text-to-speech. Very advanced, indeed.

Infocenter This is a dedicated application. It enables the deployment of a corporation's permission-based marketing strategy. Period.

Broadcaster This is another cutting edge application. It automates the delivery of personalized messages and actionable information through WAP and mobile phones, PDAs, email, Web pages, pagers, fax, and printers.

Software Development Kit It is what it says it is. It is the kit for the technically savvy to build their own custom parts for the MicroStrategy engine.

Future

MicroStrategy's future is in the part of the wireless world in what they have called "the decade of the voice." Since I cover it in Chapter 16, I won't spend a lot of time with it here, but suffice it to say, it is sexy. The idea is to use a telephone to receive voice-enabled and activated content from a website. Whoa! That is a very hot idea and between this, their product suite, and their Strategy.com initiative, MicroStrategy not only has a future, it is the cutting edge of a very exciting era.

Websites

http://www.microstrategy.com/
http://www.strategy.com/

Oracle (CRM)

Oracle is, well, Oracle. It is the sumo-sized baby of Larry Ellison and is the second largest software company in the world. With the beating that Microsoft's stock has taken in the last year, it may soon be the biggest software company in the world. It has been marked by controversy, acrimony, public battles, foresight that has been ridiculed (network computers which are now thin clients) to death, and continued growth due to what is perhaps their greatest product, Oracle, the relational database (RDBMS). Additionally, with Larry Ellison's vision of the Internet, he was smart enough to rewrite Oracle 8 to become Oracle 8*i*, which was the first entirely re-engineered, Internet-ready RDBMS. This spurred phenomenal sales leading to a dominant market position in the database world, with only IBM's DB2 and to some extent, Microsoft's SQL Server 7.0 and later, any competition at all.

Oracle CRM's most recent release has been given kudos by much of the industry. Oracle's foresight in developing CRM products, in addition to an unusual bit of strategy, has sparked substantial sales of its flagship CRM product. The unusual bit of strategy? Giving away the CRM sales component as the online service Oraclesalesonline.com (discussed in Chapter 4). The sales? Within approximately 18 months of the first release of its CRM product suite, it had captured 2.2 percent of the total CRM market, fourth after Siebel, Vantive, and Clarify. Amazing.

Strategy/Mission

Oracle's mission in general seems to be similar to Microsoft's: dominate the earth. However, its CRM mission is to gain increasing market share and do what is necessary to get it, including giving away a part of the farm. That means evolving their strategy to cover a broader area than just CRM—e-business. Oracle CRM is buried into the E-Business product matrix. To find the individual CRM segments such as Marketing, Sales, and Service, you have to pick through fields of Oracle E-Business applications such as Financials, Human Resources, Internet Procurement, Projects and Supply Chain, among others. This used to be Oracle CRM, Oracle Applications, and so on. Now it is lumped under E-Business in a clear bid to link the front and back offices for end-to-end e-business solutions. This is the strategy carried out by many of the major players mentioned in this section of the book, and for the larger enterprise players such as Oracle, it is a successful one for the moment.

Products

Oracle delivered the first version of its CRM application in 1999 on the HP platform, followed about six months later by versions for Compaq, Dell, and IBM. Since that time, their claims are that they have reduced the total sales cycle time by 19 percent. They claim that those that use their CRM software for online sales have been increasing Web sales by more than 700 percent per year. Heady claims.

They carry the full three-suite of products—sales, marketing and services. The most recent incarnation, Oracle CRM 11*i*, provides a brand new service component called the Interaction Center 11*i* suite, which supports multimedia call centers. The Oracle Call Center in fact handles complex routing they call "Advanced Inbound and Outbound." It has a powerful email workflow that fires the email to the customized versions of the proper queues.

The components of Oracle Sales (besides Oraclesalesonline.com, which is covered in Chapter 4 in detail) are

Oracle Sales Online This is a classic sales application with contact, opportunity, account, and pipeline management. Its most interesting feature is Oracle Field Sales for Palm, which enables field salespeople to take their information anywhere they go using a Palm device.

Oracle Telesales This is a singular product, unlike any I've seen elsewhere so far. It is a call-center-enabled application created for inside-sales representatives, distributors, resellers, and sales executives. It tracks, manages, and executes the entire customer sales cycle. By its nature, it allows for sharing of opportunities across channels. An inside-sales-specific product is smart.

Oracle Incentive Compensation This is an MBO sales product—management by objective. It matches incentives to business objectives, all online. It integrates the back office (financial compensation processes) with the front office (sales functions). Oracle Incentive Compensation automates the complex task of calculating, allocating, and accumulating incentive credits. Another standout product, though one emulated by many others.

Oracle iStore This provides a customizable online storefront for selling products and services and is tied to ERP systems for order and inventory management. Not truly an SFA product, but Oracle has a plan.

Oracle iPayment iPayment is a complete electronic payment processing solution that makes it easy to "payment enable" new or existing Internet-based applications or client/server applications.

Oracle Service has a lot of the Oracle ERP side built into it. With such components as Depot Maintenance, Maintenance Repair and Overhaul, Spares Management, and Advanced Scheduler, you get the impression you're dealing with a facilities management application, not a true customer service application. It does have some of the more typical service components such as TeleService, iSupport, Service Online, but this is more a field service application than a call center.

Oracle Marketing is a simple application with a lot of purpose. There are only two components, but they are *big* ones:

Oracle Marketing Online This is a classic Internet-enabled multichannel marketing automation application. It works closely with Oracle Marketing Intelligence.

Oracle Marketing Intelligence Marketing Intelligence is designed to meet the reporting and analytic needs of marketers. It can handle planning and budgeting to segmentation, campaign execution, and measurement, and refinement. These are basic analytic functions.

Future

Oracle's strategy seems to be the strategy of several of the larger players: to evolve from CRM products (at least for marketing purposes) to e-business suites. This means growing the product offerings to include more "e" versions of client/server products. Additionally, to increase the e-business offerings, Oracle is forming the necessary alliances to create an IP infrastructure that handles data, voice, email, and Web traffic and supports the integrated systems. To this end, in July 2000, they officially allied with Cisco to take the first step to bring life to this Oracle-driven backbone. The other benefit is that Cisco already provides the network and computer telephony features that can be integrated into Oracle CRM. This is most noticeable in the interaction management features of Oracle CRM, which is directly linked to Cisco's version of the same name.

Oracle's approach to creating this future seems to generally be through partnerships. They currently have support and investment from EMC, Hewlett-Packard, Arthur Andersen, Cap Gemini Ernst and Young LLC, KPMG Consulting LLC, PricewaterhouseCoopers, and the Siemens Business Solutions Group.

Oracle has not ignored the wireless world either, with a significant investment into this realm. However, they have tied it directly to a move toward hosted services as a whole. Oraclemobile.com is their wireless initiative. It is a portal that resembles many other, with dozens of hosted services for your Palm, your cellphone, your pager, your "whatever-doesn't-trip-you-because-it's-plugged-in" device. But this is only one of their hosted portals. They have others, such as oracleexchange.com. Oracle's overall thinking? As was once said by a wise sage (Pogo), "I have seen the future and it is us."

Websites

http://www.oracle.com/
http://www.oraclesalesonline.com/
http://www.oraclemobile.com/
http://www.oracleexchange.com/

E.piphany

E.piphany has a strong pedigree. When Roger Siboni, the former COO and deputy chairman of KPMG, assumed leadership of E.piphany in 1998, this just put a stamp on what was already a blue-blooded management team, board of directors, and board of advisors. Representatives from the most significant venture capital firms (Kleiner, Perkins, Byers, Caulfield, and the like) to the former senior vice president of Oracle Consulting round out this high-powered team. What makes E.piphany interesting is that in their short existence in the EMA world, they have garnered numerous accolades as one of the up and coming CRM and Internet companies. They come from a history of analytic CRM and have moved with the release of E.5 into the operational CRM world. An attempt to be all things to all people—albeit in the CRM-centered universe.

Strategy/Mission

Their corporate mission seems to be focused on making sure that what they produce controls all inbound and outbound customer interactions, and then analyzes and interprets them to the nth degree. They follow the common strategy characterized by "when you need a significant piece of expertise, acquire it." However, their acquisitions are careful. They made two major ones by mid-2000—Rightpoint, a real-time personalization engine (see Chapter 5), and Octane Software, a provider of service, sales, and marketing applications. The Octane purchase was a landmark for E.piphany. It was an attempt to take an analytic CRM, combine it with operational CRM, and make it into a front-office solution. Playin' with the big boys.

E.piphany continues to play like a big boy. In fall 2000, they announced a relationship with Sun Microsystems to make Sun the platform of choice for their software, even though they had been a Microsoft house in the past. This was the first CRM deal that Sun had participated in up until that point, so it had big implications. This is not unusual, but it confirms E.piphany's push into the front-office solutions market and out of the pure analytics CRM space and their power in landing a presence the size of Sun.

Products

E.piphany's E.5 is the latest incarnation of the product suite that made them one of the fastest growing companies in the Internet world. The core product prior to the Octane acquisition had been personalization, analytics, and campaign management, but with the move of Octane into the fold, a fuller front-office suite emerged that involved partner, employee, and customer interactions in sales, service, and marketing.

Their E.5 product suite breaks down like this:

Campaign Management E.5 covers two areas of campaign management: e-commerce and email. They are markedly different in functionality, with e-commerce working with segmentation data such demographics, click-stream, transactional behavior, and scoring time. Needless to say, this data flows to the analytic engine that E.piphany built its reputation on. For email, the functions are more toward permission-based campaigns that involve capturing information, which can be opt-out rates, click-through rates, and delivery success or failure. It also is able to send personalized email messages through the data captured and analyzed.

Real-time Personalization This is a multichannel capture engine that can make dynamic changes to personal profiles and issue dynamic, flexible responses. It grabs information from click-stream data, customer databases, transaction systems, third-party data, and other sources.

Connected Sales The E.piphany description of this SFA application is interesting: "Sales management features include lead tracking and distribution, forecasting, activity management, order entry, order status lookup, pricing, discounting, and reporting and analysis." What makes that interesting is its emphasis on order taking and pricing. Most SFA applications (as I hope you saw in Chapter 4) are not focused on order taking—that tends to be a benefit. They are aimed at opportunity closure. This is a very different emphasis than traditional sales force automation. It has a lot of the back office in it.

Service Portal This is a good idea with basic features. It is focused on customer self-service. It allows the customer to research and construct highly personalized product profiles and actually order online without the benefit of a live representative.

Service Center This is the E.5 product that provides the single view of the customer with information gathered from all channels. It is a product that a customer service representative would love. The customer can reach the representative by any means he wants. The representative gets all the information captured and, because it has hybrid sales and marketing features built into it, the customer rep can up-sell and cross-sell, though customer service reps selling isn't necessarily the greatest idea.

Enterprise Insight This is a system that consolidates and analyzes all the data on customers and customer segments, providing the business intelligence for the marketer, the sale teams, or the management of an enterprise. This is the core of E.piphany's original business, along with campaign management.

Future

This is an interesting question. The purchase of Octane was E.piphany's attempt to go toe to toe with the Vantives and Siebels of the world. That is a tall order. They are a lot bigger than E.piphany is. However, E.piphany has a good product line with the release of E.5, so we'll see if they can compete or if their toes get stepped on.

Website

http://www.epiphany.com/

Pivotal

Pivotal is a company that is now finding a domain that they hope distinguishes them from the CRM run-of-the-mill. The Vancouver, British Columbia–based Pivotal calls its products an "XML-based, demand chain network solution." They define a demand chain network as "integrating all of a company's customer-facing inter-activities and networking new kinds of business partners into its solution offerings." What this means in non-techno is automating solutions to manage marketing, selling, and servicing processes over the Internet. Their solution encompasses CRM, online sales, e-commerce, and the wireless world—a large bite to chew, but one that they claim to do effectively.

Founded in 1991 as a company to support pen computing, Pivotal has undergone a number of facelifts since then. However, their current face is perhaps the most, pardon the pun, pivotal, in their history. Why? Because of competition, the high risk of makeovers, and tricky market conditions. They are betting the corporate farm on this change. They are taking the risk that all technology companies take—that the technology they support is a keeper. It may be.

They have an impressive customer list encompassing 35 countries. Some of their customers are among the world's major players, including ING Barings LLC, KPMG, Intrawest Corporation, USFilter, NEC, Ericsson, Emerson Electric, and Nissan Motor (Denmark). Their foundation is strong, their customer list blue chip, and they've survived since 1991—a long time in the New Economy.

Strategy/Mission

As they say in big, gutsy letters on their website, "Microsoft.Net is Key to Our Vision." That is a high-risk (although lower than some) proposition to use to define an entire corporate strategy. E.piphany was like that until they made a deal to support E.piphany on the Sun Solaris. However, Pivotal has a proven track record and in fact, near the end of 2000, was voted by Deloitte & Touche one of the fastest growing companies in North America, with revenue growth of almost 35,000 percent between 1995 and 1999! They received nearly $55 million in financing shortly before that. They have 700 customers. Obviously, with those revenue numbers, and that customer base and financing, someone thinks they are doing something right.

Products

The Pivotal self-designated solutions are 100 percent Microsoft. Net-based. They attempt to "unify Internet commerce, CRM, eSelling, and wireless technologies to manage collaborative relationships between customers, business partners, and employees." Actually, they are a set of products that are linked by an Internet-based framework. As is the noted trend in these top companies, these products are attempting to go end-to-end for their clients. They are

> **EPower 2000** This is a very heavy-duty "demand chain network" infrastructure. It is the engine from which all Pivotal

activities flow. It handles messaging of the garden variety such as MQSeries actions to more exotic messaging such as Voice Over Internet Protocol (VOIP) messages. It handles workflow and event triggers. It handles data mapping and migration, personalization, embedding business rules, transaction processing, fulfillment, advisory and recommendations, data mining, data analysis, Web content filtration, and delivery. I presume EPower 2000 has also vowed to win five gold medals in the 2004 Olympics.

ESelling 2000 This is not a sales force automation product. It is more of a self-service customer interaction product that takes the customer through the entire sales process or, more to the point, the buying process. It uses the EPower 2000 engine to provide highly personalized, dynamic powerful interaction, configuration, and advisory features. The customer picks the right thing to buy with no nagging rep looking for a commission or ignorant of the products that are being sold.

ERelationship 2000 This is the core product and the product that Pivotal has been known for over the past few years. This product now resembles Onyx's in its style with three portals—the Intra Hub for employees; the Partner Hub for, well, partners; and the Customer Hub for—oh, you know. They are tied through a series of hosted Web services that Pivotal calls PivotalWeb.Net. The services read like a virtual Palm wireless service map—Travelocity, Marketsoft, Hoovers Online, New Channel, Newmediary.com, *ad infinitum.*

Other things Pivotal also packages three other solutions. The first is PivotalHost, an ASP that Pivotal has as an alternative to owning the applications. The second is Pivotal RPM (Rapid Productivity Methodology), a rapid implementation methodology—something I haven't seen claimed since the ERP heyday in 1998. Kudos to Pivotal on that one. Finally, they offer Pivotal Anywhere, their wireless version. Curiously, as of the end of 2000, they certify a number of devices, including the Palm III and V with the Minstrel modem, but not the Palm VII, which has an internal wireless modem. Odd. In any case, it is a normal wireless offering described in many places elsewhere in this book with a number of devices at the ready.

Future

Pivotal's future is probably the one in this list that could go either way. On the one hand, they have had the highest speed growth rate for the last several years. On the other hand, they are undergoing a constant reinvention, which is good if it meets market conditions, bad if it underestimates or exceeds market conditions. Pivotal is entirely dependent on the Microsoft.Net platform, which is a big question mark. But, they have exceptional well-evolved products that do their job well. Figure it out.

Website

http://www.pivotal.com/

Kana/Silknet

It's funny the way the New Economy works. Magnitudes of scale are no longer meaningful. Kana Communications was called a small software company in *Information Week* this year as it was purchasing Silknet Software for *$4.2 billion*. Small? I feel like going out and spending a couple of million in pocket change!

When Mark Gainey started Kana in 1996 with $27 million in venture money, it was an email management company. Admittedly, after a few iterations of its basic software it had unique aspects to it, such as an artificial intelligence for the email campaigns, but it was an email management application. Not more. Not less.

But Kana's strategy included multiple acquisitions. Their acquisition strategy accelerated with the ascendancy of Michael McCloskey as the chairman and CEO of the company in 1999. Let's look at asset list:

1997: Connectify This purchase gave Kana tools for direct marketing campaigns.

1999: Business Evolution This acquisition gave Kana capacity that included chat and instant messaging so that customers could be in touch with their service representatives in real time.

1999: Net Dialog This was an important one. Self-service for the customer, as well as information sent to and pushed to the customer based on their preferences were the important features of the acquired software.

2000: Silknet This was a CRM industry–significant acquisition. Kana acquired an XML-based, n-tiered architecture that used open standards and open protocols. Silknet's product managed all aspects of customer interaction so, for example, the customer representative could see an entire history of customer preferences, support requests, sales order status, and other customer history as the customer representative spoke to the customer. This customer information was gathered through multiple customer channels.

Strategy/Mission

Kana is a company that has created a multichannel communications framework to gather information from customers. Their mission is to provide enterprise relationship management (ERM) to companies worldwide. With the acquisition of Silknet, they developed a broad product matrix that would provide what they hope is a "compelling" experience in e-business. They are seen by many analysts as a tactical group that has developed a product line for B2B and B2C organizations.

Products

The Kana 6 product suite was released in very late 2000. It is their first true release since the acquisition of Silknet and reflects the completed integration of the Silknet product line. Kana is attempting to provide a fairly full service eCRM collection. They have added a stronger personalization engine to their existing applications. They have more tightly integrated their framework to tie Web customer service to the existing sales processes.

Kana 6 runs on just about any platform, including Sun Solaris, Windows NT, and IBM's AIX. They can use any RDBMS, including Oracle, DB2, and Microsoft SQL Server 7.0. In other words, with the open standards, open protocols, and flexible platforms, they are virtually platform independent. Plus, it only takes a browser to access Kana 6—any browser.

The revamped products as of late 2000 are

Kana Connect This is an electronic direct marketing solution that engages customers in conversations through permission-based email communication.

Kana Advisor This is a pretty cool application. It creates a virtual salesperson. It utilizes the customer data accumulated from multiple sources to identify what a customer wants and then recommends the options it thinks the customer is likely to want as a result of the profile.

Kana Realtime Communication Channels This allows the enterprise to engage online customers in a live interaction. It includes instant messaging and text chats between the customer and the customer service representatives. Perhaps the most interesting is the Kana Voice channel, which provides PC-to-PC voice dialog between the customer and the customer service rep. It is fascinating to me that the most interesting channel provided by Kana is one that uses the PC as a telephone.

Kana Response This is an email response management solution that enables businesses to manage inbound communications channel interactions by using agents to automate the responses. It also provides customized reports that can provide information on everything from system reports to agent roductivity.

Kana Classify This engine will take customer inquiries from any inbound communications channel (the phone, the Web, instant messenger) and categorize them by subject matter and priority. It can then send an automatic response to the customer based on the inquiry and customer history. More complex responses are routed to the appropriate customer service representatives for review, using a good workflow engine.

Kana Service Kana calls this an e-business application. This is the application that provides the "single view" of the customer for the entire enterprise by compiling a universal customer history of interactions and transactions across all communication channels and business processes. The workflow engine is very strong and provides automatic escalation and intelligent routing, extranet workflow of service requests and processes, and multimedia publishing of solutions for self-service.

Kana Commerce This is a tool for online store creation that can be tied into the back office.

Kana Conduits These are the plug-and-play integration hooks for multiple platforms and products that Kana can provide. These are powerful not only because they make up an integration toolset, but also because they are easy to use.

Kana Studio Kana Studio is the toolset for customizing the Kana applications or for developing independent e-business applications. It includes a workflow designer, business rules editor, and multimedia knowledge base.

Future

Kana, though it has seemed to have a targeted dot-com customer base, was not hit so hard by the dot-com collapse of late 2000. Over 70 percent of Kana's actual customers are Global 2000 companies who have bought into Kana's ERM vision. By the acquisition of Silknet, they signaled their intent to do what several of the other cocky up-and-comers are doing—attempting to provide *the* end-to-end e-business service offering. The Global 2000 is where Siebel and PeopleSoft/Vantive play. Can Kana compete? We'll see.

Websites

http://www.kana.com/
http://www.silknet.com/

Check Out the Lists

There are a few matrices available for your perusal. Given the constant liquid shifting and morphing of the CRM market, these lists may be outdated by the time you read them. I am recognizing those few that have added value beyond just a list, but there are several others that you could probably find. They will give you the broad scope and magnitude of this mind-boggling maze of choices, with a sometimes different and occasionally dyspeptic view of the CRM world.

Knowledge Capital Management

The Knowledge Capital Group (KCG) has a unique perspective on CRM for their matrix. The matrix resides in the KCG MarketView

128-page document entitled "CRM Redefined: Beyond the Front Office and Out to the Customer." From the get-go, you realize that this isn't the traditional outlook of operational, analytic, collaborative CRM. In fact, the matrix is divided into sections (I'm producing a very brief description of each category):

Customer Information Platform These are foundation applications such as front-office suites and data warehouses.

Spheres of Expertise These are the horizontal-specific applications such as sales force automation, EMA, analytic applications, and so on. They are focused primarily in the sales and marketing worlds.

Customer Interaction Platforms These are more in the call center world—the world of "multichannel management of customer interaction."

Channels of Execution These are channel-specific applications such as those with partner relationship management (PRM).

Consulting, Integration, and Change These are services companies that handle everything from strategic package-independent CRM consulting to package-specific implementations to systems integration.

That will give you the lingo you need to interpret their matrix. Once interpreted, this matrix gives you a fantastic broad view of what the market has to offer. Oh yeah, read the rest of the report, too. You can find the report for free on the Onyx website at http://www.onyx.com/ or at the KCG website http://www.knowledgecap.com/free_freeresearch.html.

CRM Magazine

CRM magazine, the official magazine of the Customer Relationship Management Association, issues an annual Buyers Guide that is a comprehensive listing of everything you always wanted to find out about CRM companies and then some. Its great strength is the muscle power of the magazine itself. It is a monthly biblical equivalent for the CRM world. The weakness of the Buyers Guide is that, when you get down to the core, it is a big advertising supplement. However, there is genuine value in it. To get a copy, you can go to their website at http://www.destinationcrm.com/ or write to them at 156 W. 56th St., 3rd Floor, New York, NY 10019 or phone them at (212) 333-7600.

META Group

The CRM-omnipresent META Group analyst firm has a CRM Technology Ecosystem Vendor Landscape (their name for it)—a comprehensive look at CRM vendors from their perspective—operational, analytical, and so on. It is a useful breakdown of the vendors by feature sets. To get it, contact the META Group. Their information is available on their website at http://www.metagroup.com/.

CRM Solutions Guide

For a different take on specific vendors, check out the Customer Relationship Management Solutions Guide by Jay Chang of Structured Chaos, done exclusively for Robert Thompson's CRMguru.com. It is a compendium of ideas and thoughts on specific vendors, including several of the ones that I mention in this chapter. It is a refreshing take on them and worth reading.

Chapter 11

ERP Says Hello to CRM

Enterprise resource planning (ERP) has been having a hard time saying hello to CRM. CRM doesn't seem to want to listen or, if it does listen, it doesn't respond. Both the ERP system and ERP companies have been fretting about how to integrate CRM, the Internet, and the back-office ERP. The ERP companies are trying to retool and create their own CRM solutions. We are going to look at how the ERP world is responding to the Internet revolution and how ERP and CRM products integrate.

Enterprise Resource Planning

Enterprise resource planning is a highly integrated (and highly expensive) system of back-office functions, particularly human resources and financial applications that are integrally customized and linked to all existing office business processes. In the late 1980s, SAP AG, a German software company, now the fourth largest software company in the world, came out with SAP R/2, a huge piece of software focused on manufacturing companies that were using mainframe applications. What made this a revolutionary breakthrough was the integration of best business processes directly into the guts of applications and the whole office integration of business functionality. For example, with SAP R/3, the client/server version of R/2, sales and distribution were interlocked with financials, which were intertwined with production planning, which was intermeshed with materials management. SAP had very successful sales despite an extremely high software and services implementation price (sometimes as high as $100,000,000!) and implementation times that could take up to three years. By 1998, they had more than 4,700 customers in Germany and 1,800 customers in the United States and generated $5.5 billion in revenue.

This led to dozens of real and pretend ERP companies, the most notable real companies being PeopleSoft, Oracle (with its ERP Application suite), J.D. Edwards, and Lawson Software, each aimed at different markets and each simultaneously competitive. Hundreds of other companies such as Great Plains and Macola, formerly known for their accounting packages, revamped themselves and began styling themselves as ERP mavens. Cottage industries that linked ERP packages to almost any other form of application grew up as tens of billions were being spent on implementing ERP by almost every single Fortune 1000 company. The middleware market, which had been modestly successful with products like IBM's MQSeries, Casahl's Technology's Repli-caction, and so on, was transformed when companies who had implemented these vast ERP systems realized they had a lot of data they needed to link to and use that they couldn't spend the time "translating." The enterprise application integration (EAI) market was born, with major players like Mercator and NEON entering the fray and doing very well as the EAI market expanded rapidly to many other areas.

After a banner year in 1998, which was reflected by PeopleSoft growing from a small company with $227 million in revenues in

1995 to $1.4 billion dollars in revenues in 1999, ERP troubles began to show on the horizon. All of a sudden, corporate vice presidents who had authorized millions of dollars for an ERP implementation that was supposed to take a year to 18 months were clutching their throats when the implementation just didn't seem to be able to get finished, the 18 months were turning into 24 or even 36 months, and the process was well over budget. The benefits of the ERP return on investment weren't all that apparent, either. Unfortunately, as with all quasi-revolutionary applications and changes, ROI has no metrics. So how was the senior vice president for information technology going to explain to a CFO who was concerned with both costs and return that it was very costly and the return couldn't be measured?

The climate was changing at this time too—ironically, partially due to ERP, but primarily due to the Internet. Globalization and the dramatic escalation of transaction speed irrevocably changed the way the customer looked at the supplier. Customer demand for immediate response to inquiries and rapid shipment of orders, increasing competitive fervor and the "need for speed" to market, created a new form of customer demand. It demanded that personalized goods and services be delivered almost on demand nearly anywhere in the world.

ERP wasn't suited for this. While there is a lot of value in the back-office functionality it provides, it is not designed for rapid, nimble action; it is made for integrated functionality. SAP R/3 is a good example of that. Throughout the late 1990s, there were complaints that SAP R/3 versions from 1.0 to 3.0 were inflexible and forced you to adapt to their business rules, rather than provide you with applications that could be customized to those business rules you used as your best practices. SAP retooled and by 1997 came out with SAP R/3 4.0, an object-oriented version of the product that allowed the flexibility, but the mindset took a while to change.

Despite being seriously affected by the ERP market decline in 1999, PeopleSoft recognized the change that was occurring in the marketplace. In 1996, they acquired Red Pepper, a company that specialized in supply-chain software. With that acquisition, they began to push ERO—enterprise resource optimization—a philosophy and method they claimed was necessitated by the increasing real-time customer-driven economy. Perhaps the best example of this is the current "build-to-order" model used by most of the major computer system manufacturers (Dell, Micron, Gateway, and so on).

The ERP Market Declines Suddenly

ERP entered a dramatic market decline in early 1999. What was expected to be a banner year for the major enterprises became an unmitigated disaster. Dramatic stock price loss, with flat revenue growth after nearly 40 percent annual growth, major corporate upheavals and key management changes, thousands of top employees jumping to the dot-com world where flexibility, nimble footwork, and IPOs were the order of the day all led to major soul-searching and reorganization. Stock prices plunged. For example, within a year, PeopleSoft's stock price, which had been as high as 53 in 1998, dropped to a low of around 14, though as of late 2000, due to CRM sales, it had climbed back to 45. In ERP, only Oracle weathered the stock price storm, on the strength of its database sales and its foresight into the need to retool the database and all products to the Internet, not just adapt them. As 2000 approached, the ERP companies blamed Y2K concerns and the near panic to complete Y2K projects as one of the major reasons for the decline of their revenues.

ERP companies began noticing the fast-track growth of Siebel Systems, a company that had been around since 1993 promoting CRM. While ERP enterprise-wide software went into a steep market dive, Siebel Systems began to promote, not the back office, but the front office, or customer-facing, applications necessary to meet the globalized and personalized real-time demands of customers. Siebel, run by ex-Oracle executive Tom Siebel, climbed as spectacularly as SAP and other ERP vendors fell. Table 11-1 shows revenues for 1997 to 1999 for ERP and CRM vendors and the striking changes in the applications landscape virtually overnight. Keep in mind that the fiscal year ends vary in this chart.

Table 11-1: Revenue Comparison for Major ERP and CRM Vendors from 1997 to 1999

Company	Revenue 1997 (in millions of dollars)	Revenue 1998 (in millions of dollars)	Revenue 1999 (in millions of dollars)	Growth Rate 1997–1998	Growth Rate 1998–1999
SAP	3,345.5	5,073.3	5,146.0	51.6%	1.4%
PeopleSoft	815.0	1,313.7	1,429.1	61.1%	8.7%
J.D. Edwards	647.8	934.0	944.2	44.1%	1.1%
Oracle	7,143.9	8,827.3	10,130.1	23.6%	14.8%
Siebel Systems	118.8	391.5	790.9	229.5%	102.0%
Clarify	88.2	130.5	230.7	47.9%	76.8%

The differences are startling. The winds had shifted and the market was fully aware of the impact. While the ERP market leaders still gained a bit over the long run in a very uneven roller coaster ride, other ERP companies plunged to the bottom, and only in late 2000 were beginning to return. Take a look at the CRM companies and their stock prices over roughly the same period in Table 11-2. It is amazing. The pure CRM market leaders had spectacular growth. PeopleSoft made a fairly spectacular recovery in late 2000 due to PeopleSoft/ Vantive CRM sales' dramatic growth. SAP gained all told, but that is deceptive since part of the increase in the stock price was their opening on the New York Stock Exchange in 1998. From that opening through 1999, their actual percentage increase was zero. Oracle, the smartest of the ERP leaders and the one that had a database and a CRM product to fall back on, showed major growth. All stock prices are rounded to the nearest whole and reflect a month of activity in December of the year in question. They all show what CRM was becoming and ERP wasn't.

Table 11-2: Stock Prices for ERP and CRM Companies from 1997 to 1999

Company	1997	1998	1999	2000	Pct of Change (1997–1999)
SAP	$25	$36	$52	$63	252%
PeopleSoft	$38	$17	$22	$45 (November)	–42%
Siebel	$6	$9	$42	$101 (After several splits; September)	1683%
Clarify	$10	$23	$123	$157 (bought by Nortel, no longer traded in April; March)	1570%
Oracle	$9	$12	$58	$91	644%

ERP was inextricably (and inexplicably) linked to CRM by industry press and pundits as CRM rose spectacularly. After all, Y2K-tainted data rested in the back office of financials and human resources, not the front office of sales and marketing, so the connection was peculiar.

Witness the headline and first paragraph of an article in *Information Week* on July 21, 1999:

> **Earnings Reports: ERP Down, CRM Up**
>
> Quarterly results from SAP, PeopleSoft, and Siebel Systems confirm the obvious: The market for enterprise resource planning software is continuing its free fall, while the customer relationship management software market continues to climb.

This was typical for the time.

ERP Tries to Catch CRM

Beginning in 1999, ERP companies decided that perhaps CRM was the way to go. However, there were considerations. How were these behemoths going to compete with the head start that Siebel had? How could they retool to beat the young pups that were entering the eCRM and CRM space Internet ready? Not an easy task.

They also had to look at their historic investment in their own ERP software and thousands of clients. They had an attractive base, but many of the clients hadn't yet seen any real return on ERP implementations, so they were reluctant to trust their implementation partner. ERP implementation cancellation and failure stories were rampant. However, if they moved quickly, they could reap huge benefits as they reinvented themselves for the twenty-first century. Their installed base with the fully integrated back office could also have a fully connected integrated front office. Liz Shahnam, vice president of Infusion: CRM for the META Group, said in an article in *CRM* magazine:

> Not only do [customers] value these pre-integrated solutions, but they're willing to pay a premium for them, because this integration is really hard.

CRM-ERP Integration

What does integration between ERP and CRM mean? Back during the ERP troubles of '99, another buzz acronym enjoyed a short reign of popularity: XRP. This stood for extended ERP, which was another way of looking at what the Yankee Group calls the "Extended Enterprise." While the acronym was short lived, it reflected the ERP vendors' tentative foot out the door when they realized that what they had been building for the last several years was in jeopardy.

There are two distinct chains in the corporate ecosystem: the supply chain, which covers the back office to external suppliers and distributors, and the demand chain, which extends the front office to the customers and the channel. The back office includes departments and processes associated with finance, human resources, and, often, manufacturing. It includes multiple functions ranging from inventory management to accounts receivable to shipping and logistics. The front office includes sales, marketing, and channel management and all customer service functions. Its reach is out to the customer or partner, not through to the supplier or vendor.

However, there is a lot going on between the back office and the front office. For example, a closed product sale to a customer generates a bill or invoice and creates an account receivable that has to be taken into the ERP or financial package being used by your company. This product has to be physically created and moved from inventory to shipping and distribution. All this is accounted for in the back office, though the transaction originated in the front office. If the front and back offices are integrated, this works well. Easier said than done. How do you integrate this well enough so there is not duplicated data or repetitive data that has to be entered into the system?

The natures of ERP and CRM are not at all similar. As modular and flexible as it has tried to become, ERP's foundation (which evolved from earlier manufacturing-based manufacturing resource planning (MRP) applications and its later incarnation, MRPII applications) is based on creating *internally* stable business functions and predictable process control. The concept of ERP was the integration of all back-office functions so that the bottlenecks responsible for interruptions and breaks in the processes were smoothed and the incompatibilities of the best-of-breed applications (homegrown or commercial off-the-shelf (COTS) software) were eliminated or reduced. This doesn't work with CRM, which is *external*. How can you be in command of the processes when they are based on your customers' behavior? Conceptually, one important reason for CRM is real-time (or near real-time) response to the constantly liquid shifting of customer demand, which is not controlled internally at all. It also means the psychology of the front office is quite different than the psychology of the back office. Despite all your efforts to create a uniform, employee-friendly corporate culture, you have two different subcultures functionally within. It would be like mixing yogurt and cheese. Both are dairy products; both have bacterial cultures. But together—ugh!

Integration presents a real challenge to the enterprise. Micron and Dell, with "build to buy," are the proof that integration, daunting as it may be, can work. While ERP predecessors, MRP and MRPII, functioned in the "build to forecast" world, that model is now dead. The challenge of CRM-ERP integration is, in one regard, to keep it dead.

ERP, CRM, and the Web

There were two other major problems with ERP vendors' incursion into CRM and, particularly, eCRM. Before they could enter this agile market, they had to reinvent themselves as business-to-business enablers. To get e-business panache and to actually become e-commerce-focused enterprises, they had to revamp their entire applications since none of them had Web-integrated applications of any note. For example, in order for Oracle to deliver Oracle CRM effectively, they had to convert their Oracle 8.0 database so it would work with the Web and then convert a series of other products to make them Internet ready. Since mid-1999, all of them have serious Web initiatives. The most prominent three are

> **SAP** mySAP.com is their highly trumpeted Web portal, which will be platform independent. This is not integrated to their CRM product or even their ERP product per se.

> **Oracle** They have fully rebuilt their world-class database Oracle 8i, Web-integrated their applications suite, Oracle 11i, and revamped their CRM package to be 100 percent Web integrated.

> **PeopleSoft** Through the purchase of Vantive and the complete rebuilding of PeopleSoft CRM 8.0 from the ground up, they have a CRM package in the world-class category.

ERP vendors are behind the curve. This arch is becoming more preeminently populated with eCRM vendors who provide fully Web-integrated applications that are increasingly being created in Java and are XML ready. ERP is rushing to catch up.

Options for ERP-CRM Integration

The simplest option is to hire a systems integrator to come in and integrate the systems. However, the obvious pitfall here is that they are not only dealing with ERP and CRM applications they may not know much about, they are also dealing with your legacy systems, which they know nothing about. But integrating all of that is what they are paid the big bucks for. The bucks will be big, too.

You could hire the ERP vendor and implement the ERP vendor's CRM solution. But many of the solutions remain vaporware or poorly integrated. SAP, for example, had yet to release its highly publicized CRM product when this book went to press.

The third solution is what many companies are increasingly turning to: enterprise application integration (EAI).

MIDDLEWARE

EAI applications, previously known as middleware, can be the most cost-effective way of integrating the back and front offices. EAI ranges from full-blown applications like IBM's MQSeries, or Mercator's Mercator, to adapters that are application specific such as the highly touted SalesLogix-to-SAP adapter from Scribe Software or the Intelligent Bridge Siebel-SAP Intelligent Bridge from STC.

EAI's purpose is razor thin: to integrate data between disparate applications that don't natively speak with each other. That can mean off-the-shelf applications, legacy systems, ERP, and CRM. It means virtually any data. The adaptors, which carry a lot less load, are even more specific. They move information from one specific application to another specific application. For example, Intelligent Bridge can handle up to 80 percent of the functional integration between Siebel and SAP R/3. Data synchronization works with everything from front-office sales functions to the back-office inventory and pricing. To hand-carve that level of integration could be a multimillion dollar project over months. The price for Intelligent Bridge is six figures. For basic efforts, STC offers eWay Adapters, priced considerably cheaper, for Oracle, SAP, Siebel, and such.

XML

XML is perhaps the most important emerging standard in Internet "languages." With universal applicability, it makes internal and external integration possible. Even though the standard is not complete and there are currently competing standards bodies, the promise of XML in integrating suppliers, customers, and back and front offices is monumental and could actually solve integration problems. Current XML applications leaders include WebMethods, XML Solutions, and Extricity.

ERP Vendors Deal with CRM

So how did the ERP vendors deal with the onrush of CRM? See Table 11-3 for some of the strategies. Most of them just made their pacts with the CRM devils. SAP decided to go at it internally. All in all, though, ERP ventured into the unaccustomed front office.

Table 11-3: ERP Vendor Strategies for CRM

Company	Approach	Actions
SAP	Internal development	Development team building SAP CRM with initial release planned in 2000. Integrated with mySAP.com. Announced alliance with Nortel-owned Clarify in early 2000 so they could integrate call center software into the mySAP.com offerings.
PeopleSoft	Acquisition	Partnered with Vantive, then bought them in 1999.
Oracle	Acquisition, internal development	Purchased Versatility and Concentra in 1999.
Baan	Acquisition	First to see CRM as important with purchase of Aurum in 1997. Created Baan Front Office.
J.D. Edwards	Partnership	Siebel strategic partnership in 1999 and announced integration of ActiveERA software with Siebel eBusiness suite in 2000.
Lawson	Partnership	1999 partnership with Siebel and use of Siebel Sales, Call Center, and Field Service as part of enterprise relationship management.

The ERP Players Take Center Stage

Who are the ERP vendors in the running for possible success? We're concerned here with the four who are developing or integrating internal ERP solutions. That means goodbye to Lawson and J.D. Edwards, who are simply partnering with Siebel, which is amply covered throughout this book.

Oracle

Oracle knows how to be a player. Oracle Customer Management integrates e-commerce with more typical eCRM functionality. It is entirely Web integrated and soon to be fully integrated with other Oracle offerings. For example, not only is there an Oracle Sales module, but there is also Oracle *i*Payment, a module traditionally lumped with e-procurement solutions such as those presented by Commerce One, Metiom, and Ariba.

Each of the Oracle Customer Management modules has a series of subsets within it. For example, Oracle *i*Sales contains the following:

- ▶ Oracle Sales Online
- ▶ Oracle Telesales
- ▶ Oracle Field Sales for Mobile Devices
- ▶ Oracle *i*Store
- ▶ Oracle Sales Compensation
- ▶ Oracle Order Capture
- ▶ Oracle Sales Intelligence
- ▶ Oracle Configurator

Comprehensive, to say the least.

Big Five systems integrators and consulting firms are working closely with Oracle on their eCRM solutions. For example, KPMG successfully implemented Oracle CRM at PBS in 2000. The Oracle 8*i* client base is a terrific foundation for Oracle to be the most successful of the ERP vendors to enter the eCRM world.

SAP

The SAP CRM initiative is intimately tied to mySAP.com and to some degree represents the most ambitious of all the projects and the one that has had to fight to get out of production and to market. In a roundabout acknowledgment of their difficulties in bringing their product to market, in June 2000 SAP announced an alliance with Nortel-owned Clarify, a leading CRM call-center vendor. SAP will integrate various Clarify call-center components with its mySAP.com e-commerce portal offering. It will continue to develop the non-call-center CRM components that it announced in 1999.

PeopleSoft

PeopleSoft did it the "easy" way. They acquired Vantive, now called PeopleSoft CRM. Vantive was one of the top CRM applications on the market (third after Siebel and Clarify) when PeopleSoft took the plunge and purchased the company in late 1999. They saw an immediate increase (68 percent) in Vantive revenues from the third to the fourth quarter of 1999, while PeopleSoft sales rose 37 percent during that same time period. While there was an issue of whether the cultures could commingle, that became minimized buzz with the release of PeopleSoft 8.0 and Vantive eArchitecture 8.5 in July 2000. These are both Web-based architectures, rebuilt from the ground up, for back and front office functions that could fully integrate the offerings. There is more on Vantive architecture in Chapter 10.

Baan

Oddly enough, troubled ERP vendor Baan was also perhaps the most CRM foresighted when it purchased Aurum Software in 1997, far ahead of any other ERP company in the CRM game. Baan's CRM has been totally acquired, with the CRM suite from Aurum Software, product-configuration software from Beologix of Denmark, and sales-force support software from Matrix in Holland. Unfortunately, "Baanvision" has been blind to market reality. Baan has not done anything substantial in either the ERP or the CRM worlds for two years. In April 2000, Baan announced that, contrary to all other ERP companies, it was spinning off its CRM applications. As with everything Baan, analysts questioned the whole idea. By comparison, SAP, Oracle, and PeopleSoft were integrating their CRM applications into their overall offerings. Baan's approach flew in the face of conventional wisdom, another odd move from this seriously shaken company. Baan was acquired in early 2000 by Invensys, Plc. so, more or less, it is now out of its misery.

Chapter 12

Why Does Your Company Need CRM?

The costs of CRM in dollars, personnel, and time can be steep. CAP Gemini recently released a study that found that the average total investment in a CRM implementation is $3.1 million. The payback period is 28 months. The most significant cost may be in impact on staff, which is reflected in an 8 percent turnover increase in year one and 16 percent in year two. This is a heavy price to pay in an era of increasing labor shortages. Yet, to retain customers who can get "it" cheaper, often via mouse click, is not easy. CRM implementations aim at solving this conundrum. But, how do you convince the corporate officers and other stakeholders to do the deed?

In order to successfully persuade these internal targets to approve and support your eCRM project, it is necessary to understand what the key internal metric(s) should be for the eCRM implementation. While each company has a set of ideas and ways to measure those ideas to define their customer success story, ultimately, it falls to customer response. That means that the first measurement, whether the company is conscious of it or not, should be the increasingly popular customer lifecycle management (CLM).

Customer Lifecycle Management (CLM)

Customer lifecycle management, also called Customer Relationship Planning (CRP) by the Gartner Group, is mapping customer data to define customer behaviors so that the processes of a company are fully occupied in acquiring, selling to, and maintaining a long-term relationship to a customer. The "engagement" is long term, and modifications of the responses to changes in the behaviors are done in real time. Although CLM is inherently a strategic issue, most companies manage their customer relationships tactically, which means the transition to a system that centers on the customer and organizes processes, technologies, and channels around that customer may not be easy.

CLM defines the full spectrum of customer interaction. The META Group defines CLM as "engage, transact, fulfill, and service." The purpose of CLM is to envelop the customer so deeply in your corporate mesh that they are captured and retained for an eternity, optimally. While the intricacies are sophisticated, the pieces of CLM are easy to define. They involve an optimized, intermingled conglomerate of methodology and process, technology and tools that will add to customer lifetime value (CLV) or, minimally, help define CLV. When you become customer-centric, you can build a CRM strategy that encompasses the CRM ecosystem described in the Introduction and Chapter 1 with CLV-measurement tools, analytic applications, and customer services, providing a full lifecycle management system for your customers. Ultimately, they are captured and kept as long-term friends of the company. The tools are myriad for this and technologically can involve business intelligence tools, data warehouses, and customer-facing technologies via the Web.

Customer Lifetime Value (CLV)

CLV is not just another acronym. It is a measurement of what a customer is projected to be worth over a lifetime. CLV is also not a new concept—it is a staple of one of the earlier incarnations of CRM, database marketing, and has been calculated by direct marketers for years. Its importance has increased due to contemporary customers' freedom of choice. It is also due to the vicious competition to acquire those same customers. It is a measure that allows you to allocate a weighted version of your resources and focus on a specific customer depending on the projected CLV of that customer.

E-Acme.com spends $1 million on a series of email promotions sent to 100,000 qualified email addresses. The cost of their email list is $1,000 per thousand addresses. They pull the Forrester Group study-determined click-through rate of 5.5 percent (see Chapter 5) on the emailing. This generates 5,500 sales at $69.95 for their Videocam package. Historically at this company, the CLV of customers acquired through email is a total dollar expenditure of $400 and a profit of $80 per customer. By dividing the $1,000,000 by 5,500, the acquisition cost of each customer is $181.81. Those 5,500 Videocams at $69.95 each generated $384,725 in revenue immediately. A big loss: $615,275 on the cost of the campaign minus the revenue generated. However, each of these customers, due to the anticipated CLV, will generate $440,000 in profit on $2.2 million in revenues, thus turning an apparent loss into a big gain. The presumption is, of course, that these customers remain for their "lifetime," which is a given number of years determined by corporate metrics. The company's ability to understand and employ these CLV metrics creates a valuable tool in the successful management of their marketing actions.

Needless to say, this is a gross oversimplification. There are a substantial number of factors that will determine the final CLV for any group of customers for a specific company: actual customer retention rate, the average dollar value of an order per customer and the number of orders per customer per year, the costs of customer acquisition, other direct and indirect costs, profit per order, and net present value (NPV) considerations. The simplified example doesn't consider the fact that some groups of customers are more valuable than others.

One of the most complete CLV methodologies belongs to Mei Lin Fung, a managing director at Wainscott Capital, an early stage VC fund with offices in the Silicon Valley, New York, and Washington, DC. For example, in a paper that she wrote in 1998, Ms. Fung identifies how you can determine which leads become the most profitable customers:

> *Assuming you have a process in place*: Measure Cost of Acquisition, Selling Cost, Customer Care Cost, and Revenue. Then calculate Net Profit for those you think are your most profitable customers. When you've looked at your top 5–10 most profitable customers, examine how you acquired them. We anticipate you might be surprised. Some of the most valuable lead generation activities occur by happenstance and not by design. Some are repeatable, some are not. Look at the repeatable ones and design programs to repeat them. Look at the happenstance and see what you can do more of, to be ready to respond to and take advantage of unanticipated opportunities. Profitability is dependent on good follow-up, not just at the prospect stage, but through the very latest encounter. *The Price of Profitability is Eternal Vigilance.*

> *Assuming you don't have a process in place, for example, a new sales channel like the Web, or a new business*: Describe the most profitable customers that you would like to have. What will it take to find them and keep them? Define the Acquisition, Selling, and Customer Care process. Calculate the ROI on these "ideal case" customers. After checking that they really have the potential to be profitable, you now have defined a process for finding the most profitable leads.

> The framework helps you see how to decide what to do next, based on your calculations. Here you are "staging the customer experience." Discordant effects not in harmony might annoy or frustrate the very people you are trying to build relationships with. Starting with the people you already are satisfying gives a sound basis for understanding what people like and come back for. Divide into the three sections: Acquisition, Selling, and Customer Care. Don't forget the impact of referrals. Prospects who never make a purchase themselves might make referrals that bring a steady stream of profits.

All of this lead generation is based on a sales pipeline plus an awareness factor that anticipates the level of sales needed to get to a goal. Then, based on historic data, it identifies the number of leads or opportunities needed in January, for example, to achieve objectives in May.

Thus, your customer relationships become qualified, rather than amorphous; your objectives clear, rather than vague. For more information and considerably more detail, please refer to Appendix B, a primer on CLV by Ms. Fung.

Once the CLV is established, it is considerably easier to design programs that can escalate the customer-type's CLV. That can take the form of increased revenue from the customer through up-selling, building exit barriers so that the customers will remain a customer, and cross-selling to expand the customer's "revenue horizon."

Many of the analytic applications are designed to help identify the obvious and hidden factors that determine CLV. Knowing and using CLM and key CLV metrics are essential to successfully managing marketing efforts and resources. These metrics become critical when you are trying to justify and sell a CRM implementation in-house.

Convincing the Stakeholders

Most companies have internal procedures to evaluate proposals for large projects. Such a project could be a major internal IT project to improve the overall sales analysis and forecasting process or creation of a new factory or distribution facility. It also could be a decision to invest in a customer management project that promises long-term return. One step in securing approval for your project is to identify the potential decision makers for the project and convince them that the company needs to make your proposed investment. Frequently, the approval process for substantial projects involves several different functions—the CxOs within your enterprise. The rest of this chapter will take a look at the minds and eyes of two of the decision makers—the president/CEO and the CFO, with a more cursory look at the VP of sales. The idea? Letting you get a picture of how to sell this to these mission-critical decision makers.

President or CEO

This is probably the most difficult person to convince, aside from the CFO. The president is the strategic thinker, the person who is responsible for it all and, for the most part, the board of directors' fall-person if something goes wrong with revenue. So the metrics and projections, benefits and pitfalls of an eCRM implementation are particularly sensitive to him. Since he is the man who has the relationship with the outside world, how the internal implementation "looks" is actually a very important consideration.

Scott Fletcher is president and COO of epipeline, an Atlanta-based e-commerce provider that has a Web-based platform for the sourcing and management of government-related sales opportunities. He has a considerable background in implementation planning and execution as the vice president of technology services for PeopleSoft and EMA vendor Annuncio.

In an interview conducted in late 2000, Mr. Fletcher said:

> CRM systems have great promise, but no system, CRM or SFA or ERP, is good unless it provides better information or improved business processes. Hopefully, both.

The drivers are business considerations, not technical.

The rule of thumb for an implementation of a packaged application is that it has 80 percent of what you want and needs 20 percent customization. Mr. Fletcher stated:

> Many of the CRM packages are integrated with best practices, much as ERP was. If your proposal calls for too much customization, then you might want to revisit how you are dealing with your customers, or if it's an SFA implementation, how you're managing your sales force. I'd be looking to see if you need to change the customer processes or if you are simply choosing the wrong package.

The system should differentiate the company from its competitors. When push comes to shove, the top companies in a particular domain produce a similar enough product or provide contemporaneous enough services to be not all that distinguishable. In the IT world, product lifecycles are so short that your competitor's product can leapfrog over yours every six months. "The real differentiator is how you reach back to the customers," said Mr. Fletcher.

Internal Implementations Are Very Competitive

Mr. Fletcher emphasized the importance of the relationship to the vendor. "If your main competitor is using vendor X, what impact would the system have if we used vendor X instead of another system?" There are a variety of vendor points to look for when you are getting ready to produce your dissertation to the corporate stakeholders.

- ▶ Is the relationship your competitor has with the vendor strategic? (In other words, are they a key beta partner or does the competitor run the user community?)

- ▶ How does the competitor understand the technology?

- ▶ How much is the competitor's use of the technology written up in the press?

- ▶ Can you become a strategic partner of the vendor so you can implement key new features early that then allow you to get to market earlier than your competition?

This may seem an unusual view of what is apparently an internal implementation, but the purpose of these systems is to provide the level of customer interaction that drives significant revenue so that you are number one in your domain. The CRM system is one of the key management systems for differentiation from your competition in the New Economy. Customer participation is that driver of success because in turn it provides the foundation for the revenue growth. That means features such as Web enablement are very important to the system. If your competition uses the same system and is a strategic partner, they will know how you work since they are using the same processes you are. The flip side is, of course, also true.

Mr. Fletcher continued:

> As president of epipeline, I put less emphasis on the cost of the project than I do on the payback for acquisition and retention of customers. I look at Dell and how they handle their customer processes and then look at Compaq and realize that Dell wins hands down—and it shows. The one or two million that it might cost for the project is not critical. Does the application have features that are beneficial? Is the vision of the vendor similar to the vision of epipeline? These are factors that matter to me. They are strategic because of the ROI that we will get if it succeeds and they are the things that I want to know.

A well-known ERP vendor, in its earlier, more carefree days, had an account management program where they assigned one account manager per 15 customers. When they were small, this worked well. They grew to a client base of thousands and this became unmanageable, so they went to a well-known CRM package. However, rather than take advantage of the excellent features of the package, they simply created a redundant system that tried to do what the account managers did rather than view the implementation of the new CRM system as a means to effect significant and important change throughout the company. It was a disaster. No one worked the system, and the account managers kept the information to themselves and never really updated the system. In other words, rather than an agent of change, the system became the equivalent of a dumb terminal.

Stated Mr. Fletcher:

> For the eCRM system to succeed, it has to be seen as an agent of change and integrated into the culture of the company so that it can transform the culture. The recognition of the eCRM system as a change agent would be something I would be very alert to when a proposal comes to me. Several years ago, Paul Strassman wrote a book in which he took companies and correlated the size of their IT investments to their success. There was no correlation at all between expenditure and success. If you are proposing putting an eCRM system in to mirror current practices, then it won't make it past my door. Customization to the old is not good. The use of the system must be forward thinking. This could mean things like enabling the customer with the capacity to track his own call status and call logs, it could mean that training becomes Web enabled, it could mean the creation of customer communities, or a large number of [other] things.

In summary, said Mr. Fletcher:

> The bottom line that you need to convince me of is how it gives us strategic competitive advantage and how it will help revenue generation. If all you are looking to do is use the eCRM implementation to automate current practices, outsource that to an ASP or something like that. eCRM is strategic, not back office.

CFO

How does the CFO think? Time, money and "energy densities" (productive, efficient uses of time and money) are thoroughly intertwined in any project—both short and long term. Craig Thompson, a seasoned CFO, identifies what it takes to convince a CFO of the value of a CRM implementation. Mr. Thompson has seen the process from several viewpoints:

▶ As an external consultant with Accenture creating justification analyses and helping senior management validate justification analyses

▶ As a CFO reviewing investment proposals

▶ As a CFO making proposals for key information systems

▶ As a general manager sponsoring projects

Mr. Thompson says:

There are three questions that need to be answered to make the general business case. One: What is the sound reason for the investment? Two: How consistent is this CRM proposal with the longer-range corporate strategy? Three: Is the execution plan sound?

According to Mr. Thompson, the key point in considering eCRM for most companies is probably not a question of *if*, but of *which* (technology) and *when* (to do it). eCRM is the current electronic frontier. The ease of use and instant response available to your customer also can put a wealth of information in your hand immediately. Not only do you get data in electronic form, you get your customers to enter most of it for you, you get it instantly, and you get it in a structure that matches your product and customer identification structures. What a deal! Further, if you don't figure out how to grasp this data and effectively turn it around to better meet your customers' needs, don't worry—your competitors will show you how.

Why Invest?

For the CFO to give his stamp of approval, he needs to see a credible benefits statement. According to Mr. Thompson, benefits from a successful CRM project can come from two major areas. First, internal cost reductions from new efficiencies. For example, will the CRM system provide the capability for better inventory or manufacturing production scheduling? This often occurs as a result of improved customer demand information through faster order capture or customer requirement forecasts. Can it improve sales and support activity cost metrics by eliminating customer support tasks through Web-based customer self-help features?

However, cost reductions should only be a small part of the CRM justification.

Growth Is a Good Thing

As a key component of the marketing process, the CRM should provide clear advantages for customer retention (thereby improving CLV). It should also increase competitive position through ease of use, enhanced customer response times ("anytime, anywhere"), and other differentiation features. A company's "product" is not just the tangible service or product that is delivered, it includes the "wrapper" of how your customer interacts with you and how satisfied they are with that interaction.

Accordingly, the second class of benefits—longer run marketing effectiveness—should be the most compelling. The advantages provided by a successful CRM implementation should lead to a stronger competitive position and higher revenues. That could include:

▶ Enhanced customer retention by means such as electronic bonding, enhanced customer satisfaction, and so on. For example, once you have all of their profile data and ordering history and have trained them through repetitive use, why would they ever want to leave you and start that process all over again? Your history of their interactions with you is a marvelous tool for you and them. Use it internally and present it back to them for their use. My local auto repair store has me as a customer forever because they know what they have done on my three cars for the past five years. I can't afford to leave them—do you think I want to manually track that data?

▶ Stronger marketing differentiation through "wrapper" characteristics such as ease of use, anytime-anywhere interfaces, and better channel support features (market electronically to end-users, but sell through your channels).

▶ New customer acquisition opportunities through electronic ordering/payment options. Leverage the automation available through the Net.

▶ Unique features that can be created out of your interactions that meet key needs of your customers or your channel's customers.

Mr. Thompson points out that the metrics used to identify these benefits vary from industry to industry, and among different business models within industries. He continues:

> However, companies should know which metrics are relevant to their success based on their business structure and should be using those metrics in day-to-day reporting and in their planning models by the time they are ready to propose a CRM implementation.

You need to look at the historical statistics and then quantify the degree and timing of improvements based on the functionality of the proposed system.

To a CFO (and a CMO), a broad CRM application can be very effective for both direct and indirect customer channels simultaneously. One example Mr. Thompson mentions is how a major U.S. chip manufacturer used eCRM to directly support end-users and keep their distribution channel happy:

> They put up a Web-based system for key end-user decision makers (PC board designers—not purchasing managers) that gave them anytime-anywhere access to chip specs and even samples for prototypes. However, the ultimate purchase of the chips used in the manufacturing production runs still came through the distributors, so that the direct and indirect channels were both serviced.

In fact, the high level of service provided to the decision point probably helped cement the final production orders. How should the proposer measure the proposed benefits? What are the metrics? Mr. Thompson makes it very clear what wins his support:

> The metrics have to be clear and specific. These can be things like revenue per customer, sales rep quota loading, reduction in complaints per customer, marketing efficiencies of varying sorts, pure sales numbers, or increased market share. But above all, they have to be credible, meaning reasonably quantified and specific. Guarantees of future results are not necessary or believable. We are looking for well-thought-out analysis that is consistent with the company's management process. All investments involve risk and uncertainty. We know that.

Executive Ownership

Another key factor to the CFO is clear executive ownership of the enhanced metrics. Are the relevant department heads whose performance is expected to improve in agreement and endorsing those improvements? Mr. Thompson answers:

> You need to demonstrate that this has been thought through, the right executives have bought in, that the deliverables are owned by the appropriate people and that the promoters are clear on what the enhancements to our business will be with the successful CRM implementation. You tell me why this will help us. I assume that you've done your homework. Stand up for what you are going to deliver. Additionally, it's linked to the budgeting and planning systems. The expected benefits will be reflected in improved metrics on the next business plan cycle.

Strategic Consistency: Business and Technology

In an overlapping, CFO/COO hybrid vein, Mr. Thompson, who has served as general manager in several companies, identifies another key decision point. Is the proposed application consistent with the company's strategy in both business terms and IT infrastructure terms? Are you building platforms that move you in the right direction? A CRM system is not an easy or quick implementation and certainly would be very difficult to change. Half the battle of implementing a key infrastructure system is getting the technology to work with the rest of the IT systems in place, but the other half can be even more daunting—institutionalizing it within the company. Institutionalization may include:

▶ Integrating the CRM system with management practices and philosophy. The metrics from the CRM system should become a part of the ongoing management reporting process.

▶ Day-to-day staff in the company should be familiar with how the system works, should direct their activities using data from the system, should immediately be aware of any deviations from norms, and should use the system and its data in wide-ranging ways.

The larger the company, the more time- and more energy-intensive the CRM implementation. However, there are huge benefits on the backend. Changing it would be a nightmare.

On the technology side, says Mr. Thompson, the CRM system should not be a data island. "The prevailing principle should be enter data once, use it often." Data consistency provides the foundation for the single customer view throughout the organization. On the technical side, there are several obvious "shoulds" that apply to most systems:

Strong, reliable vendor You don't want to spend three times as much as the system cost to implement it and then have the vendor wash out.

Standards-based open architecture This means that future changes to the architecture or expansion of the system is easily done, rather than the nightmare of a new architecture or a different standard.

Open APIs or other integration hooks By using an open API, you can customize the basic code provided to your specifications.

Flexible reporting tools Reporting is the basis for so many corporate decisions that easy construction of reports with lots of options means smarter decisions and improves that "single customer view" considerably, by providing the same reporting information to different groups within different departments.

Mr. Thompson continues:

I would see a higher risk component if we are talking about implementing version 0.9 of a new eCRM application. There would have to be very clear differentiating factors for doing so. We don't want to bet our business on a risky application. We have enough challenges modifying our practices to meet the system structure, training our people, training our customers, etc. Adding application risks on top of that simply increases the "failure risk." We are betting our marketing image and customer relationships. The implementation plan would have to recognize those risks and have appropriate pilots and checkpoints built in. The vendor that would reduce our risks has a stable application, a stable corporation, referenceable sites, and proven business application for his software.

Mr. Thompson would be unmoved by a proposal that sells technology "gee whiz" factors, cutting edge or not, rather than deliverable benefits and results. The expectation is that you are buying current technology. There is a time and place to implement technology, but the justification for doing so is still in the benefits to be obtained. You don't improve your company's share value with technology, you use it to drive successes that produce tangible value.

Execution Control

Mr. Thompson wants to see an execution plan that will deliver the expected benefits on schedule. To do this requires a crisp, clean, credible implementation plan. Risk points should be identified and managed. A lot of the considerations here are based on the quality of the implementation plan and the team's track record. There are specific elements that the budding eCRM promoter needs to be alert to when his CFO questions him. The CFO is going to look to see if the execution plan:

- ▸ Is thought out and disciplined in its approach
- ▸ Has an adequately seasoned technical and functional team who can handle issues appropriately (and if not, what outside resources are required?)
- ▸ Has executive ownership
- ▸ Has adequate checkpoints and review points
- ▸ Has sufficient team membership to involve all key users
- ▸ Has a phased implementation approach

According to Mr. Thompson, a phased implementation plan with milestones that can get phased return value is much easier to accept than a "big bang" implementation approach.

> Big bangs are not wrong. They are just more risky financially and operationally. Virtually all of the implementation costs are committed before any payback is seen and any success measured. That is high risk. It might be necessary sometimes, but requires a very experienced team, lots of overview and very careful validation of each step. You only get one chance to succeed. Phased implementations allow learning curves to be looped back to the implementation team and small direction changes made early. Early success also builds acceptance throughout the company.

The CFO's decision-making is affected by the track record of the implementation team. If they've done it many times, the deal could be a rubber stamp. If it is the first time that they are implementing anything, much less something with the complexity of eCRM, the risks are higher. Additional resources are committed (such as outside consultants who have "been there, done that") or the schedule and business justification have realistic provisions for schedule slippage and corrections. This is no different for the overall company and its management. If the company has frequently implemented core applications, it already has change management experience, and the new system will be easier to implement. If the eCRM system is the first major system, especially if it is the first major Web application, this will be a demanding project. Many existing paradigms are changed in Web-based applications. The management processes have to be crystal clear before the CFO will say yes, especially in this circumstance. States Mr. Thompson:

> A strong implementation plan generates a higher success proba-
> bility. If you can make me comfortable you can do this or have
> taken appropriate risk management steps, I'll be comfortable
> with the risk.

Mr. Thompson further cautions that the credibility of the implementation plan and the inherent risks identified in that plan affect the
phasing expectations. Factors that create higher risk are things like limited company experience in larger projects, limited individual history,
limited funding, and political risks. In these cases, smaller phases are
suggested—"microbursts, rather than big bangs." Build success patterns
and confidence increases. If you practice bursts of clean execution and
the implementation strategy looks like it will be successful, the CFO—
and, in fact, all the executive stakeholders—will buy in a lot more
confidently.

In summary, Mr. Thompson says:

> As a CFO, I'm looking for a clear reason to do this implemen-
> tation, a well-defined measurable set of expectations, and a
> consistency with the company's overall business and technol-
> ogy strategies and value propositions. I will expect to see the
> appropriate metrics associated with that in the proposal and
> the deliverables in the implementation plan. With that and the
> other less tangible factors clear to me, I'm far more comfort-
> able in the success of this eCRM value proposition for the

company. Recognize that I am a backer of key projects. Not doing an eCRM project because of a poor justification could be the biggest failure of all. A company needs to move forward, or be left behind in the "also ran" category. Tools like eCRM are essential parts of that progress. I want to do this, just do the homework to educate the management team and we will back you, risks and all.

Mr. Thompson has been involved in the implementation of numerous IT applications and company management platforms in several companies. He served as a consultant in a leading IT consulting firm, an implementation team leader, a sponsoring executive, and an executive on the approval team. He has an extensive management background in the IT and telecommunications industries. He can be reached at mail@craig-thompson.com.

Vice President, Sales

The VP of sales is easier to convince. If it impacts the bottom line with increased sales and more revenue per salesperson, plus cost savings, the vice president of sales is a happy camper. However, there are going to be concerns that this VP has, among them ramp-up time for each salesperson to learn the system, which takes away from the time they are selling (as does pretty much everything but selling). They have to see the long-term benefit because of the potential short-term difficulties.

The Sales Cycle

At Live Wire (my company), we've ascertained that roughly 24 percent of the salesperson's time is spent on any particular client sale, with only 5 percent in front of the client. Roughly 35 percent of the time, the salesperson is involved in administrative work of some sort, ranging from deal sheets to updating the client files, to surfing the Net for intelligence and opportunity. That means roughly one third of the time, the salesperson is doing paperwork and not prospecting or mining, so to speak. Lot of gold lost here. eCRM will reduce this administrative time significantly, allowing increased customer contact, opportunity mining, or whatever else the salesperson can do to develop more sales.

Reduction in Ramp-up Time

In sales there is a period that is called by many sales organizations "ramp up." This is the time needed by a new salesperson, either rookie or experienced, to learn the company processes, corporate style, how to deal with clients that are handed off to them from the previous salesperson, and products or services offered, as well as time to master the collateral material and understand the compensation structure. Depending on level of experience, this often can take several months. Most companies write off the ramp-up period as one with little performance results. eCRM implementations, since they embed much of the information such as business rules, methodology, easily accessible client information, and pipeline forecasting, reduce ramp-up time considerably. The newly hired salesperson has easy access to what he or she needs, rather than chasing down managers or other salespeople or endless database mining. There are a few things, including getting to know the clients personally, that cannot be fully resolved by the eCRM applications.

Customer Incident Solution Time

If your eCRM implementation involves automated customer service such as call centers, there is a significant time reduction per incident or transaction due to a variety of time savers. (See Chapter 9 on call centers.) These could include automated self-service, Voice Over Internet Protocol (VOIP), easily available customer information or information on past incidences with a client onscreen. It could mean time efficiencies because there is a single accessible customer view regardless of what department is looking at the customer records. This eliminates redundancies and information "translation" problems.

Manager Involvement

The managers are the trackers—the ones who are watching the sales pipeline, tweaking the sales forecasts, and often determining the qualifications of a sales opportunity. With eCRM, the qualification process is quicker and, because there is more customer or potential client information available, more effective.

Costs

Prior to Live Wire's SalesLogix implementation, we initially looked at the potential return with the following parameters:

- ▶ Normalized cost of sales. For us, this meant the cost of sales in 1999. This included basic cost of the salesperson's salary and cost of the recruiter's salary, multiplied by the anticipated labor time in mining, qualifying, chasing and closing the opportunity, travel, phone bills, and a myriad of other cost factors, and then multiplied by the anticipated rate of change of costs in 2000—the latter, a very small percentage increase.

- ▶ Expected hourly rate per consultant on a time and materials project, or the expected average hourly rate for a consultant on a fixed price contract with unpaid hours built in. This was multiplied by the expected paid hours. We also took the costs of the consultant into account, such as travel, accommodations, food, local transportation, phone bills, and other incidentals. Our gross margins were gleaned from this final number.

For a business such as ours, due to its intensely competitive and time-sensitive nature, any reduction in administrative time meant increases *hourly* in dollars. So time reduction and energy-dense time efficiencies were our main objective. Cost saving, except for the fact that we were self-funded, was less of a concern.

However, as we moved through the internal trail of implementation planning, we began to realize that there were a significant number of other costs involved. The implementation cost was obvious, but also there was a dislocation cost while the system was living a dual existence with our legacy Outlook address books and the other contact managers used by the staff. There was anticipated downtime while the data mapping and translation was going on. There were anticipated (and sadly, unanticipated) system crashes as we found out what SalesLogix worked well with and not so well with (on the whole, not bad at all). There was the ramp-up time for the software and use of the software on the Web. If our salespeople used ACT! 2000, data mapping was no problem since the founder of SalesLogix was also the co-creator of ACT! so that the translators were built into SalesLogix. But if they used the robust Daytimer 2000, there was an ASCII flat file that had to be created, and that didn't work nearly as well. In other words, there were hidden costs that we had to allow for in this implementation.

Another cost that we anticipated was that there was significant customization that had to go on. For financial relief, we did it in a phased way. First, we put up the basic plain-vanilla, out-of-the-box system. We used it while our MIS department began a well-planned months-long customization features inclusion. That helped keep our costs spread and manageable.

One cost we didn't anticipate was a very good salesperson who decided that he didn't like the system. The time spent in working with this valuable employee was a significant budgetary drain, but ultimately worth it. Cultural dislocation and even sheer cussedness can take a real toll on the company implementing eCRM. Remember that statistically, 8 to 16 percent of employees leave within two years when eCRM is implemented.

Each of these is either an anticipated or unanticipated cost that could lead to serious cost overruns. So how can you measure revenue gains to mitigate the cost and persuade (or dissuade) the CFO to approve the implementation?

ROI

Normally, the simplest ROI for an eCRM implementation (or any implementation, for that matter) is the impact on the bottom line. How many more sales closings per salesperson will it create due to timesaving? A single time and materials "deal" for Live Wire is about $100 per hour for four months (total revenue value). In those four months, the consultant is expected to work around 640 hours. That means around $64,000. Multiply by 3 to annualize the revenues and you get roughly $192,000 per salesperson per year with a single additional closing per period. If we have five salespeople, that means roughly a million dollars to our bottom line. However, it means a few other things as well. First, this is the average value of a deal, not the actual value of a deal. Could be more, could be less. Second, this isn't the margin. Third, this assumes seasoned, ramped-up salespeople from January 1. Fourth, this isn't a net value that presumes any ending of deals or fall-offs for any reason. Fifth, the costs of the project are up front while this (speculative) value is gained over the year. For a self-funded company, up-front costs are the biggest possible problem, since cash flow is always an issue. Sixth, the savings are anticipated, not real, until they are real. Finally, the quality of the deal has to be taken into account to see the actual value.

However, a "real" ROI for a CRM implementation is far more complex and impacts a variety of departments and divisions, much as ERP did in its heyday. Let's look at some examples of that—how analytic applications within the CRM implementation might affect the departments directly affected by the implementation, sales and marketing.

It is now 28 months since the eCRM implementation, and the sales reps are up and running on the SFA component of the applications. They can access sales data via the Web on their PDAs wirelessly. The benefits that evolved were quicker response times to opportunity, reduced administrative time, shared best practices, more accurate forecasting for the sales pipeline, and better deal tracking and problem solving. The resulting ROI is more deals per salesperson due to a shorter sales time, better risk management, less administrative time, and shorter closing time. Of course, that means more deals per year and more revenue.

In marketing, due to the marketing performance analysis and campaign management software, all senior marketing executives are able to track the success rate of any particular campaign, with multiple opportunities to slice and dice the data in infinite variety to see who, what, when, where, and how a campaign is successful. The metrics for success in marketing ROI identify the more profitable customers (CLV), more revenue derived from more highly focused types of campaigns, improved cost savings, and improved product/services profitability.

Ultimately, as in all good ROI, customer acquisition and long-term customer retention leading to increased revenue is the bottom line best answer to the effectiveness of a CRM implementation. When you are convincing your president, CEO, VP of sales, or CFO the measures that could make your business great are the measures that need to be justified to implement eCRM or CRM.

Now that you've been so convincing, on to the implementation and who is going to provide it.

Chapter 13

There Really Is Value to You and Yours: CRM/eCRM Service Offerings

The saddest thing in the world occurs after you've bought CRM software. You have to implement it. Well, actually, *you* don't have to implement it. In fact, you don't want to implement it. You have to find some company that will do it for you. Otherwise, if you do attempt to implement it yourself, with rare exceptions, you'll have wasted a lot of money on software and you can actually harm your company more than help it. The question is who should do it?

It's great to have CRM software and the hardware that is used to carry it. However, it's estimated that the cost of installing and configuring CRM software to enterprise specifications is two to three times the costs of the software itself, at least. That's why the choices for how the software is implemented aren't as easy as they seem at first. Will a professional services company do it? Will the vendor do it with their professional services division? Will internal MIS staff do it? If a professional services company does it, will it be large or small? Not only are all of these issues, but often the choices made can mean dramatic things to a career—whether it's promotion or termination. Many a job has been lost due to cost overruns because of the wrong choice of implementation partner or the idea that to "save money," implementation can be done internally. These are momentous decisions.

Several years ago, I was involved in a bid with Lotus Development Corporation for a Lotus Notes implementation. A government agency issued the request for proposal (RFP). The only competition was a company, the incumbent, that specialized in a groupware product that was not much like Lotus Notes, but which had workflow capabilities. It was called Viewstar. Within the specific agency, there were proponents of Notes and proponents of Viewstar. The internal battle that went on was so ugly that there were threats of termination, threats of quitting, backstabbing, mysterious internal leaks that were designed to hurt some of the agency personnel, and external resources brought in beyond the scope of the RFP to champion one or the other. Ultimately, the budget was cut and no one got anything, but the internecine war was horrible to behold. People still lost jobs and quit over this issue, despite the fact that nothing happened. All due to which software was going to be used! Unfortunately, I've run into this situation more than once over my career. Think about that in a larger context. How important is the choice of software at a workplace to a life, really? Yet, this was a deadly serious struggle. That's how important these choices can be on the service side, as well, because services are even more costly than software. There is also a lot more that can go wrong with the wrong choice. Human foible is a much larger category than software bugs.

The need for CRM services is increasing with implementations for CRM software that can be long and costly, as I've outlined throughout this book. For those of you with short memory, that means between $1 million and $5 million. In terms of cost benefits, however, they are well worth it. Customers are fully aware of these benefits and are rapidly moving toward purchasing and implementing CRM and its eCRM Web-brother. The projected proof positive is that IDC is anticipating a $125.2 billion market by 2004. Yet, the availability of CRM-skilled personnel is low despite major investments by dozens of companies in developing those skills. The very large services companies, such as the Big 5 consulting firms, IBM, and EDS, are pouring millions into creating CRM practices to handle the CRM work that is currently available—at similar levels and speeds to the ERP implementation practices they all created in the 1990s to install and customize SAP or PeopleSoft or Oracle applications. Look at this blurb from *Information Week*'s online news in the fall of 2000:

EDS Prefers a CRM Crowd

Trying to keep up with aggressive customer demands, EDS is partnering with no less than seven CRM-service and software companies, including Siebel Systems, Inc., and NCR Corporation. Backed by the group, which also includes Avaya, McHugh, Retek, Servicesoft, and ServiceWare Technologies, EDS plans to bill itself as a single source for automated-marketing, business-intelligence, knowledge-management, and fulfillment-and-distribution services. One EDS customer sees the service provider's new a la carte approach as bringing CRM technology to the masses. "We couldn't afford an Oracle or SAP implementation," says Brian Harris, VP of technology and operations for Click-well.com, a Dallas seller of dietary products. EDS's hard push into CRM services follows similar, if slightly smaller scale, moves by competitors Deloitte Consulting, Pricewaterhouse-Coopers, KPMG Consulting, and Art Technology Group. In May, Deloitte Consulting teamed with WPP Group plc and BroadVision, Inc., to form Roundarch, Inc., an independent company specializing in Internet-based CRM.

What's interesting about this announcement—typical of others that are becoming more commonplace daily—is that the level of service is end to end. EDS is not only allying with the various CRM vendors, but is also providing strategic consulting, systems integration, and ASP services—in other words, the full gamut of CRM-related services. This is not an unusual move. Part of the global agreement between IBM and Siebel involves an extensive services component that is tied to IBM Global Services. IBM Global Services is providing 2,500 professionals for CRM services as a whole. EDS is going to provide 10,000 CRM services pros! Wow! If you need a job, call IBM, EDS, or the Big 5.

The e-services companies are recognizing not just the value, but also the necessity of providing CRM services, even in the specialized spheres, to simply stay with the state of the market. Deloitte & Touche is training 200 consultants in E.piphany's customer interaction software. Two hundred is not a small amount for a niche market application, even if it is a significant one. The CRM services world is exploding and as the corporate world increasingly recognizes the need to "love their customers," it will get even bigger.

The Choices

If your company decided to go with a CRM package, what kind of service provider would it be? Vendor? Large consulting services company? Smaller implementation partner? Let's check it out.

The Vendor

The vendor seems to be a logical choice. After all, who knows the software better than the software provider? However, you have to keep in mind that often product companies don't want to be anything but product companies. Their professional services department is a courtesy to those customers who want the comfort of extremely knowledgeable engineers. These companies often look at the engineers and their professional services departments as marketing overhead. However, there are a number of vendors who have fully staffed professional services organizations that are as good as any consulting services organization. They are companies such as Oracle, PeopleSoft (for Vantive), SAP (for SAP), Siebel, and Nortel (for Clarify).

Many other vendors depend on partner programs to give the customer qualified, certified partners who can do implementations. Companies like this include Interact Commerce Corporation, whose business partner (implementation partner) programs are strict so that certification is something a partner earns. Their largest partner is Deloitte & Touche. There are some questions you should ask a vendor and criteria you should examine to determine if their professional services organization is just a marketing courtesy, an umbrella "shell" for outside contractors brought in, or a legitimate, going concern. The umbrella "shell" is often a reality. I know this well because staff members from the last three companies I've been associated with have often been used on vendor-supported projects to fill in for vendor personnel. Live Wire made millions of dollars doing this sort of staff augmentation. Normally, the way this works with a vendor is that staff augmentation divisions of companies like Live Wire will fill some of the technical or functional roles during the lifespan of a project, but the vendor does the project management.

Some of the questions you should ask are

What is the size of the professional services group? This gives you an idea of what investment the company has made in services. Carrying a bench (a nonworking group of consultants) is an expensive proposition.

What are the utilization rates of the services group? This will give you an idea of how frequently the services are used and what your chances are of getting a capable team from the vendor when the time comes.

Can I get customer references from the vendor for similar-sized projects? It is not worth your time to get references for much larger or much smaller projects since the scope makes a huge difference in how the implementation is handled.

What percentage of the projects is handled by partners, what percentage by the vendor company? This is important because the partners aren't under the project control of the vendors except officially. The reality is however, no matter how much contractual control a vendor has with its partners, the partners' employees don't feel particularly loyal to the project or the vendor, and only somewhat loyal to their company interests.

What's it going to cost me? Very often the cost of vendor professional services are high because you are getting "at-the-source resources" that can be counted on to know what they are doing. Even those coming from partners are screened prior to their joining the team. Superior product knowledge advantages can be obtained elsewhere, especially with the larger professional services organizations (such as KPMG). Lower cost and increased customer flexibility can be attained through the smaller vendors.

The Small CRM Services Company

The small CRM services company is a vastly different animal than the vendor. The small services company can be defined as a company in the $3 million to $75 million range, though this is a subjective definition. I remember SAP identifying the midmarket as companies between $200 million and $1 billion. I wish my company were that tiny! Normally, the small company is either a totally dedicated CRM company (at the lower end of the revenue spectrum) or has a strong CRM practice of perhaps between 15 and 50 people. By no means does it have the resources the large systems integrators do or expertise in the large enterprise market. It is often focused on the midmarket for its implementations. Many of the small companies even specialize in small market companies. They are expert in eCRM and CRM software such as SalesLogix or Onyx, which are aimed at the less-than-2,500-seat implementations, while perhaps the larger institutions focus on Siebel and Oracle CRM. However, as we will see, even the larger consulting companies are aiming at the midmarket and implementing SalesLogix and its competitors. Smaller companies also may specialize in niche market segments such as enterprise marketing automation or even are product specific with practices that implement applications such as MicroStrategy eCRM 7.

The advantages of smaller companies tend to be straightforward: price and knowledge of the market they are part of. Small companies understand the problems and culture of the small market. Waltham, Massachusetts–based Live Wire, Inc., a small market SalesLogix Technology Partner that specializes in both CRM and back-office e-commerce services, is typical of an excellent small services provider. Live Wire provides CRM midmarket implementation services at under-market pricing—either fixed price or time and materials. What they also do, unlike the larger enterprises, is provide staff augmentation services. This means that if you are doing an internal implementation using your own staff, Live Wire provides individuals who fill the skills holes you have. This is strictly at time and materials pricing.

Cool. Time and materials pricing. Okay, what does time and materials or fixed price mean? They are pricing scenarios used routinely in the CRM services industry specifically and e-commerce services world generally. Time and materials is the combination of an hourly rate that includes the labor costs of individual consultants and expense costs. The expense costs can be built directly into the hourly rate, but more frequently, they are billed separately. There is no great advantage to the customer with time and materials pricing unless the services vendor finishes the project under the projected time of completion. The biggest customer advantage is the likely use of an iterative methodology by companies that use time and materials pricing. What that means is that the customer is involved in each stage of the project and can suggest changes in the application or project routinely and see them implemented in each stage. Each deliverable is reviewed by the customer. The services provider doesn't mind, because the charges are by the hour, so changes are accounted for by simply being billed as additional hours. Typically, Live Wire will charge rates ranging from $90 per hour per person to roughly $150 per hour per person, depending on the skills necessary. These rates are considerably lower than the larger professional services firms or the vendor rates, which range from $125 to $300 per hour, again, depending on the skills acquired.

Fixed price and/or fixed term pricing is much more advantageous to the customer. Essentially what this means is that if the cost of the project exceeds the specified price or the specified time, the services provider eats the continued cost. The advantage to the customer is obvious. The customer can manage his budget prior to the implementation and the risk lies with the services provider. The services provider's advantage is finishing ahead of schedule, which still nets them the fixed amount, increasing their margins. As I will show in more detail in Chapter 15, the processes and methodology for a fixed price implementation are far stricter than time and materials-based projects. Normally, prior to the signing of the fixed price contract with the services company, there is a clear-cut statement of work (SOW) that outlines specifically what is to be done for the fixed price. There is also an agreed upon written step-by-step change management process that details what the costs and caveats are for changes in the SOW. This is a critical difference between the relatively footloose time and materials contract and the very strict fixed price contract. The risks for the services provider are much higher for fixed price. Time and materials shifts the burden to the customer.

Staff Augmentation: Nice Name for What?

Staff augmentation is a tricky part of the CRM and e-services landscape, because, when it is stripped to its essence, it's the sale of the labor power of a body. Because the number of small enterprises focused on staff augmentation is huge, it is a minefield. Yet it is an explosive industry that has engendered some multibillion dollar enterprises in IT staff placement alone, as with Modis or Maxim Group (a subsidiary of the much larger temporary agency, Aerotech, not to be confused with the rock group with a similar name). However, most staff augmentation companies are very small and can be as small as one-person operations. In this case, size really doesn't matter, but quality does.

If you do a lot of your own CRM work and have not farmed it to an ASP, at some point you will need a skill you don't have and don't want to hire due to the short-term timeframe you need it for. For example, you may need a functional expert in campaign management who is working with you on your Annuncio implementation. Possibly you will need an Oracle database administrator (DBA) to work with you on the backend for your Siebel implementation. This is where companies such as Live Wire can help. They provide you with temporary (three to six months) labor for a time and materials price. But don't fool around here. Normally, the labor you need is a critical short-term need, so the quality of the individual is essential. Because there are thousands of companies that do this staff augmentation work and a lot of them are not as reliable or have the quality of Live Wire, you should be taking certain precautions and asking certain questions of the small companies, especially if they are not being recommended to you by a friend or business acquaintance.

Here is the information you need to find or know:

How many actual employees does the company have? How many technical consultants? Often, particularly in staff augmentation, the consultants that will end up on your project are either independent contractors (called "1099s" after their IRS status) who have been interviewed by the staff augmentation company, or consultants that come from other vendors and are being passed through. The best of these companies have hired their own technical consultants whom they carry on the "bench" (a euphemistic expression for being willing to carry consultants on the payroll even when they're not working so that quality individuals are available to customers). Press this question pretty far, because often the lower end of the staff augmentation business—the appropriately maligned "body shops"—will hire consultants as full-time employees for the length of a contract, basically to increase margins and to be able to say that they are employees. In truth, they are independent contractors who are being given a W-2 status (again, an IRS designation). This is an important distinction because staff augmentation companies have no control over either 1099s or other vendors' consultants. There are project accountability issues that can come up, such as tardiness, communication problems, or poor development work. The vendor that doesn't truly employ these contractors can't control them either, so they have their hands tied when it comes to resolution of these issues. I've seen it time and time again in the industry—contractors who don't show up the first day of work, because they took a different contracting job and forget to let you know. That is not a terribly unusual circumstance. Be afraid. Be very afraid. These issues will come up. You will have to make sure the path to accountability of your vendor/partner is pristine and sharp at the edges.

What kind of margin is the vendor getting? The vendor doesn't have to reveal this information and is not likely to. Optimally, it would pay for you to strike a deal with the vendor where you pay them a fully loaded rate (as is often the case in government contracting). That means the vendor's total costs—overhead, administration, cost of the consultant, and so on, plus an agreed-upon margin. Typical margins that are considered reasonable in a normal time and materials deal are 30 to 45 percent over the cost of the consultant. That means overhead and everything else is included in that number. Beyond 50 percent is genuine gouging, except in unusual circumstances, none of which occur to me now. Don't expect to get the margin information unless you have a very close partnership with the vendor or are doing substantial volume with them. It may be worth a shot in asking about it, though, if you feel comfortable.

What kind of experience has the vendor's consultant(s) had in doing the specific job? Keep in mind, this is staff augmentation we are talking about here, not project work. *The vendor's experience is less important than the experience of the individual who is going to be your resource.* Since, presumably, you are project-managing this one, the vendor's project management experience is not critical. What is critical is that there is a qualified resource being placed on your job. Don't forget to ask this one.

Who are some of the vendor's clients? This is not the simple question it seems. There are a lot of fly-by-night outfits in the small CRM services world that do staff augmentation. They are characterized by really not having any true end clients. What they do is provide contractors to vendors who have end clients. They tend to be middlemen—in other words, body shops. They never know the end client's representatives at all. Their contractor is running through another vendor. Or two. Or three. That puts all accountability something akin to the level of the sixth degree of Kevin Bacon: distant, indeed, almost nonexistent. The better vendors that do staff augmentation have sales forces that go to end clients that do business with them. For example, Live Wire has 25 to 30 end clients that we do business with. Many of them have been our clients for the life of Live Wire (three years). They trust us. We trust them. Rush jobs are done on a handshake, without protracted contract negotiations. This is CRM at the functional level: true interaction and trust between the customer/client and the vendor. That is the advantage of the "end client model." So you should be asking the question, getting references. The body shop will often use the end client's name though it isn't their client. Thus, the references become *very* important.

With all this precaution, why even use the small CRM services company for staff augmentation? First, most large CRM services companies don't do staff augmentation, though large companies who are IT generalists, like Modis, do. Second, small company overhead and administrative costs are lower. Small companies are more nimble, and they have a more intense desire to establish themselves. Thus, the small company will provide you with excellent prices for qualified individuals and still be happy with their margins. Ultimately, you're responsible for your own project. Being under budget and on time is a good thing. Small companies can either do it for you or aid you in the process.

What About the Big Boys?

CRM practices are popular in the larger consulting services companies. The commitment of the giants range from dozens to thousands of consultants dedicated to various CRM services. Often these are product-specific services ranging, for example, from Siebel and

SalesLogix to the more specialized E.piphany and MicroStrategy product lines. Additionally, there are vendor-neutral consulting services or multiproduct consulting services that the larger CRM service companies provide.

Who are these giants? They are the Big 5: Deloitte & Touche, KPMG Consulting, Accenture, PricewaterhouseCoopers, and Arthur Andersen. They are systems integrators such as Cap Gemini (which bought the consulting services unit of Ernst and Young), IBM Global Services, and EDS. They are spin-offs of the Big 5, such as EYT who broke free of Ernst and Young in 2000, setting up a consulting services business, an ASP, and a hardware/software reselling business. All in all, though, they are characterized by hundreds of millions or billions of dollars of revenue, thousands of technology consultants, an end-to-end service offering, and premier expertise at a premium price.

Since the big guys are pricier, why would a company want to go with them? It'll cost more without a doubt and perhaps even take longer. Besides, they might be using some of the personnel from the smaller CRM companies and just passing them through.

There are several good reasons. Table 13-1 outlines the strengths and weaknesses of each of the types of companies.

Table 13-1: The Pluses and Minuses of Small and Large CRM Consulting Services Companies

Small Consulting Company	Large Consulting Company
Pricing is considerably cheaper.	Pricing is expensive.
Staff augmentation services available readily.	Staff augmentation rarely available.
Hungrier for business—more flexible terms, willing to negotiate to win the business.	Fixed pricing schedules, set methodologies, often inflexible in terms, though attempting to be more nimble in the twenty-first century.
Post-implementation maintenance not usually part of the plan.	Post-implementation maintenance more likely than in small company.
Specifically vendor/partner-focused or niche market-focused. Strategic consulting not usually a service offered.	End-to-end services including vendor-neutral strategic consulting, reducing the need for multiple companies.
Significant problems handling midstream personnel changes, if they occur.	Very large services organizations that can handle midstream personnel changes.

Table 13-1: The Pluses and Minuses of Small and Large CRM Consulting Services Companies (cont.)

Small Consulting Company	Large Consulting Company
Generally fewer and smaller implementations experiences.	Solid implementation experience that leads to a consistent methodology, often reducing implementation times (in its best moments) and stabilizing change management processes.
Size works well for the midmarket and small market companies, due to the experience of being one.	Best suited for large enterprises or the upper end of the CRM midmarket, which, according to definition, could amount to a $1 billion revenue company.
Best on time and materials projects. Fixed price projects are not the forte of the small company, though this should not be construed as a blanket statement.	Can do fixed price, fixed term contracts very well, with statements of work that can be exceptionally detailed and parameters that are well defined.
Project management skills are limited for the smaller companies in this range.	Varied, but potentially excellent project management skills (see below).
Will partner to do the job, if necessary.	Will partner to do the job, if necessary.

As you can see, the larger companies have experience and depth on their side. You pay for it, but it is in your interest to do so if you are a large enterprise or a large midmarket company. If you are small or on the lesser-sized end of the midmarket, it might pay for you to consider the smaller company.

A lot of the same questions you put to the small company apply to the larger consultancy. There are a few more you have to decide upon as well:

How is the project management going to be handled? This is almost a matter of preference on your part. The largest consultancies will bring their project managers with them on the project, especially if it's a fixed price. Their project manager will see to it that the project is completed in a timely fashion, because if it isn't, the consultancy eats the remainder of the cost, which is devoutly *not* to be wished by the consultancy. The good project manager is a specialist in three things: relationships with the customer, bringing fixed price projects in at budget or under, and—related to the other two—change management. This means you should interview the project manager to see if you're going to get along with him or her as you move forward through the project. One thing is definite: there are going to be very rocky periods where you will not be happy with something going on. The project manager becomes the pivotal individual in these situations, so you'd better be sure that this PM is your person of choice before anything gets started.

What about the Statement of Work and the change management process? This has been the doom of many a project. I participated in an implementation of a large ERP package at a fairly small agency that had a clearly defined statement of work, but an undefined change management process. My company had submitted a fixed price bid to the client. The vendor was doing the project management, due to unusual terms in the vendor contract, though my company did the actual project. The project manager committed to a midstream (in the middle of the statement of work deliverables) product upgrade for free to the customer, without our direct knowledge or participation in the change and commitment process. The change screwed up the completion of the project and cost my company a nearly six-figure amount because there was no clear change management process that said midstream upgrades, well outside the scope of the statement of work, are an additional cost that will affect the time. Consequently, there was a considerable amount of acrimony, though we, in good faith to the customer, did the midstream upgrade. The project finished roughly two months behind schedule, since the upgrade was not a small task. While this may seem to be a benefit to you as a customer—after all, a free upgrade—this is actually a major problem because of the friction and delays in getting up and running. So query the consultancy representatives on how they handle change management. It may save you a fortune later.

Who makes up the proposed project team? Often, the larger consultancies will take advantage of the smaller consultancies' willingness to do staff augmentation work and will augment their project teams with small company consultants or independent contractors. This isn't necessarily bad, if the technical and social skills of the contractor or small company consultants are good. It's just better to know upfront and make your decisions with full knowledge. After all, this is likely to be an expensive and long-term vendor, especially as CRM goes from competitive advantage to business necessity.

Are there partners involved? If there is an RFP issued by the soliciting company, the response will often include a partner or two because they can round out the holes in the necessary skill sets. Having partners is not a bad thing, but it is an additional factor for you to consider, since the partner's company comes into the mix for compatibility.

None of these questions are overkill for the small consultancy doing staff augmentation or a smaller CRM implementation or the large consultancy doing a major project. Keep in mind that your decision making can literally mean your promotion or your dismissal. It can mean the difference between a successful, productive company and a counterproductive collapse. ERP failures were notorious, with hundreds of millions of dollars lost in failed implementations. All of a sudden, these questions seem important, don't they?

Chapter 14

Implementing CRM: Easy as 1, 2, 3, 4, 5, 6, and so on

Once the stakeholders are convinced, the budget is set, the software is chosen, and the integrator/implementation partner is hired, then comes the work. The software must be implemented. This is not a simple matter. Implementation doesn't just mean installing the software and hoping it runs well. It means understanding how the software must conform to the business model and the style of the company. Implementation is always required, regardless of how much or little it is. Very rarely does a SalesLogix 2000 or a PeopleSoft CRM work right out of the box. If it does, it is more of a miracle than design and means the likely canonization of your IT director for this nearly celestial choice of CRM application.

The Caveats of Implementation

There is no such thing as an easy implementation. Even installing
Microsoft Word or Excel can be problematic on a network for multiple
users. CRM and eCRM are very complex implementations involving
multiple elements and, frequently, back-office integration. It could
involve commingling with multiple software packages that are already
installed in the corporate system. Issues such as scalability—can the
software handle the amount of use and number of users it is going to
get—are paramount even prior to the selection of the software. Some
CRM applications are focused on the smaller and midsize companies,
others on the Fortune 1000–sized enterprises. Large companies with
multiple locations have a different set of problems than small companies with a single location and multiple users. Because each company
has a different process and culture, each company will have a unique
set of issues to solve with the implementation—technical, functional,
and cultural. Even a perfect technical installation and carefree customization can fail if you have snippy employees who don't take to
the system.

Guess what? You have to plan to resolve all of these issues for an
implementation to be successful. You thought getting management
buy-in was tough? Wait until you find the salesperson with 25 years
of experience continuing to do it "the way he does it," when you ask
him to do it another way. Good luck.

The Implementation

If you'd prefer to skip this chapter, do so at your own risk. If you
attempt to implement a CRM package without knowing how implementations work and the likely problems you will face throughout the
project, you could be in for a fall—and a big one. Even job termination. The statement of work and the change management processes
have to be clear prior to even starting the *installation*. Forget about
planning it in the course of customization. Figure it this way. The
industry rule of thumb is that the implementation services will cost
you at least double to triple the price of the software itself. Something
that costly needs your attention. For this chapter, I'm going to use the
example of a typical midsize implementation, based on the methodology often used by Interact Commerce Corporation (IACT) for their

SalesLogix 2000 installs. There is some variance from their strict mode, but their implementation methodology is a classic example of a thorough approach, so it serves as a useful model for the chapter. Implementations on a larger scale are not covered here—they are more complex in scope and methodology. They have a different set of problems and often a larger team. For example, you'll notice in this chapter, I don't identify a program manager—just two project managers. The program manager is often necessary as the person who tracks the cost, schedule, performance, and risk factors involved in the project. In smaller projects, this isn't really a necessary position. A senior project manager can do it. Another example: it isn't necessarily wise to have a formal steering committee in a small project. However, in a large implementation, such as a PeopleSoft/Vantive implementation or Siebel implementation, it is often entirely necessary to have a formal steering committee that consists of the stakeholders, program manager, project managers, and so on who would review the project as it moves through the implementation stages. It is far more complex and beyond the scope of this chapter to look at a Fortune 1000 CRM implementation. If you are interested in a larger implementation, please feel free to contact me (see the Introduction for contact information) and I will refer you to experts in this.

Now time to get to the first step. Let's look at...

Pre-implementation

The timeframe on this one varies from several weeks to several months according to the depth of preliminary work your company needs to do. For example, in this timeframe, the decision is made to go with a CRM/eCRM implementation. The criteria for this are those questions the CRM software functionality needs to answer and those corporate weaknesses the software and processes need to address. (See Chapter 12 for some of these questions.) Additionally, this is the phase where the stakeholders at the executive level are identified and engaged.

This also is the phase where software selection occurs. The market is spitting out new CRM choices every day. They can get confusing. If your selection criteria are sharp and if you have some reference (such as this book) to help you identify the established vendors—or if sexy and new is more your speed, the cutting-edge vendors—your path will be considerably easier. The road less traveled can still be the road identified by the markers. Some of the criteria for the selection are

- ► Scalability of software

- ► Toolset flexibility for customization

- ► Stability of the existing CRM application code

- ► Compatibility of the CRM application with legacy systems and Internet systems

- ► Level of technical support available during and after the implementation

- ► Upgrade support

- ► Availability of additional modules such as EMA complementary to SFA (marketing module complementing a sales module)

Pay attention to the criteria. Projects fail, and they fail quite often and easily. The average loss in a typical enterprise-wide IT project is $4.2 million, according to Effy Oz, an associate professor of management at Penn State, quoted in the October 31, 2000, *Computerworld*. There have been projects that have been monumental disasters. For example, one manufacturer spent $112 million on an ERP implementation that failed. Gasp. What would happen to your job if that were your recommendation? So please don't underestimate the selection criteria for both the software and the implementation services. As an executive or someone with authority on this software selection, your and the other corporate stakeholders' acceptance of "buck-stops-here" responsibility must happen. You define the criteria and then choose the software. Accept the consequences of what you define and choose. In other words, there's a hell of a lot at stake here and no company can afford the price of failure. There is no room to be in what Bruce Webster of PricewaterhouseCoopers calls "the thermocline of truth." A thermocline is the area between the hot- and cold-water bands in a lake. In the IT world, it is the area between the corporate executives who think the project is going great and the underlings on the project teams who know the project is failing.

Once the selection is made, you move on to…

The Kickoff Meeting

This meeting is where it all gets real. This is where the implementation partner—be it the vendor, a large or small consulting services firm, or a systems integrator who is doing more than just the implementation—meets with the customer to figure out the customer's needs. This meeting, which should take one or two days, is where the customer and the partner decide which responsibilities are assigned to whom. The team members meet each other and the chemistry for the implementation is established. Be wary if you notice friction right away, because ordinarily, there is a honeymoon period before problems set in. Early friction can be a harbinger of bad things to come.

What should a typical vendor or partner SalesLogix 2000 (or other midmarket eCRM application) team look like?

Project manager (PM) The project manager is responsible for all aspects of the implementation, including cost control, quality and testing, and customer satisfaction. Since the PM may be managing several projects simultaneously, the time that he is on the site is not usually 40 hours a week. Don't expect that. Be grateful, too, because he tends to have the highest billing rate of any of the staff members on the project. If there is a problem, the PM is the person to speak with and expect to work the solution. The project manager is the one with the connections back at the Interact Commerce Corporation headquarters and his own company's HQ, if he represents a consulting services partner or a systems integrator. If there are changes to the statement of work (SOW), it is the project manager who must work out the details with the customer. There should be a change management process in place that is approved by both the customer and the implementation services company.

Implementation leader Sometimes this person is called the technical lead. He is responsible for technical aspects, directs the system engineers, and is usually dedicated to only one project at a time. He tends to be onsite full time until the end of the project. His strength is a combination of people skills and technical knowledge. Often, he is a CRM architect who takes a hands-on role in the project. He assists in preparing the statement of work with the project manager. However, he does not resolve the problems of the project. That is the project manager.

System engineer(s) Sometimes they go by their particular titles—Java developer or functional sales specialist or whatever the company that employs them wants to call them. Their primary role is to do the coding. Period. They are onsite at all times, unless there is work to do at home. In many implementations, you have technical and functional expertise necessary for them to do their work. CRM implementations are complex. For example, to work with the SalesLogix Architect tool, it's important for the systems engineer to know how corporate sales processes tend to function. They don't necessarily have to know how the particular company's specific processes work, just how the sales workflow functions.

Okay, that's the implementation partner's team. It's now time for introductions and assignments for the customer's team. Yes, you do have to have a team. Not the stakeholders. These are "merely" responsible for the project so that there is smooth sailing among the executives. Remember, if there are to be cost overruns, it's probably a good idea to have the CFO on your side. Then again, hopefully, there won't be cost overruns. However, you do need a team that will be working hand in hand with the implementation partner for a number of reasons. First and foremost, your team is the one with the knowledge of how the company works and is expected to impart that knowledge. Second, your team needs to know how SalesLogix 2000 works. When the implementation is done, the partner will probably not want to hang around and maintain things for you, unless you acquire their company to do that. Therefore, someone has to learn how SalesLogix 2000 works at the technical level. That would be your team.

Who's on this all-important customer team?

Project manager This PM owns the project from the customer's point of view. That means the PM is the liaison with the partner's PM and is also the one who sees to it that the statement of work developed by the partner PM is adhered to. This project manager filters any suggested changes in the SOW prior to a discussion with the partner PM on changes. This PM also is the one who approves (with stakeholder acquiescence) the pricing for the changes. (No, changes are not free.)

Systems or business analysts These employees are the functional experts. They provide input on business processes and flow that are enterprise-specific. In the ideal world, they will be assigned full time to the project and not leave it until it is complete. That happens sometimes. The rest of the time, they are onsite when they can be, which doesn't necessarily dovetail with when they *should* be. That can create serious headaches, if not major problems for the implementation's completion in a timely fashion. Here is where some variance might also be the case. This is the typical midmarket implementation as represented by SalesLogix 2000. However, if you are doing a PeopleSoft/Vantive CRM project with a Fortune 500 company, there may be some differences in the way the project is staffed. For example, there would also be functional expertise on the implementation partner's team in the guise of "business analysts." This would not mitigate the need for the enterprise-process specialists. It is just that the larger CRM packages have enormous specialized functionality best understood by a functional specialist who has background in the area and who also knows the product being implemented.

IT staff These are the administrators of the system, the people who are maintaining and setting up the network and its software. They have to see that there is no significant downtime or problems during the implementation period. Actually, they have to do this all the time. Because a good deal of an implementation is working the bugs out of it, the stress on the system can be great. The administrators, who have enough stress in their lives as it is, are under greater pressure during this critical period.

Integration expert This person guides the integration of the SalesLogix system with other information systems. These people are very specialized. Who they are is entirely dependent on what the other information systems are. For example, someone who is integrating midmarket PeopleSoft 8.0 with SalesLogix is going to be someone who knows how to make the hooks, find the APIs, write the scripts, whatever is necessary to make this work. This person is going to be different than the one who is integrating SalesLogix 2000 with Annuncio Live! so that the SFA package talks to the EMA package. Integration, covered in Chapter 11, is extremely complex, now that the prevailing wisdom is apparently moving back to best of breed, rather than one big package that does it all. Companies in CRM or ERP and the like who are trying the "all things to all people" approach are having more difficulty than the "one size fits one" schema.

Heads of nontechnical departments They provide input and approval on aspects affecting their departments. Don't kid yourself here—these folks are important to the implementation beyond what may seem to be their official standing. They can make you or break you. They can make the implementation succeed if the partner implementation team members understand that they are nontechnical, which means patience and explanations are necessary. They can make it fail if the non-techies think that they *are* technical (which happens pretty frequently) and want to tell either technical group their job, or if they have insufficient explanation of what is going on. This usually leads to a misunderstanding and a wrong decision. This is a very important group of team members.

Now both teams are established, and the kickoff meeting is underway. What are the expectations that have to be resolved? It's important to concur on what the system is functionally and technically going to do. For example, both teams must agree that it will allow forecasting in the sales pipeline that can be managed against the steps of the sales process. It also means agreeing that it will run under Windows 2000 when the company upgrades in 2001—or that it won't run under Windows 2000 when the company upgrades. As long as the agreement is there, either answer is fine.

There also has to be an understanding of what the software can and cannot do. During implementations that are going south, the refrain, "I thought the software could do that," is often heard. Not good. Prior to the project ever beginning, it is important to frame the limitations of the software, whether you are the partner or the customer. That way, expectations have boundaries and excess isn't expected.

The final task of the kickoff meeting is to create the initial timeline so that each deliverable is scheduled for some date. SalesLogix PMs call it the "need-by" date.

If the meeting was successful, there will be signoffs on what the system can and can't do and what the expectations are for each person. These can be formal or informal, depending on the relationship between the two parties and their preferences. I would suggest formal. There should be excitement and everyone should be ready to go. The next phase is...

Requirements Gathering

Requirements gathering for a SalesLogix-sized midmarket implementation should take about two to three days. The length of the
requirements gathering can markedly change if the scope of the
project is significantly bigger. That can be a quantitative reason:
there are a lot more people to interview. It can be a qualitative reason: the complexity of the project means the requirements phase is
more complicated. Regardless, this is the phase where meetings happen with the stakeholders, users, other corporate decision makers,
and the IT staff. In other words, all those who are going to use the
system. This could be five people, fifteen people, or twenty-five people. The in-between number tends to be midmarket-sized implementations. This requires that departments cooperate, since the
CRM implementation is going to affect the interactions of every
appropriate department in the company. Marketing, sales, finance,
and so on all have a direct need to input the teams during the
requirements gathering phase.

What actually happens during requirements gathering? Is that like
hunting and gathering? There are a number of actions during this
procedure.

Legacy systems need to be analyzed. That is both a technical and a
functional issue. This is where there is analysis of the enterprise's
sales methodology and the business rules that define the company.
This is also the time for some corporate soul-searching. How successful has the sales methodology been? What can be changed? A
good requirements analysis will bring out these issues and some
of the answers, though certainly not all of them. Ultimately, whatever the customer wants to carry forward will be architected into the
CRM system. Most CRM packages are fairly flexible in their toolsets,
allowing for wholesale or small changes to the business rules that
govern the customer's corporate life. One of the major complaints
about earlier ERP packages was the inflexibility of the embedded
business rules. If you wanted ERP, you did business their way. When
the ERP packages were built using object-oriented methodologies
and languages (SAP R/3 4.0, for example), the ability to alter the
best practices and business rules implanted into the application
became a simpler matter. CRM packages have all learned from the
mistakes of ERP past.

Once the requirements for the front-office practices are gathered, the next step is the identification of the inputs and outputs. This is the way the users will interact with the system. Some of the questions to be answered in this phase include:

- Which screens will be needed to input data

- How information will be retrieved from the system

- How the customer wants to work with the system

- How many users the system must accommodate and how they will connect to it (LAN, individual remote users, remote offices, Web)

While this is being done, there is a lot of other work to do. For example, what would be the system's optimal functionality if everyone had their wishes granted? The difficulty of this part, though necessary, is twofold. First, the users, unacquainted with what the system can technically do and not do, often ask for functionality that is impossible. Nonetheless, it is noted. However, a briefing on the basics of SalesLogix 2000 or other CRM application prior to the requirements gathering is often useful in narrowing the field of dreams. As the project proceeds, the functionality list narrows significantly. Obviously, the plan is to include as much as possible to keep the customer happy, but the technical boundaries and the interactions of the proposed functionality have a lot to do with the ultimate restrictions on what gets implemented.

There is a lot more to be done, with the identification of what data must be imported to the system and what must be exported. That means both the one-time efforts that must occur and the ones that will be recurring throughout the life of the system, such as financial data gathered from invoiced sales and the like.

To make the requirements gathering go smoothly, it is important to obtain all information possible about the existing system and thus provide a foundation to see how the legacy system and the CRM implementation will fit. This means a look at the legacy system's functionality and how that will conform the CRM functionality, the usage level, the scalability of the CRM system, and the workflow of the system.

To get this information, nondisclosure agreements and all other necessary paperwork need to be signed during this phase. The

nondisclosure agreement states that neither the implementation partner nor the customer will disclose each other's information given
during the course of this project to anyone outside those identified as
the ones who "need to know." This agreement is binding for the life of
the project and usually a term of one year after that and, on occasion,
longer than that. That way, both the partner and the customer can get
the data and confidential information necessary to start the project
work, including the system detail from the customer and some of the
SalesLogix or other information from the vendor or partner.

This leads to the next phase, which is…

Prototyping and Detailed Proposal Generation

This is where the actual hands-on work begins—with a prototype.
The purpose of the prototype is to develop some of the key functionality for the customer to examine before the rollout. By doing it
in a prototype, the amount of difficulty in the achievement of the
functionality and the issues it brings up are all on the table before a
complete implementation to all users is done. For example, if the
customer wants to be able to click a button in SalesLogix that would
populate a custom reporting system, it can be examined in minute
detail. This confirms that it can be done or not.

The same goes for the creation of mock screens. With the creation
of the screens, the workflow can be demonstrated ("click this button
and this happens, taking you to here…"). This allows the user to
participate at each step of the workflow and prototype development.
In most circles, the methodology that gives the users the maximum
participation and input on deliverables as they are delivered is called
the "iterative" method. The idea is that the users are involved in all
iterations of the application. The result is happy customers because
they not only verified the workflow and, often, the look and feel of
the screens, but they are also giving input to the team at all times,
hopefully with a clear understanding of the scope of the statement of
work. The prototype can clarify the customer needs by visualization.
This means when the customer sees the process work or the workflow and agrees to what he or she sees, the development team and
the customer team are of like mind, making the project work go that
much more smoothly. The prototype can be demonstrated to varying departments, each with their own agendas and ways of viewing
data, and can be worked by the development team, even if the data

presentation from department to department is conflicting. This process generally takes about two weeks.

Not all customization requires prototyping, though that is less likely. On occasion, the requirements are clear and the processes already work well or are embedded in the out-of-the-box version of the software. Also on occasion, tornadoes are known to have lifted cows 350 feet in the air and put them gently back on the ground unscathed.

Once the prototype is done and demonstrated, and the proposed changes to the workflow and functions are acceptable to both the customer and the development team, a formal project proposal that states the deliverables, timelines, and final costs is written for the client. This document can run as small as perhaps ten pages or as large (in the SalesLogix midmarket domain) as fifty pages. In the larger PeopleSoft/Vantive world, these proposals can be one hundred pages or more.

These midmarket CRM projects are often divided into four phases:

> **Phase I: Sales module customizations** The product catalogs, the sales process embedding, the account and contact databases, and the sales pipeline management criteria, among other things, are developed.

> **Phase II: Marketing module customizations** They are no different in technical process than sales module customizations. It is merely different in what needs to be customized.

> **Phase III: Integration with external applications** This is where there are certain possible difficulties. The "as is" review is often done in the beginning of the requirements gathering. This is an analysis of the existing information technology infrastructure and the network functionality. This work identifies the integration points between the legacy systems, the CRM application, and the possible installation and customization of other new non-CRM applications and systems. This is always done after the customizations of Phases I and II and a third intermediate phase of other CRM modules if need be (for example, PRM customization—see Chapter 7).

> **Phase IV: Reporting integration** Oddly, this apparently innocuous phase is one of the most important points in the

process. Reporting is a vital function, especially for businesses that are scattered beyond one office. The customization of those reports and their generation are critical to corporate success. There are often problems when information isn't appropriately structured or appropriately routed—problems that are corporate life threatening. By making sure the appropriate templates are created and the right reports are autorouted to the right recipients, the danger of incorrect decision making is reduced dramatically.

Once there are the appropriate signoffs on the formal and final proposal document, the next phase is…

Development of Customizations

The time length of the customizations varies widely, with five to seven weeks being typical, and depends on a substantial number of factors:

- The size of the project.
- The complexity of:
  - The interfaces
  - The workflow
  - The functions
- The availability of employees/users to work with the team to improve the customizations at a given iteration.
- Technical problems unrelated to the implementation that affect it. These can be resolved by creating an independent environment for development, testing, and eventually production.
- Midstream workflow and rules changes for the customization, necessitated by changing corporate business processes. This is something that can be managed, but will affect the timetable and the price.

These are a few of the many reasons the project can exceed its five to seven week anticipated timeline.

The elasticity of the application is very important in the ease of creation of the customized application. SalesLogix, for example, has an open architecture, a large third-party integration base, and a very flexible toolset, making the customizations fairly easy. Other products in the same broad CRM category or in the more specialized subcategories such as EMA or PRM may not have the easily usable toolset or may have a proprietary architecture, making the application customization very difficult.

The next step is to assign tasks to developers. These developers may not be, for example, SalesLogix 2000 toolset specialists. Rather, they may be Oracle database administrators, PeopleSoft and Vantive integration specialists, Java developers—whatever is needed to ensure the project's success.

An effective implementation partner will then set up a development environment that mirrors the customer site as closely as possible. Needless to say, an exact mirror isn't possible. There are differences that will have to exist, simply because the machines used are not identical. What can be done is a database that is the same as the customer's and a system that is about the same as the customer's. So a copy of the customer's sales/accounts database—for example, in a Microsoft SQL Server 7.0 environment with 25 users—can be reproduced. This means that success in this environment will mean success in this system. The processes initiated in the customization phase will be known to work on the customer's system, simply because they are working on a mockup of the customer's system.

The project manager is responsible for a project plan at this phase also. This is a checklist of what developers and team members are assigned to what tasks. Based on the hopefully successful checking-off of these tasks, status reports on the state of deliverables can be given to the customer in agreed-upon timeframes. Depending on the formalities of the project, these can be phone calls or formally written documents with the specific successes (and caveats and failures).

Throughout this customization period, the development team is demonstrating the functionality to the customer and soliciting customer response. *It is important that the customer is engaged at all times in the project.* Doing this manages "scope creep"—a scary term for a project potentially inching out of control. With a clear statement of work, strong change management procedures, and the constant education of the customer, scope creep likelihood is reduced significantly. There is simply no way that changes to the original, agreed-upon statement of work won't occur. So the change management process is there to both control costs and time loss. It can satisfy the customer without succumbing to the client feature-lust that is often the case when the client realizes how much more powerful and interesting the application is than they expected. This is universal to almost every project ever done. If you are the customer, take one piece of advice. More stuff costs more money and loses time. Be sure the features you want are for the benefit of the corporate CRM, not just fun for you alone. That said, the consulting services company or implementation partner will attempt to accommodate you with what you want. If they work well, they will tell you the truth about incorporating a Web connection to the Starbucks delivery unit, rather than the sales forecasting tool. With this level of communication and control, even the project time can potentially be reduced and everyone is happy.

If there are changes to be made, several things must be done prior to that. As mentioned earlier, a clear-cut change management process has to be in place so that both the contractors and the customer can accept the changes. That change management document should include the understanding that changes to the statement of work in function or scope will incur extra costs, will increase the delivery time and due date of the total implementation, and that there is no liability to the implementation partner for that. It also must include a workflow that identifies who is the authority who can sign off on the changes and thus add them to the budget.

One very valuable implementation lesson is to "routinize" it as much as possible. In the customization phase, writing data import routines using the CRM toolkit can save days of effort and manual entry. The time saved is inestimable and critical.

Finally, the data routines are written, the screens developed, and the other customizations are done. The final part of this phase is development team testing—making sure the basic system works. If that is a go and signed off, the next phase is…

Power User Beta Test and Data Import

This is where the star users (usually called "power users" since they are among the nontechnical people who "get it") get to play. They get involved in finding the systemic discrepancies that crop up when the customizations are moving to completion and the data migration is being prepared. *The more experienced users involved in this phase, the better.* This is not a case of too many cooks spoiling the broth, but of a need for two, three, or many Emeril Lagasses. By involving power users, verification and acceptance of the system are ensured.

The first major step in this two- to five-day process is to create a testing environment at the site. There are often dangers that seem to be inherent in this. What if the testing environment crashes the system? Usually, the customer in progress purchases a server that can be isolated from the important operational systems and work side by side with the legacy system, but not as part of it. Very often, systems with the most extensive customizations exhibit the fewest problems in beta testing because they have been checked so extensively during development. To get to this exalted state, however, there has to be a close working relationship between the development team, the internal implementation team, and the IT staff (which may overlap with the internal implementation team to some extent). Meetings with the IT team focus on how to implement and support the system. With some implementation methodologies (such as SalesLogix), this is the beginning of knowledge transfer, with the customer IT staff performing a beta implementation. The success or failure, strengths and shortcomings of the IT team's beta attempt determine what kinds of backup resources are necessary, what kind of procedural automation is still needed, and what kind of training will be paramount when the time comes for the vendor/consulting services company to leave the premises.

Once the beta installation is complete and analyzed, then comes a very tough part: the test data import. Before the system goes live, there has to be a full-scale test run. The run will identify the usability and accuracy of the data. *This must be done with the full participation of the customer.* The customer must verify the integrity of the data transfer. This is a sensitive part of the implementation.

It is now time to gather last-minute usability requests. The good thing about beta testers is that they often have recommendations for improvement that go beyond simply finding bugs.

Now comes the final part before actual rollout. There is a consistency check for everything ranging from look and feel of the screens to spelling. Rollout is prepared as the system moves from beta to production. But as the departments gear up to rollout, there is...

Training

Training time depends on the number of users and available facilities for training, and typically runs about two days. There are four parts to training:

Basic training There are no pushups in this training. This is the plain vanilla training for users on the application. Normally, this is run by the vendor. There are two ways to do it, depending on which is the most cost effective. You could send your users to Scottsdale, Arizona, for example, to get SalesLogix training at Interact Commerce Corporation headquarters. That means you'd pay the cost of the training plus the cost of hotel, food, airfare (unless you're in the training facility's location), and other incidentals. You could also have a trainer come to your facility, often the cheaper alternative if you have a significant number of users. However, be smart and have the training worked out and put into the original contract and statement of work. This can be a surprisingly costly part of the implementation.

Customization training This is done by the now-trained employees who have been engaged in the project, though it doesn't have to be. The reason that it is best done by the internal project team is their familiarity with the system to begin with. The internal project team cost is what it has taken to get them up to speed on the basic CRM system training and their ordinary labor costs. One other plus with the internal staff is that they have had the benefit of ongoing knowledge transfer throughout the implementation process. Knowledge transfer, for those of you never involved in IT "techspeak," is the continuous education on what has been learned from the vendor/integrator to the customer team who will be using the knowledge in an ongoing fashion. It is ordinarily built into the proposals, contracts, and statements of work that are the basis for the implementation. It is very important that the knowledge transfer is an intentional written part of the statement of work.

Documentation Another vital part of the process. The vendor or consulting company's implementation team has full responsibility to provide documentation on the customized system to see that future use is assured. Often, as part of a team, companies like IACT will provide documentation experts (who can be doing something else on the team as well) who know how to piece together useful documentation. Bad writing is endemic to the IT world and making sure that a bad writer isn't writing the documentation is something that, while sounding funny, is deadly serious. Take a tip here and look at some disclosable past documentation written by the person or people who are going to be writing your documentation. Have the documentation deliverables sketched out in detail in the statement of work.

Additional training Some companies, such as Interact Commerce Corporation, recommend additional training. Two highly recommended courses are train the trainer and an integrator course.

> **Train the trainer** As the name implies, whoever you send to this course will be the one to train the users on your staff. This is a major time and money saver.

> **Integrator course** This course teaches your IT staff how to make their own customizations to SalesLogix or to the other vendors who have such a course.

While the training is ongoing, it is time for the Big Kahuna, the...

Rollout and System Hand-off

This is it. The final phase. End of days, though hopefully not Armageddon. It is the time when the production environment has to be installed at the site. The production environment is the one your company is going to use.

The final phase is both delicate and a huge task. If anything goes wrong, with ample opportunity for that to happen, by the way, it could mean a disaster. The legacy system has to be shut down. The data migration has to convert all data into the format of the SalesLogix or Vantive or Siebel databases, which could be Oracle, MS SQL Server 7.0, Interbase, or any number of other or proprietary formats. When this is done and acceptable, the new system is powered up.

Normally, this process takes one or two days, and usually occurs on a weekend so there is no—or, at least, minimal—disruption of the actual workweek. If it extends beyond the weekend or can't be done on the weekend, alternate arrangements are planned and executed so that the disruption remains minimal. One to two days is midmarket data size. Large implementations of a PeopleSoft CRM Fortune 1000–sized operation could take a week or more. Tools to do nothing more than data mapping and migration in a large environment in a few days are so important, that companies think nothing (well, that may be an exaggeration—they think something) of spending often tens or even hundreds of thousands for this tool that they will throw away when it gets the data migration completed.

The other significant part of the rollout is remote user and satellite office preparation. This differs according to different software and different methodologies. For the sake of consistency, I've been following a midmarket SalesLogix 2000 implementation. Please be aware, though, that variances in both methodology and preparation are related to the individual company and, very often, to the scale of the project.

Each remote user is given a copy of the general database installed on their desktop or laptop. Each of them will be customizing it as they move through a given day. Initially, all users are guided through the use of the system by trained implementation personnel who, if physically possible, will walk around and work with each person in the hands-on use of the system, answer any questions, and increase the overall comfort level in using the system.

This is now a production environment, which, no matter how good the effort has been, is different than the beta environment. That means a developer stays onsite to deal with unexpected problems. Often, the initial problem is not part of the CRM system, but is rather the interaction between the system and the network. One place that normally has some problems—though they are mostly mechanical—is data synchronization with remote users. The sync-up doesn't always run smoothly in the first few moments of the production environment. But when products have good data synchronization engines, these problems get solved very quickly.

Finally, the rollout is complete and the installation/implementation team is, gulp, going away. What's next? Well, to keep the hands held there is…

Ongoing Support, System Optimization, and Follow-up

This is all optional, of course. There are a substantial number of companies who opt to not follow through on support after the rollout. As I've pointed out elsewhere, one of the disadvantages of small companies doing the implementation is their limited ability to provide post-implementation maintenance and support. In any case, the level of service needs to be there, and it is wise to arrange for post-implementation support. Incurring cost is better than incurring systemic failure simply because you did something wrong and didn't know what you did.

The implementation partner has some liability here, too. What that liability is needs to be part of the contract before the implementation ever starts. Finger-pointing never solves problems and, besides, it's impolite.

Presuming who is responsible for what in the post-implementation era has been decided, the implementation partner must be ready to provide the customer with rapidly turned-around support. This has to be there until the client can swim. Even then, it is good CRM to contact the customer to make sure they are happy and functioning. Occasional onsite assessments should be done after the customer has been habitually ensconced in whatever procedures they have changed and are now using for the system. This lets the implementation partner assess whether the customer is getting maximum benefit from the system.

A Couple of Good Cautions

Make sure you keep your databases from growing too large for the power of your equipment. This can happen if you do too much data importing. Prepare in advance for growth by having more machine power than you need.

When there is an update available, work with the implementation partner to ensure that the customizations aren't overwritten with the update's installation. That is something that could easily happen if you aren't careful.

The End?

Sad to say and happy to say, it is never the end when you've installed a CRM system. Maintenance is ongoing, but that's because a successful implementation means that happy sales and marketing staff, executives, analysts, and anyone else who has a stake in how customers relate to your business are using the system productively.

To sum this up, take a look at the implementation timeline in Figure 14-1.

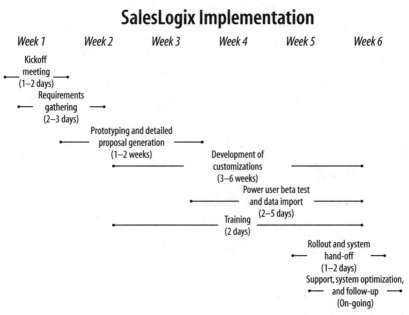

SalesLogix Implementation

Figure 14-1: A typical SalesLogix 2000 implementation timeline (Copyright 2000, Interact Commerce Corporation. All rights reserved.)

Chapter 15

The Host with the Most: Application Service Providers and CRM

Hosting is hot. Very hot. It is less of a headache for a client because someone besides you maintains it, apparently inexpensive, and 24/7. Sounds ideal, but there are pitfalls. Is this a viable means of handling your CRM needs? There are significant pluses and minuses, and because of the immaturity of the application service provider (ASP) market, the strengths and weaknesses at this time tend to be extreme.

Yet, there are hundreds of ASPs to choose from, so the choice is confusing. Wall Street recognizes that the ASP market is here to stay, despite its failure in a different incarnation as a sub market of outsourcing in the mid-1990s. Hence, the high valuations investors are giving ASPs. For example, one major ASP who has other business units had the following ratios for their valuation, based on a multiple times gross annual revenue. For their hardware and software sales business, they had a ratio of 1.4 times revenue. For their professional consulting services division, they had a ratio of 2.6 times revenue. For their ASP division, which at the time, unlike the other two, didn't even exist yet and so was based on estimated revenue, the ratio was 41 times revenue! That's no typo. Not 4.1 times. Forty-one times revenue for a business that didn't exist yet! (Note: It does now and it is a good one.) Two existing successful businesses got them little. What part of the business would you emphasize? That, of course, is one of the reasons there are so many ASPs. The lure of the dollar and the smell of high valuation can do that to a company.

ASP in a Nutshell

Put simply, an ASP is a company that hosts a software application and rents it out for a monthly fee. The basic value proposition of an ASP is twofold. Firstly, to outsource the headaches and expenses associated with managing a business application, thereby allowing its customers to free up resources for more strategic initiatives. And secondly, to enable its customers to conserve capital by paying a monthly service fee instead of having to make the large up-front expenditures required to bring enterprise business applications on line. The economies of scale that an ASP can leverage for their customers are dramatic. Most companies simply can't afford to implement the levels of redundancy, reliability, and security. By using an ASP, even the smallest businesses can gain access to leading business applications and world-class information system infrastructures.

Break Out Your Bell-bottoms, the '70s Are Back!

ASPs may be the new buzz of the IT community, but they are far from being a new concept. In the 1970s, centralized data processing centers would "rent" computing power and software to businesses that needed to run applications but lacked the capital and technical skills required to acquire and maintain these systems. Terms such as time slicing, teleconnect, account partitions, and kilo-character usage reporting were in vogue. Many hardware and software platforms of this era were designed specifically for multitenancy—in other words, for multiple companies to use the same machine at the same time while remaining completely autonomous. This model worked well because it allowed companies that would otherwise be unable to afford computing power and software applications to share the costs with other companies. To truly appreciate the value of this time-share model, one has to reflect back on that era when it could cost $500,000 to obtain the computing power of a modern wristwatch!

Fast-forward 30 years. Disco is dead, Laverne and Shirley have retired, and nobody carries that big stupid comb in their back pocket anymore. But centralized computing is not only still here, it is red hot. In the 1980s, hardware and software costs plummeted and skilled labor supply was in line with demand, so most companies were able to move information systems in-house. Then in the mid-1990s, the Internet created the e-everything frenzy and the picture changed once again. Software has become infinitely more complex and there are many more pieces to buy. Insatiable demand for e-solutions has created a global shortage in IT professionals and has driven the costs of labor through the roof. Outsourcing non-core competencies in general has always been a sound business strategy, but current market conditions have forced many a do-it-yourselfer enterprise to reconsider the value of managing their own information systems. Thus, the market and economic conditions that set the stage for an explosion in the emergence of ASP-modeled vendors. Industry analysts estimate annual spending by U.S. companies for ASP services ranging from a low of $2 billion to a high of $33 billion by 2003. This wide variation is inevitably a result of the newness of the business world's focus on ASPs.

To ASP or Not to ASP

Like any important decision, choosing whether or not to use ASPs for your business starts by taking a high-level overview of their advantages and disadvantages. The value proposition of an ASP is targeted mostly toward small to midsize companies: ASPs give your business access to leading business applications, implemented rapidly and painlessly, deployed on world-class infrastructure, supported by a fully staffed remote IT department, all for one fixed monthly fee. Wow, that sounds like a dream come true for smaller businesses. And it is. But life is a series of tradeoffs, and ASPs are no exception. Following are the basic advantages and disadvantages that need to be contemplated before deciding to use an ASP.

Advantages

Why should you support an ASP with your hard-earned dollars? There are some compelling reasons to do so.

Rapid implementation ASPs implement the same products on the same platform over and over again. This enables them to become extremely proficient at this task, even to the point of being able to automate the most repetitive parts of the process. Because the implementations all happen within the ASP's data center, certain application components can be predeployed and/or shared among multiple applications, to further reduce the human effort and total time required for the implementation.

Lower cost of entry and ownership ASPs rent applications for a monthly fee. This enables their customers to defer the large capital expenditures traditionally required to bring applications on line. Because ASPs are able to leverage tremendous economies of scale by centralizing and sharing of resources such as network connectivity, hardware, software, facilities, and human resources, they are able to pass additional savings on to customers and still maintain substantial profit margins.

Reduced people headaches Let's face it, good people are difficult to find, difficult to recruit, and even more difficult to retain. This has always been true, but never as prominent a problem as in today's IT job market. ASPs directly address this business pain point by effectively outsourcing their customer's IT department, or at least the part of the IT department required to manage each respective application.

Availability Most ASPs advertise 7/24/365 uptime for their customer's applications. To put it another way, "online all the time." This is typically backed up by a service level agreement (SLA), which essentially guarantees that your systems stay up and running or you start getting portions of your money back. This is an especially significant guarantee for mission-critical applications. Try convincing an internal IT staff to start paying their salaries back if the systems they manage experience downtime!

Scalability The very nature of the ASP business requires that they use high-performance, scalable technologies. Leading ASPs have invested millions of dollars to develop a scalable infrastructure because they must be ready to accommodate the needs of the new economy's companies. Because it is already in place, all customers small and large get to enjoy the same world-class infrastructure.

Disadvantages

Why shouldn't you support an ASP with your hard-earned dollars? Reasons here are compelling too, but not as compelling as the advantages.

Limited choices ASPs typically provide a very limited number of brands when it comes to applications. They are forced to do this if they are going to be able to produce repeatable, scaleable results. For example, USinternetworking only offers Siebel's CRM product, so if a customer wanted the Clarify brand they would have to choose another ASP. Because most ASPs are completely reliant upon the marketing efforts of the actual software vendors to drive brand loyalty, they are likely to host only the products with greatest market share. These products are not always the best solution for a customer's business problem, just the safest bet for the ASP.

Integration with other applications Because ASP applications are hosted outside the enterprise, integration with other enterprise apps becomes challenging. Even though actual data connectivity between the enterprise and the ASP can be reasonably robust, the fact that the applications (and the experts who manage them) are not part of the enterprise's core IT function makes integration efforts more complex.

Security For all practical purposes, data held at an ASP is very safe—arguably safer than data held within an enterprise because ASPs must go to extreme measures to protect information in a multitenant environment. However, discomfort still exists with many CIOs and IT managers because not only their job, but the viability of their company depends on the safety of enterprise data. Simply stated, no matter how you slice it, if the data is located offsite as it is with an ASP, it is outside their direct sphere of control.

Connectivity If an application is operating within the enterprise, it would take a LAN failure to break connectivity to the application. LAN technology is very stable, and in the event a problem does occur, it can be fixed directly by the enterprise. When using an ASP, there are several more variables introduced into the communication loop, including telecom companies. And everyone knows that if there is a problem with a telecom company you are 100 percent at their mercy and the fix will not be quick!

In summary, for most small to midsized businesses, the advantages of an ASP substantially outweigh disadvantages. ASPs outsource the "low value" work, allowing smaller companies to focus their limited resources on more strategic initiatives that create competitive advantage and drive revenue. For larger enterprises, the use of ASPs is likely to be very limited.

Types of ASPs

Even though ASP was a relatively new space two years ago, there are already hundreds of companies who have positioned themselves in this space. Because shakeout and consolidation has not yet hit this space too hard, ASPs currently vary wildly in their offerings. Analysts, investors, and the business world in general at this time are still struggling trying to come up with an effective segmentation for these companies. For the purposes of this writing, ASPs will be divided into two high-level categories, PASPs and NASPs.

The first category, PASPs, are *packaged* application service providers. These are companies who rent brand name software applications to their customers. PASPs effectively outsource all integration, planning, and maintenance for these applications. The large majority of ASPs fall into this category.

NASPs, the second category, are *network-native* application service providers. These are essentially hybrid-software companies who develop their own applications and provide them as a hosted service on the Internet. Where the PASP is more of a services company, the NASP is more of a software company that has simply chosen to deliver its product over the Web.

PASPs Provide Full-service Outsourced Business Applications

The majority of ASPs are PASPs. These companies purchase name brand applications and rent them back to customers. Because PASPs offer high-end enterprise solutions they typically provide substantial integration services and ongoing professional services. Qwest Cyber.Solutions (http://www.qwestcybersolutions.com/), a KPMG/Qwest joint venture, is an example of a PASP. Cyber.Solutions leverages the inherited strengths of its parent companies to provide a soup-to-nuts solution. Telecommunications and infrastructure expertise is provided by Qwest Communications, while enterprise application integration and processional services are provided by KPMG. Cyber.Solutions is a complete outsource solution offering a full range of IT services, including infrastructure, software, application development, implementation, maintenance, and enhancements. Cyber.Solutions provides products from Siebel for their CRM solution. Another leading PASP is Corio. Similar to Cyber.Solutions, Corio provides products from Siebel and PeopleSoft for their CRM solution and offers end-to-end implementation services.

To any CIO, the PASP model is a welcome relief from the nightmares of implementing and owning enterprise applications. However, this relief does not come cheaply. PASPs provide full-blown implementations of brand name enterprise applications and services. Even with the economies of scale provided by the ASP business model, there are significant unavoidable expenditures to acquiring and implementing these large, complex applications. While pricing among vendors in this space will vary dramatically, you can anticipate spending $2,000–5,000 per user per year to rent popular applications. Additionally, any significant integration or modification work is commonly billed as time and materials at Big 5 style rates. While taking the PASP approach may reduce overall cost of traditional application deployments, at the end of the day it is not likely that cost will be the primary consideration for electing to use a PASP, but rather, the incredible values associated with eliminating the headaches of running an IT department.

Even though the PASP market is relatively new, differentiation is almost nonexistent among current vendor offerings. They, of course, will argue that point, but let's consider the facts. Corio, Cyber. Solutions, Applicast, Bright Star, and USinternetworking all offer the exact same Siebel product as their CRM application. They all tout supremely scaleable infrastructure, rapid integration, application expertise, guaranteed system uptime, and the promise of reduced IT headaches. While each of these vendors may have some particular specializations in their offering, there is very little room for true innovation and differentiation in the PASP market. The inability to differentiate typically drives a product or service into becoming a commodity, whereby differentiation based on price becomes a prevalent strategy. Great for customers. Not so great news for PASPs.

To compound this, the vendors have decided to become ASPs in their own right as they grow. Also, the major consulting services companies are adding their own ASP data centers. IBM and the Ernst and Young spin-off, EYT, have their own 24/7 hosting services for CRM. PeopleSoft is now providing ASP services for Vantive, the leading CRM solution they acquired in 1999. As Table 15-1 shows, there are several ASPs who are not vendors or even that huge necessarily that are providing CRM services.

Table 15-1: Leading Packaged Application Service Providers

Company Name	CRM Application	URL
Applicast	Siebel	www.applicast.com
ArtistaSoft	Clarify	www.artistasoft.com
Bright Star Technology	Siebel	www.brightstart.com
Corio	Siebel, PeopleSoft/Vantive	www.corio.com
Cyber.Solutions	Siebel	www.qwestcybersolutions.com
Interliant	Onyx Software	www.interliant.com
Usinternetworking	Siebel	www.usinternetworking.com
Push	SalesLogix	www.push.com
ScionASP	SalesLogix	www.scionASP.com
IBM	SalesLogix, Siebel	www.ibm.com
Quaero	Microstrategy eCRM 7	www.quaero.com
KBM	Microstrategy eCRM 7	www.kbm.com

Watch Out for the NASPs!

Network-native application service providers (NASPs) are in an incredibly exciting space. While PASPs closely resemble a services company that simply transfers the burden of the same old enterprise applications from your IT group into its data centers, NASPs are a revolutionary approach to software delivery in a networked economy. Basically, NASP applications are designed for you, as a customer, to simply hit their website, sign up, and begin using the application instantly—while costing the NASP almost nothing to bring your business on line. This is possible because NASP applications are designed using *Net-resident, multitenant* architectures. Oops, too much techno-speak? Let me explain. Multitenant applications are designed to run many customers (tenants) using the same server. One of the byproducts of this design is that it enables user self-registration and automatic resource provisioning, just like signing up for an email account at Yahoo!. In addition to being multitenant, NASP applications are Net-resident, meaning that they were designed explicitly for delivery over the Internet, not within an enterprise. Most enterprise applications will never see more than a few hundred users, but Internet applications must be ready to deal with tens of thousands or even millions of users. Net-resident applications are also designed for access by any Web browser, making them available to tens of millions of users with a simple click, while many applications provided by PASPs require installation of additional client software.

"So what?" you say? Well, these technical advantages translate directly into tremendous business advantages for a NASP. To give an example, when a PASP acquires a new customer they typically follow a traditional sales cycle for each individual prospect, play phone tag, negotiate the deal, sign contracts, wait for the PO, then purchase and configure hardware and software, and finally install and configure the software. If the customer is lucky from the time of their first phone call, they may be up and running in 30 to 60 days. Not only do these issues create a severe scalability problem for the PASP and time-to-market problem for their customers, but the cost for these human-intensive activities and capital purchases must inevitably roll down to the customer. In sharp contrast, it is possible for dozens (or hundreds) of sales prospects to simultaneously hit a NASP site, sign themselves up, plug in a credit card number, and be using the application in minutes. Because the entire process is automated and the same hardware is leveraged to service all customers, the incremental cost to acquire these customers is essentially zero. This is a slight over-simplification of the process, but very realistic. Given the different models, NASPs will be able to scale their business exponentially faster than PASPs while providing products for far lower prices.

The NASP market is in its infancy, and most companies in this category are immature, lacking refined products and a sturdy customer base. However, salesforce.com is a good example of a reasonably successful NASP in the CRM (or CRM-related) space. salesforce.com provides a true multitenant solution for sales force automation (SFA). By simply visiting the salesforce.com website, you can create an account and begin using the system immediately. As of this writing, salesforce.com advertises its pricing as $50 per user per month with the first five users free for six months. Their product is remarkably robust for a hosted solution, providing almost all of the features that are found in larger enterprise SFA products. Features include collaborative account management, task management, scheduling, real-time forecasting, "canned" and customizable reporting, integration with content management sites, synchronization with Palm and Microsoft Office and data import/export tools.

Another NASP example is instantCRM.com, which—evident from its name—is a hosted CRM solution. The instantCRM.com product provides the tools for small businesses to manage their post-sale relationships with customers. Features include collaborative customer account management, customer issue tracking, contact management, automated customer portal, customer email management, and data import/export capability. As of this writing, instantCRM.com is advertising pricing as $50 per user per month with a one-time activation fee of $1,000.

Other interesting examples of NASP vendors that provide eCRM or eCRM-like solutions include TouchScape's customer interaction management (http://www.touchscape.com/), Oracle Corporation's hosted SFA (http://www.oraclesalesonline.com/), and Agillion's hosted collaboration solution (http://www.agillion.com/).

ASPs a Passing Fad or Here to Stay?

The crystal ball is still cloudy on the future of ASPs, but they are without a doubt emerging as an important evolution in the Internet economy. While there are early indications, opinions are still mixed on what the profile is for companies who will embrace ASPs in the long term.

ASPs provide small businesses with the opportunity to leverage world-class information systems solutions as never before possible. This is a good thing. Most analysts agree that the basic principles and advantages of the ASP model will ensure their survival, but the next couple of years will be definitive in identifying who the real customers are, and who the surviving vendors will be. With a bit of luck, ASPs will remain a viable alternative for application hosting, their service quality will go up, their prices will be driven down, and disco will remain nothing more than a dark chapter in musical history.

Chapter 16

The Future's Not Hard to See

Wireless devices that are linked to customer information via the Web and respond to voice commands. Intelligent agents that listen to customers and proceed to act on their behalf. The Internet as a channel rather than a phenomenon. The semantic use of XML/XSL and the development of a CRM-specific XML standard. And much more. There are several trends that have emerged in late 2000 in CRM (that overlap into the global e-commerce world), which are more than just cool, they are productive. This eCRM future fits squarely into a new digital, mobile universe.

While there is no holographic projection of you that can be transported onsite to a customer to handle a meeting, there are a few initiatives specific to CRM technology that are both interesting and have their own unique acronyms in a world rapidly running out of letter patterns.

Wireless Is More

Look at one day in the life of "The Real Market," a CRM-focused online daily report (see Appendix A, or to subscribe go to http://www.RealMarket.com/. It's worth it.):

> **Sprint Helps Interact Commerce Go Wireless** Sprint and Interact Commerce announced a partnership that will offer selling professionals access to sales information and Web services available through Interact.com by using Sprint PCS Internet-ready phones. Selling professionals can use the Internet-ready phone to schedule Web conferences, receive news on clients and prospects, and review their calendars.

> **TeamShare Offers TeamTrack Mobile** TeamShare has devised a way for its customers to access live TeamTrack information utilizing their Palm-powered handheld computers. The new product, TeamTrack Mobile, must be used with either tTrack or tSupport and is currently available for purchase or on a free, trial basis.

> **Delano Adds Wireless Support** Delano announced it is integrating real-time wireless interactions into its e-business platform, enabling customers to develop and deploy e-business applications that extend email and Web-based communications to mobile phones, two-way pagers, personal digital assistants, and other wireless devices.

> **StayinFront Announces WAP Support** StayinFront announced the delivery of WAP support for the Internet CRM and e-business application Web Works. StayinFront's HTML-based Web Works system can now also process WML. WML is the markup language that allows Web Works users to gain access to CRM and e-business information from the new mobile WAP devices.

It all reads wireless. Mobile and miniature are the business-to-business, business-to-consumer, and business-to-employee future. Imagine customer service, customer acquisition, customer retention, and marketing analysis, all through a handheld device that you sequester in your shirt pocket when not in use. Imagine part of your program for customer service and retention involves giving each customer a fully loaded Palm or Jornada or Handspring Visor so there is wireless, two-way, Internet-based continuous communication with you. What a future!

Some Wireless Statistics

In 1999, more mobile phones were sold than PCs and automobiles combined. In 2000, there are 300 million wireless subscribers—primarily through cellphones. By 2002, it is estimated that there will be 529 million. Not a bad leap in two years. However, only a very small number of that 300 million—200,000—are wireless Internet users, and perhaps 10 million are wireless email users. By 2002, that number is expected to jump to 4 million wireless Internet users and 50 million wireless email users. By 2003, Jupiter Communications anticipates 79.4 million browser-enabled cellphones will be in use in the United States. Those are continuous orders of magnitude jumps in wireless use and in Internet bandwidth. However, even before the anticipated leap, a small startup called NextWave tools around in cars with their technology and sets up conventions and exhibitions with wireless fractional T1, an exciting idea that implies an answer for that incredibly large anticipated jump in wireless usage.

Says Michael Simpson, chief marketing officer at Interact Commerce Corporation:

> The biggest reason for any major jump in technology adoption, when it comes to end-user tools, has always been convenience. That convenience and resulting business efficiencies will override the monthly costs of wireless access for corporations. This is leading to a gigantic push in creating wireless mobile-friendly applications that can still provide rich data to the salesperson, the customer, and the manager despite its small venue.

Field people will still require a PC for office and home use (and wireless charges will *far* outweigh the cost of the device over time). The issue isn't which device people will use, but rather, how many? As users become more mobile, their needs change throughout the day, and thus their choice of device. While at a customer's site, your wireless Palm may be the most appropriate tool; while in an airport lounge, a Web browser; in your car, your Web phone; in your hotel room, your laptop. The issue for vendors is providing the appropriate data to the tool that is best suited to particular tasks.

Mr. Simpson continues:

> There will be several more phases the wireless device world will undergo as it matures to commonplace use. First we had basic synchronization from hard-wired devices to a PC. Now we are starting to see Web-based synchronization across multiple devices simultaneously. Wireless access to live data is happening

as well, and the holy grail will be when you don't realize when you are online and when you are not. Caching data on a local device, based on usage rules, while automatically updating across a wireless link is where we are going; but it may take a little time for those standards to emerge. The devices will soon be able to handle the storage. And when the two converge, reliability and performance will increase dramatically.

The trend toward a wireless world is the trend toward a portable transaction economy. Business will be conducted as you walk down the street and, in effect, from your pocket. While that is not the subject of this book, the possibilities are fascinating and endless. The cellphone and the handheld revolutionized the "small is better" transaction world. Mobile eCRM is about to make your business and consumer life a much richer experience (given the limitations of the corporeal world).

Soon, a salesperson will be able to close a deal onsite, give specific guidance as to availability, place the order in their Palm, and have it not only registered in the CRM system back at headquarters, but to trigger manufacturing and billing and have the product in shipping before she gets back to the office. Now, that's customer service!

mCRM

Who knows KnowEx? Not me, particularly, until recently I ran across their mCRM technology—a wireless, mobile CRM that allows two-way interactivity between the customer and the vendor continuously—whether in an office or walking down the street. KnowEx has either developed or is utilizing something that solves the protocol and hardware differences that plague the wireless world. They use content and chat streaming to accept and deliver communication between devices—cellphones, PDAs, or clunky desktop PCs. So all lines of communication are open. This is coupled with KnowEx Wireless 2.5, an eCRM solution for wireless that KnowEx calls mCRM—mobile eCRM. Imagine a secure chat, database integration, group and private chat, streaming media push features, and access to customer service histories—all on your Palm. Slick stuff. The example that KnowEx uses in their advertising is, "Imagine being able to change your flight, with your travel agent offering you the best fares, right from your Palm Pilot. Once you get the information, all of it is instantly updated to your date book, and a map is pushed right to your screen. No laptop, no phone, just a Pilot." This is a terrific use of sales force automation in the small.

But this is just a partial view of what the future holds in CRM/ eCRM. The larger picture is even more exciting and far more daunting. It involves the ultimate integration of customer acquisition, maintenance, retention, and service wherever you are, twenty-four hours a day, seven days a week, and the direct interactivity of vendors, partners, and customers so that business problems are solved immediately. However, this is not going to be a smooth drive. The road is paved with broken glass.

Some of the issues that one major telecommunications company faces as they attempt to implement a wireless CRM solution are represented here. Take a look at them, because they are not just technical, but also cultural. The nature of the customer is changing and the need for speed in delivery is accelerating. Problems are much larger when both infrastructure and thinking have to be simultaneously overhauled. Imagine these issues on a national scale with an expectation of millions of customers, and the vast nature of the questions becomes clear:

▶ Simplifying the customer experience in obtaining and using the information received over the phone.

▶ Capturing this experience in a way that can be used within a CRM system for management of the customer.

▶ Dealing with mobile customers who are calling about technology related to the phone—how to use the appliance, why it doesn't work the way they expect it to, coverage problems, features, and so on.

▶ Dealing with contacts about the more traditional areas such as billing, adds, and deletes.

▶ Dealing with a new class of Internet-phone-related calls concerning how to get at information more concisely, faster, and unobtrusively in their mobile environment—for example, how to get the information with a very limited keyboard and almost nonexistent pointing device.

▶ Creating CRM systems to help identify, track, and understand customers' experiences rapidly enough to offer solutions to their problems when they call using a mobile phone.

▶ Offering services and technology (phones and accessories) that address mobile characteristics.

▶ Dealing with the culture shift in the customer who behaves in a different way when conducting business via a PCS phone than he or she does when making contact through more conventional non-wireless phones and email.

▶ Debugging or solving a problem a customer is having "surfing the Internet" via a PCS phone—an experience unlike its PC-based cousin.

These are not easy issues to deal with. They call for new expertise, new customer relations, and a new culture. It isn't just a matter of eliminating cables. However, if telecommunication companies resolve these questions, the future is huge.

The Voice of eCRM

Natural language speech recognition (NLSR) and interactive voice response (IVR) are also important to the future of eCRM.

IVR is something that has most likely frustrated you, as you've hit one and two on your touch-tone phone and gone to more menus on one phone call than you'd care to count. Unfortunately, that's IVR's current state. But the technology holds huge promise for eCRM, especially with call centers. The transformation of call centers with some IVR to full-service, multimedia-based customer interaction centers (CICs) is something we can look to in our immediate future with some excitement.

Customer Interaction Centers: Speaking to the Future

Call centers and IVR have gone hand in hand for a number of years. The more sophisticated versions ask you for some sort of identification number that is transmitted verbally, read back by the voice, and then queried against a table that identifies the number as belonging to you and responds appropriately.

In the optimal IVR world, there would be a complete integration of voice and data, using multimedia (video and audio) across multiple channels to route a call or inquiry in some other fashion to an appropriate call center (or centers in a network of customer interaction centers). META Group anticipates the latter by the year 2005. Aside from the clear customer convenience, there is a very justifiable cost savings. It is estimated by META Group that a typical live agent interaction cost ranges from $15 to $35. The IVR interaction, though more primitive and less complex, costs less than $1. While there is never going to be a substitute for live agents, the IVR interactions can be used for less profitable or lower-maintenance customers. On the other side, this opens more time for live interaction with higher-maintenance or higher-profit customers. Saves money, increases customer satisfaction. Good trend.

InterVoice-Brite is a player in this domain. While it may not sound that exciting, their AgentConnect product is a step toward a truer customer interaction center. While it is a strong, multifeatured system, there are two features that move the CRM world closer to the real customer interaction companies crave. The first is Inbound Call Management, which processes inbound calls and routes them to IVR applications, call center agents, or other system resources. It is not much of a stretch to see this work across a network of call centers and do multiple routings. The other feature is Agent Messaging—intelligent agents that obtain information from the inbound customer without live action and, through "permission" from the customer, responds to unique customer questions or prompts and then uses Inbound Call Management to route the calls appropriately. What Intervoice-Brite lacks is the multimedia capabilities that CICs will call for in the future. A great plus is strong Computer Telephony Integration (CTI) features with the system, host, and database, allowing access to very large numbers of customer records. This is a promising product that skims the surface of a CIC future.

Even more interesting is Live Contact Service that is being offered by WebTelecom. Voice, video, text chat, and co-browsing are offered so that customer service can be live and activated on any website for a monthly fee. With these services, you could call into a customer service center in Houston, see the live representative on the Web so the costs are down, hook into a technical support center in Los Angeles (or even London), and be directed to a third website that has a technical FAQ that you need. All local. All via the Web. Echopass, Precision Response, and Servicesoft offer similar services. The level of live customer service offered means deal closings at two to four times the existing rate for a company and a 10 percent increase in completed sales through shopping cards, with the completion rate going up from 35 to 45 percent.

eCRM: Spoken Out Loud

Natural language is a seductive technology. In the early days of DragonDictate and IBM's ViaVoice, the two commercially recognizable text-to-speech programs, the use of language for computer commands was both discrete and speaker-dependent, and primarily good for dictation. Not only did you have to train the program to recognize your voice patterns (and heaven help you if you had a cold when you were training it), but you had to pause after each word. "How…are…you" was the only way the programs would recognize what you said. This was an irritating waste of time that was not particularly useful since you could type or write the words that you were speaking in less time than it took to verbalize. Plus, training and refining the language database took hours and even days to get to a recognition level of 95 percent. While 95 percent seems pretty successful, imagine if you misspelled 5 percent of all the words you wrote and had to erase each one and correct it—and the eraser didn't work very well, so multiple erasures were necessary.

By the late 1990s, with companies like Dragon Systems, IBM, and Lernout & Hauspie evolving the language recognition engines, there were two breakthroughs. First, the language of the programs went from discrete to continuous. Your natural speech patterns—speaking in normally cadenced sentences in a normal tone of voice—achieved 98 percent accuracy with the newer programs. Additionally, Lernout & Hauspie in particular developed a reasonably priced speaker-independent engine, which meant that training was no longer necessary. The engine would recognize almost anyone's voice as it was spoken. With Lernout & Hauspie and other vendors, the engines evolved from text-to-speech dictation to speech recognition—the ability to act on the commands that were presented to the engine by voice. There is a neat product on the market that uses this Lernout & Hauspie engine called HAL2000—which stands for HomeAutomatedLiving 2000—a home control product that uses your voice commands to turn on the lights, dim them, and control the thermostat. It can also let you know the traffic, weather, and sports scores, downloaded regularly from the Internet. It reminds you of what you have to do, controls your TV, DVD player, your garage, sprinkler—all through your voice commands, either directly or even over a remote telephone. Imagine the complexity of technology for such a mainstream and inexpensive commodity!

What does this have to do with CRM or eCRM? Plenty. When you make those IVR calls, in what capacity do you normally make them? As a customer. CRM is probably the system that benefits the most from advances in voice technology.

"The next six months are the first months of the voice decade," says Christian Hernandez, the narrowcast product manager for Micro-Strategy, a personalization specialist, (see Chapter 6 for more on MicroStrategy), "Interaction through a personalized voice is simple and easy to understand. We all use cellphones and we all use the old-fashioned IVR systems, so the learning curve is minor." Micro-Strategy believes so strongly in the "decade of the voice" that they have created a telephony application service provider (ASP) Voice Bureau that handles the traffic for their voice-enabling site, http://www.speaker.com/. Here is the blurb from their website:

> Speaker.com enables businesses to narrowcast to their customers, partners and employees via voice. Your e-business can send customers over the phone content that is from the same source as your website's content. As a gateway between data and the public telephone network, Speaker.com expands the reach of e-business to the most common communication device, the telephone.

This is an approximation of what Motorola's VoxML voice markup language is attempting to do and to standardize. It allows you to use servers, phone lines, APIs, the Internet, text-to-speech software, and XML to speak to websites and get responses to your inquiries.

VoiceXML

Imagine being able to query a website over the phone and getting a voice response from the website! With VoiceXML, anyone with a traditional, circuit-switched cellphone will be able to query a data source verbally and get a text-to-speech response. Motorola, the VoxML parent, started working with the idea that XML would store the business data, XSL would write the scripts to format the data for wireless devices, and VoxML would then do the speech translations. VoiceXML is the latest incarnation of Motorola's work in VoxML. Other big players such as IBM, AT&T, and Lucent have joined Motorola to drive the VoiceXML standard. Since the recent release of VoiceXML Version 1.0 in March 2000, it is rapidly coalescing into an industry standard. (For more information, see the VoiceXML Forum's website at http://www.voicexml.org/.)

What does that mean in practical terms? It is pretty straightforward. As of now, most airlines have websites that keep up-to-date information on flights and their status. That is perhaps the only way that to get this information other than a live attendant. With VoiceXML, you'll be able to call the website directly and get your flight status from the website. VoiceXML, combined with a telephony application service provider, creates a "voice browser" that hooks you up to an Internet or intranet website to get the necessary data. When a company writes Web applications with voice response, it no longer needs the proprietary development environment that traditional IVR calls for. The result is an automated interaction that is data-driven, deeply personalized and fits a general standard used across the Internet. Customers of these services will be able to rapidly and efficiently access information and thereby earn the customer's loyalty and repeat business.

XML + eCRM = CPExchange

XML is a tricky standard, since it really isn't much of a standard yet. It has many flavors, down to the level of Ariba and Commerce One, two e-procurement companies creating competing versions. A substantial number of XML standards are being developed that use industry specific data type definitions (DTDs) and meta-tags. What this means in ordinary language is that the financial services world, for example, is developing a generalized means of reading their specific jargon (for example, stock has a meaning in their world different than the world of food services and it can be read differently by search engines) when it is built into a Web page. This gives search engines universal access to those terms and definitions. Beyond that, at a much more complex level, is DAML—DARPA Agent Markup Language—which is attempting to give semantic meaning to XML through the addition of ontologies added to XML meta-tags (see http://www.daml.org/). The reason? This way the different definitions of stock won't be beholden to industry specific XMLs, but will be part of a palette of choices attached to the word/tag "stock." You can pick the right definition when it pops up and asks you to. This is supported by none other than Tim Berners-Lee, the creator of the World Wide Web.

However, the profound value of XML is not in dispute. The flavor of the millennium for CRM is CPExchange—Customer Profile Exchange—an XML standard for the CRM world that is being evolved by a consortium of companies that include Siebel, IBM, Vignette (the originator of CPExchange), Oracle, and Compaq, among others, and is sponsored by IDEAlliance (http://www.idealliance.org/), the research arm of the Graphic Communications Association. This is an ambitious standard that actually is XML based, but does not stop with a markup language. It is an attempt to fashion a standard that would create a unified view of the customer that would be singular, simultaneous, and holistic and could be that across multiple enterprises, regardless of the CRM applications in use. CPExchange attempts to solve the problem many companies face in attempting to service their customers: the "left hand doesn't know what the right hand is doing" dilemma. In this scenario, for example, a customer who just purchased a product now calls for technical support, and somehow the information from the sales department never makes it to the support department, forcing the customer to re-identify himself in gory detail. Few things are more frustrating for customers.

What makes CPExchange particularly appealing is how much more extensive it is than just some DTDs and meta-tags. If successful, it will include a data model, transport and query definitions, and a framework for privacy safeguards. The privacy model embedded in the standard is designed to accommodate any privacy policy from any jurisdiction, and also provides for the customer to have some control over what information about them is distributed—a very important question, as we will see later. It will be applicable to front-office, back-office, and Web-automated CRM applications. The group creating the standard will also create software libraries that will be available as open source, thus giving the standard to whoever wants to facilitate or develop it free of charge. Data transport to any venue would be increasingly fast and effective since middleware or other forms of mediation would not be necessary, making the data transit almost instantaneous, regardless of where and how it is created. According to Brad Husick, vice president of Standards & Evangelism at Vignette:

> CPExchange will give customers a new level of comfort in knowing that the privacy protections promised by the company they do business with are indeed fulfilled. It gives these companies new insights into satisfying their customers needs, and opens new opportunities to vendors for e-business solutions.

Another advantage of CPExchange is its interoperability with other XML schemas such as Internet Content Exchange (ICE) and BizTalk, the Microsoft XML version of business network communication.

Introduced in October 2000, CPExchange changes the landscape of e-business and eCRM for the better.

CPExchange Standards

The CPExchange specification is more comprehensive than pure XML. (Reprinted here with permission from the CPEX Working Group, the IDEAlliance, Alexandria, Virginia.)

The following are the design goals:

- ► Platform, vendor, and application independence

- ► Message transport layer independence

- ► Scalability for mission-critical, enterprise-quality use

- ► Flexibility to work with many types of applications, including legacy apps

- ► Extensible for future applications

The following are the specifications:

- ► Data Model for real time and batch information

- ► Transport architecture for query and interchange (transactions)

- ► Privacy enablement model across the entire network

- ► Open source reference implementation

The following is the implementation guideline:

- ► Draft specifications available to CPExchange Network members only and will be published as completed

The following is the data model:

- ► Descriptive information about a customer

- ► Deterministic information (name, address, phone)

- ► Demographic information (age, gender, family)

- ► Transactional information (interactions, declared preferences, behaviors, purchases)

- ► Relative information (relationship to others, groups)

- ► Inferred information (affinity groups, category scores, life time value)

- ► Extensible

The following addresses the privacy issue:

- ▶ Data exchange will occur more frequently

- ▶ Multiple privacy standards will emerge

- ▶ Internet Advertising Initiative—good start, but doesn't go far enough, for example, doesn't cover offline data

- ▶ Must include opt-in, granularity, full notification of transfer if desired by users

- ▶ A unified, transitive data privacy model will accelerate the fair handling of information

The following are the privacy requirements:

- ▶ Applicable at a granular level

- ▶ Transitive through multiple interchanges (onward transfer)

- ▶ Works for intra-enterprise and extra-enterprise environments

- ▶ Support multiple levels of privacy

- ▶ Coordination with P3P, EU, IAI, FTC, and other initiatives

- ▶ Extensible for future standards

- ▶ Will facilitate individual's ability to access, evaluate, and control profile

Globalization Is Really Personal

Visionaries come in multiple packages. Often, there is a corporate strategic analyst who could have pretty much any title and is focused on the broad future and the company's role in it. There are the corporate technical leaders who are designated as those that will produce the products to move the company into the forefront of the trends that are foreseen by the analysts. These are the product managers. Product managers have to have a keen grasp of the direction of the marketplace to ensure that their product lines are appropriately out front of the market. Their vision of the future is clear and unadulterated. Product managers like Christian Hernandez of MicroStrategy and Paul McCauley of Interact Commerce Corporation are both sharply focused on the trends in CRM and eCRM.

Says Mr. Hernandez:

> True customer relationship management will become a *customer-driven* process, rather than a marketing-driven one. The movement is toward the customer telling me what's important to them and helping me act on it. In the next three to four years we will see a change from a commodity-product economy to one that is based on customer experience and tangible value exchange based around a customer's preferences. Customers will shop around for higher perceived levels of service and will be willing to share their personal information in order to acquire it.

Interact Commerce's McCauley echoes this:

> We are delivering highly personalized Internet services now with Interact.com, but we are doing it through the applications and tools people use every day, not forcing them to switch to an online-only, browser environment—which is way ahead of the game. But this is the sort of thing that is the natural evolution of applications and thus CRM. The individual and the control that the individual has over his own consumer or business destiny should be the focus of most of the CRM world, but since the consumer data is scattered about an organization, that will require that vendors' solutions work together. The single-vendor solution of customer information is a fallacy—it just needs to look like it to the consumer. The key is to not only provide a single view of the customer within your organization—we must all strive to provide a consistent customer experience regardless of who or what they happen to be interacting with.

But there is a dilemma. Customer data is growing to extraordinary sizes. Company databases are growing to multi-*terabytes* of customer data that they have to sort and analyze each day. MicroStrategy has 40 clients with at least a terabyte of customer data. This is financial information, demographic information, purchasing decisions, billing and invoicing information—hundreds of thousands and even millions of customers that are each looking to be personally recognized. This is a major conundrum for any company that has yet to unlock the value of all the data they've been collecting. What's a business to do? How can a business provide the appropriate level of personalization to each customer and gain intelligence from its vast information repositories?

MicroStrategy's answer to this problem is both at the cutting edge and representative of the market's future. They call it "narrowcasting."

It is several steps beyond simple customer segmentation analysis and the attachment of business rules to customer "type," which is the way that many CRM vendors do it now.

Says Mr. Hernandez:

> In the current paradigm, information is sifted and analyzed within the corporation to be able to provide superior customer service. In the financial world, for example, large amounts of customer data are analyzed every night, and personalized emails are sent to each broker with information regarding their customers' stock activities, [which] provides the broker with a recommended approach—a broker "hint" if you will, on how to treat that customer. This is, in today's world, a tangible leading-edge CRM application. The future leverages that information beyond the organization, directly with the customer.

> Narrowcasting takes this several steps further. It is the embodiment, at the most significant levels, of permission marketing, with the customer telling you what he wants you to do. It creates a true dialogue with customers, enabling them to profile themselves, indicating how and where they want to be serviced. The current marketing-driven version of CRM becomes truly customer-driven, proactive, and permission-based. You serve the customer the way they want to be serviced via the communication channel that they desire—PDA, email, fax, live representatives.

Narrowcasting is representative of the most personalized of all possibilities through CRM—the customer is actually empowered.

What makes CRM technology a fascinating venture is the transparency of the technical. The customer is getting increasingly important control over his own online destiny and it is due to a technical foundation that is not seen or felt or heard, but it is used. One of these technologies, intelligent agents, is part of this future to a degree not even conceived of by its early cheerleaders. Both Mr. Hernandez and Mr. McCauley see the use of these intelligent agents as central to the personalization that is coming to a wireless device near you.

What is an intelligent agent? It is a software "buddy"—a set of rules that are attached to your name that indicate an automatically triggered course of action when the conditions established by the rules are met.

For example, your bank alerts you to the fact that your checking account balance has gone below $500. The rules set that you created says that if your savings account has at least $2,000, transfer funds to bring your account back up to $501. If the savings account is below

$2,000, then go to the credit line and pull the money to bring it to the $501 level. What you see is a notification that the account has gone below $500 and should the agent proceed to make the necessary transfer? If you say yes, you will get an email notification (or whatever you have chosen as your transport) that the account was credited with *xxxx* dollars and the *yyyy* account was debited for *xxxx* dollars.

Says Mr. Hernandez:

> The intelligent agents are given permission by the customer to take these actions on their behalf. An intelligent broker, for example, knows the portfolio of the customer, their risk threshold, their stated preferences. This agent can sift through comprehensive analyst research, and recommend securities that fit the customer profile. The customer has control over this process. They decide what type of stocks they are interested in, how they want to receive this information, and based on what conditions. For example, if the market drops by over 10 percent, analyze the technology sector for stocks that fit my current risk profile and which have lost over 30 percent of their value but still have an analyst rating of "Strong Buy." Send me the list on a daily basis to my email and pager with a summary. The customer has a Web-based portal where they can view this information or change their profile. However, what makes this really attractive is that the notification procedure can be proactive. The information can come to you via any device, wired or wireless, and can incorporate intelligent recommendations on the course of action. Narrowcasting analyzes vast amounts of data checking for each individual's preferences, personalizes the information and delivers it via any media channel, and finally allows the user to act on that information on the spot. That is powerful!

Activated Data, according to Interact Commerce's McCauley, is a similar trend that reflects the drive toward highly personalized customer-controlled information and proactivity. It is a rules-based notification engine that adds business rules to data that resides in a repository on the back-end. Says Mr. McCauley:

> It is proactive rather than reactive. It actually goes pretty deeply into the customer's activity. It can reach the level that notifies a sales representative in real time via their cellphone when a particular customer opens a specific document or proposal, providing the means for immediate contact.

This is not the far future. The CRM world is in the development phase of this intensely personal experience for the customer. The level of interaction between the customer and the corporation is getting deeper and deeper. With the inclusion of rules-based personalization that is delivered across any number of channels, it is also getting very portable.

Mr. Hernandez continues:

> It is a matter of permission, personalization, and delivery across multiple channels. The value of information will continue to grow for the next three to four years. The ability to use this information will provide tangible monetary benefits.

There is another step to this increasingly personalized experience.

ROI: Changes That Meet the Future

The transformation of the world by the Web economy and in the eCRM space is so dramatic that ROI measurements need to change. While traditional ROI has been undergoing transformation for years with metrics such as those proposed in the highly acclaimed *Balanced Scorecard* (by Dr. Robert Kaplan and David P. Norton, HBS Press, 1996), in late 2000 Accenture (formerly Andersen Consulting) proposed an eCRM-specific metric for ROI that is significantly different than anything else out there.

Accenture's proposal, coming when a number of Big 5 firms are creating several benchmarks for ROI (such as KPMG's "e Valuation") is particularly important due to its timeliness for the CRM marketplace. Yes, CRM is a system, and yes, CRM is a philosophy, but first and foremost, CRM is a business. Thus, there have to be some measurable return metrics for this business. The March 27, 2000 *Industry Standard* says that it costs e-commerce companies roughly $250 in marketing to acquire a single customer. The gross income (margin) for that customer is $24.50 for the first quarter, and $52.50 every quarter thereafter, making that customer profitable if they hang around for 1.5 years. Unfortunately, nearly 65 percent of online customers make a single purchase in the same place and that's it. To maintain the customer is about $\frac{1}{6}$ the cost of acquisition at the absolute worst and is often better than that.

That means that an ROI standard for CRM is not easy, since the value of the return is not easily discernible by the high price and long payback period of customer acquisition, one of CRM's major goals.

The stakes are high. Accenture indicates that a $1 billion company can make as much as $130 million more in pretax profit if it manages its CRM performance well. This means being aimed at a 30 percent performance increase over a predetermined time period. However, in the New Economy, the numbers that get to the $130 million mark aren't the only measurements. There is much more than just the cost reductions, revenue increases, and market share indicators that are classically used. Customer satisfaction, perhaps measured by the retention of customers over time, the mix of revenue, reduction in time spent with customer complaints, and the ability of the customer to manage his own CRM destiny are all measurements being considered in a new ROI.

Accenture, to deal with all of this, developed a weighted series of measurable benchmarks and performance indicators. Their indicators can be grouped into five categories:

- Customer insight
- Customer offers
- Customer interaction
- High performance organization
- Enterprise integration

These five categories are broken down into twenty separate groups that are weighted according to the highest profitability impact:

- Motivating and rewarding people
- Customer service
- Turning customer information into insight
- Attracting and retaining people
- Building, selling, and service skills
- Strong value proposition
- Partner and alliance management
- eCRM
- Sales planning
- Key account management
- Advertising
- Customer retention and acquisition

- ▶ Managing product and service mix
- ▶ Promotion
- ▶ Ability to change the organization
- ▶ Measuring profitability
- ▶ New products and services
- ▶ Channel management
- ▶ Segmentation
- ▶ Building service culture

(Source: Accenture, from article entitled "Andersen Consulting Identifies Key CRM Drivers of Profit," ECCS website, http://www.eccs.uk.com/.)

Note that the top four measures are people-oriented and the top three categories are people oriented. CRM is CRM no matter how you come at it.

Whether this works as a set of ROI benchmarks is still questionable, but it's the first serious attempt to redefine ROI with CRM's real value proposition—which may seem intangible, but has real, tangible results on the bottom line.

Online Can Be Cost-Free—If You Want It That Way

While a lot of the technological shifts are aimed toward the "small and wireless is better" school, the business model is also changing dramatically. Low prices are embedded in the landscape as the days of ERP-like pricing begin to fade. The trend has been toward cheap or free online sales automation packages and inexpensive subscriptions to online services like Interact.com. This is what twenty-first century marketing has been aimed at. We are cheaper, better, quicker to the Internet than our competitors. Both Oracle and Siebel have a model that allows them to give away the "limited enterprise" version of their SFA packages online, such as Oraclesalesonline.com, (see Chapter 4), or Siebel 99, a single user sales force automation package that imitates a good deal of the functionality (without the power) of the large enterprise Siebel eBusiness 2000 applications. The hope, in all cases, is that the user will get so enamored of the tools they have at their command that the larger packages or additional packages will be purchased by their companies.

In mid-2000, Oracle rolled out http://www.oraclesalesonline.com/ as freeware. It aimed at some of the most typical sales force automation tasks: calendaring, contact management, forecasting, opportunity management, and pipeline management. The purpose is competitive. Lure them in with the free SFA application. Make the customers realize how valuable it is. Get them to buy the other (fully integrated) Oracle CRM applications. Cut into Siebel's base.

Oracle figures that either extensions to the SFA application—such as sales compensation CRM modules or associated CRM modules like their EMA module—paid for via a fee-based pricing model, will handle the cost of giving away the SFA applications. Oraclesalesonline.com is the first eCRM-focused application suite Oracle has released to market. Their Oracle CRM applications have been traditional CRM.

Oraclesalesonline.com targets midsize companies, although Oracle is certainly open to smaller businesses as well. The Internet model and the pricing make this an attractive option for resource-strapped companies, though that isn't necessarily Oracle's intent. But it does indicate a pricing trend in the CRM world.

Even here there are danger signs. Because of the late 2000 collapse of the dot-coms on NASDAQ, the days of no-profit Internet plays are over. Very over. Thus there is some pulling in of the free CRM site reins as this book is going to press, with a rethinking as to the validity or future profitability of the give it away as a loss leader model these sites are following.

There are other pricing models that are thus becoming popular. Many online services work from a basic subscription model, which is trendy. Basic subscriptions are often free (as with salesforce.com), with a premium subscription offered that provides a considerable increase in services. Interact.com offers basic and gold subscription levels for its services as it increasingly integrates with a multiplicity of CRM software—even its rivals.

As CRM moves to eCRM and beyond to mCRM or wireless versions, the need to charge for software becomes increasingly unimportant. Software is becoming a transport for services, even as the Internet itself evolves. "The Web moves from a phenomenon to just one more interaction channel," says MicroStrategy's Hernandez. The implications of that statement are staggering. "Buy it on the Web, and return it to the store" is actually a very important objective, states Mr. Hernandez. "I am the same customer. Why aren't you the same store? The loop has to be closed here."

Appendix A

Places to Go: Websites That Make It Worth It

The number of websites devoted to CRM are inter-minable, and many of them are nothing more than rehashed content designed to give some "substance" to marketing for a particular company. What I've done is pick out the best sites on the Net and the ones that have substantive content and the will to live for a long while on the Web. Hopefully, these nine sites will be as valuable to you as they are to me.

Interestingly, there is no real competitiveness or meanness of spirit among the CRM Internet sites. They each see the complementary value of the other, and the result is a cooperative nature that is actually remarkable. For example, CRMGuru.com will tout searchcrm.com. CRM-Forum.com gives marketing information to CRMGuru.com. A very interesting approach.

eCRM Communities

Communities are what they sound like. Gathering places, watering holes without alcohol (except maybe virtual alcohol) for the cogniscenti or the blue collar of the specific targeted groups they aim at. There are thousands of communities on the Internet, most with some specific purpose in mind, some of which escapes me. However, the CRM communities' purpose doesn't escape me. They are the places where the CRM-initiated and those who want to learn about CRM go. I'm going to show you the best here.

www.CRMGuru.com

This is one of the best CRM websites on the Net. Run by a contributor to this book, Robert Thompson of Front Line Solutions, it is a veritable cornucopia of CRM delights, including white papers, news, interactive discussions, newsletters, and Webcasts. One unique feature is a moderated discussion group called CRM.Talk. CRM.Talk is the most informative and interactive discussion group in the CRM sphere. It covers all parts of the CRM map, beginning with basic discussions on the definition of CRM and progressing to more advanced topics. Witness this recent excerpt from CRM.Talk:

> **Question:**
>
> Can you point me to topical areas or hot buttons that have a direct marketing slant?
>
> **Answer:**
>
> [from an answer by Jérôme Paradis] Here are few areas direct marketers deal with: (1) front-end: call-center, customer services, e-commerce site, CTI, source-code based data entry, (2) back-end: fulfillment, predictive inventory management, returns and refunds, delinquent accounts, (3) e-marketing, permission marketing, opt-in, opt-out lists, viral marketing, personalized or one-to-one communications, (4) marketing automation: media planning, list management (rentals, house files), segmentation, selections, merge-purge, address accuracy, database marketing, predictive modeling, data mining, (5) data warehousing, (6) metrics: ROP (Return on Promotion), ROI, break-even...

The material on this site go far beyond the ordinary. Live discussions with CRM thought leaders, white papers on CRM implementations, discussions with technical experts, a large searchable archive of articles from publications, and materials that are privately developed for the site by CRM industry leaders all provide low-hanging fruit for the discerning surfer. There is an available stable of CRM gurus available for topical discussion with the site members. They include:

- Naras Eechambadi, CEO of Quaero, LLC, who specializes in enterprise marketing automation (EMA)

- Robert Thompson, president of Front Line Solutions, who specializes in partner relationship management (PRM)

- Bill Brendler, who runs the Ebusiness-erm.com site and who specializes in organizational change and implementation

- Mei Lin Fung, another contributor to this book, managing director at eFrontier Ventures and a specialist in customer lifetime value (see Appendix B for her primer on CLV)

- Dick Lee, consultant and author of *The Customer Relationship Management Survival Guide*, who specializes in CRM strategies

- Jay Chang, president of Structured Chaos, Inc., who specializes in customer interaction channels and software evaluation

- Tony Craddock, founder and managing director of CRM, Ltd., who specializes in whole-company CRM strategies and CRM in Europe

- Jay Curry, chairman of the Customer Marketing Institute, who specializes in CRM for small businesses

This is a "practice what you preach" site. Membership increases through programs that are designed to reward referrals and word of mouth. At the corporate level are the CRM.Talk Advocates—companies like Interact Commerce Corporation (the CRM company formerly known as SalesLogix) who attach the CRM.Talk button to their websites so that visitors can sign up for the moderated discussion email group. In return, CRMGuru will give them featured status in the CRM.Talk newsletter.

CRMGuru.com also sponsors contests for the most referrals by an individual, with various CRM-related prizes such as books to the winners of the referral contests. CRM.Talk was expected to reach 24,000 subscribers by January 1, 2001, an indicator of the program's success.

CRMGuru.com blatantly advocates partner relationship management (PRM). Robert Thompson, founder of the site, is a PRM expert; thus the emphasis. To that end, there is a newsletter that goes out weekly to site subscribers called "On the Front Line" that focuses on PRM, though it also carries other useful CRM news.

The site is easy to navigate. Registration is free. Use this site.

www.CRMcommunity.com

To say the least, this is a *dense* site. Chock-full of white papers, news, and what site masters call "community news" (aimed more at mergers, alliances, and other "internal" CRM activity), CRMcommunity.com is a good site to find out what is going on within the CRM neighborhood. One interesting feature is the direct participation of its members in the evolution of the site. There are the usual interesting discussion groups. More importantly, the site members write featured articles that are posted for registered members to read or download. The involvement of the members gives this site a democratic feel.

One unusual facet of CRMcommunity.com is its enterprise resource planning (ERP) coverage. For some reason, it liberally sprinkles the latest ERP news throughout the site.

There is registered membership for the site that gives you access to multiple additional services—a reward for being more than a casual user. Besides a plethora of white papers, there are several significant advantages to the free membership. First, the CRM Journal, a genuinely useful online CRM magazine. Article coverage is wide and deep, with topics from "Influencing Behavior to Positively Affect Customer Loyalty" to "The 'People Consulting' Behind a CRM Engagement: Seven Insights for Achieving ROI." Additionally, premier members can chat with specialists and access a huge directory of CRM vendors. There are also many useful resource Web links, though in a quick survey, I found a substantial number of dead links and one-sentence discussion group responses.

This flaw aside, CRMcommunity.com is an important site for both the CRM researcher and the business executive trying to get a handle on CRM.

www.CRMassist.com

Called an ITPortal Toolbox for CRM by its founders, CRMassist.com has a Yahoo! look and feel, down to the color scheme and the smiley faces. Behind this grinning symbol is an informative site that was spawned from series of Net nodes, beginning with ERPassist in the mid-1990s, which led to EAI, Oracle, SAP, Networking and, of course, CRM-focused Web ventures.

What makes this a very interesting site is the user's ability to carry on a technical discussion in many topical areas. Some of the covered subjects:

- ▶ Siebel
- ▶ Clarify
- ▶ Vantive
- ▶ Oracle CRM
- ▶ Chordiant
- ▶ Vignette
- ▶ Data mining

Other areas of interest covered in detail:

Call center Monitoring, resolution, voice

Cross-application Print/fax, workflow, reporting

Front-office/CRM packages Siebel, Clarify, Vantive...

General CRM information Software comparison, employment

Implementation Project management, testing

Industry-specific Communication, consumer goods

Integration Back-office integration, EAI

Marketing Campaign management, customer

Sales force automation Sales analysis, sales forecast

Service tools Call routing, interactive voice

Other neat site features include a job bank and a CRM stock index.

www.eccs.uk.com

Self-styled "the European CRM portal," it is described well. It covers all matters European-CRM-related. This is a graphically pleasing site that goes for quality over quantity. For example, there is a small glossary of useful CRM terms. There is a small directory of useful, fully functional websites for CRM users or interested parties organized by categories ranging from publications to advice to event organization.

Uniquely, there is a product search function available to members that will find you the CRM product you are looking for. The detail required is just enough (the information I used is in parentheses):

▶ The country you are searching from (United States)

▶ The type of product (marketing automation)

▶ The general functionality of the product (campaign management)

▶ The platform you are using (Windows 95/98, NT)

▶ The number of users (up to 1,000)

▶ The monetary size of the project you are interested in implementing (500K to 1M)

The results were mixed. I got ten responses: Onyx, Selligent, smartFocus, Visual Elk, and six versions of Caspian. Noticeably absent were major players such as Siebel or Interact Commerce Corporation, who certainly fit the description given. So there is limited value, but some usefulness with this feature.

The best section of this website is the CRM Advice. This section carries a frequently asked questions (FAQs) list on CRM and best-practices guides, among other things, that have universal value.

www.DestinationCRM.com

CRM magazine handles this baby. This site is useful in all the ways print publications are useful. News in a well-organized format. Industry events that are pending. A "business solutions center" that highlights the *CRM* magazine platinum partners. E-broadcasts, questionnaires, and a career center. Expert advice from the largest collection of experts in the industry. Since *CRM* and *eCRM* are the industry standard publications and very good magazines, and this site is an extension of those publications, I wouldn't miss this site. It provides excellent coverage and translation of the publications to the small screen. Registration and membership are free.

www.CRM-Forum.com

This is a great medium for those seeking a career in CRM or those already in the CRM community. Comprehensively focused on the CRM world, CRM-Forum is the meeting place for CRM professionals. Not only are there internal discussion groups, but there is an extensive (paid) yellow pages of vendors, consultants, and service providers. A career center provides a place to do an anonymous posting of your résumé or of a job opportunity—something many patrons of the site take advantage of. Additionally, the news covers CRM IPOs, mergers and acquisitions, hiring and firing of key executives, alliances formed and broken, events, and a treasure trove of other CRM industry-related news.

www.Searchcrm.com

This is a search engine for CRM. It is part of the techtarget.com series of industry-specific search engines such as searchwebhosting.com or searchdatabase.com. Because the content tends to be governed by other sites, the aggregation and construction of the content is what makes this site stand out. It is almost a one-stop shop for CRM needs. The editors' picks allow the discerning surfer to get what the searchcrm.com pundits consider important (and it is the most important material). Additionally, there is a marketplace to purchase CRM-related books (including this one). A centralized vendor repository lets you find websites for all the CRM-related vendors in the areas that interest you. They even run a CRM "virtual trade show" that highlights vendor "booths" that the vendor/exhibitor buys on the site. For the cost of the "booth," the vendor not only gets a comprehensive description, but also links to press releases and news related to the vendor and a link that lets the visitor request a quote for a job and/or make contact with a key person at the exhibitor's company. All in all, a clever and convenient way to advertise.

The search capability works decently. Powered by the Inktomi engine, a search turns up total Web pages. For example, a search in the news area for Kana turned up 1,005 Web pages, many of which were the Kana site pages. So the search function works as well as any of them do these days. Some of the Kana information was useful, some unfathomable.

It is a worthwhile site, though it takes some navigating to get a grasp of it.

Other Websites

The sites here aren't communities. They are websites. That means that they provide useful, updated information about CRM and specific facets of it. There are literally hundreds of those, but the two that I mention here have impact. That's why I think you should go see them.

www.CPExchange.org

For the CRM professional and those who see the boundless future of CRM, this is a mission-critical site. CPExchange.org keeps the more-than-casually interested CRM party updated on the current state of the specification (see Chapter 16 for more on CPExchange).

www.RealMarket.com

RealMarket.com is another site for the CRM professional. It is both an active news site for information on CRM doings and a "permissioned" email newsletter for those who don't search the site daily. It is concerned with contracts signed, partnerships announced, executives hired, and other internal CRM news. It's been invaluable to me as a tool for keeping up with the CRM world.

Appendix B

Customer Lifetime Value

For the business leader who has recently become a stakeholder in a CRM implementation, determining customer lifetime value (CLV) is essential. With companies discovering automated customer service and with customer acquisition and retention a contemporary mantra, having a means to benchmark the value of a customer or customers is a tremendous tool in determining what level of priority to give a customer. Despite the fact that we'd all like to give all customers equal time and treatment, since customers are not candidates and companies not ordinarily TV networks, equal time and treatment is not usually part of the deal.

Look at this comment on the true customer relationship from Mike Simpson, chief marketing officer at Interact Commerce Corporation:

> Many people claim that relationships are built on trust, but I disagree. I have business and personal relationships with LOTS of people I don't trust. Of course, most positive relationships are built on trust, but that's a different issue. A relationship, at its very essence, is a memory of past interactions. You have no relationship with someone you have heard about, but haven't spoken to. Once you have that first interaction, every subsequent interaction will build from the previous. Your relationship is based on what you remember from those experiences. So, from a corporate perspective, that's where most companies fall down with their customers, and that's why true salespeople (more than mere order takers) will never be replaced by software.
>
> When a customer buys a product from a salesperson at a company, or even a website; they feel they have a relationship with an entity. They judge that business relationship as they judge all their other relationships—how well do we know each other. When they call tech support, and they are not aware that customer just spent a million dollars, or is a long-standing customer, or has already spoken to five people, they get upset. When you go to a Ritz-Carlton and they remember what kind of newspaper you like in the morning and when you stayed last, your relationship with the company strengthens, although you may never see the individual that shared that information again. And in contrast, when accounts receivable doesn't know you have an open support incident and you might kick their product out, that call to harass you to pay your bill just took your relationship down a notch.
>
> A consistent customer history leads to a consistent customer experience. Every individual's relationship with the customer or prospect must contribute to and complement the others.

That customer view needs support. The customer history is the other side of retention. How consistently has the customer purchased products? How continuously and at what magnitude has the customer produced revenue for the company? What customer segments are providing the most bangs for the buck?

Mei Lin Fung is a managing director of eFrontier Ventures and a pioneer in CRM. She worked with Tom Siebel at Oracle several years ago, when the first CRM systems were being developed and was directly involved in their development. Ms. Fung has become a recognized expert on both customer lifetime value and the "math" of marketing. Her CLV primer, reprinted here with her permission, provides you with a benchmark for determining customer life cycle value. Use it in good (corporate) health.

Customer Value Model, a Primer

Can Customer Retention Be Converted to Financial Value?

The following are useful definitions and explanations:

- ▶ Net present value: Valuing cashflow over time in today's dollars

- ▶ Expected value: Probability of event × outcome of event

  - ▶ Measuring the expected financial benefits from retention and referrals provides for sustained investment in customer care. Moves beyond good will and lip service.

  - ▶ Quantifying the expected results provides metrics for measuring the impact of customer care programs and actions. Turns data into knowledge that can be acted upon.

Simple Example 1: Calculate the Expected Revenue from a New Customer

Let's look at the two-year history of revenue from customers as shown in Table B-1. Suppose we find that 60 percent of customers come back and make a purchase the next year, while 40 percent of new customers never return. On average, how much revenue do you get from 1,000 new customers over two years?

Table B-1: Example of Expected Revenue Calculations for New Customers

	Year 1	Year 2
New customers	1,000	
Expected number of customers = 1,000 × retention rate of 60%		600
Average size of sale for each customer	$1,000	$1,000
Revenue	$1,000,000	$600,000
Expected revenue from 1,000 new customers, cumulative	$1,000,000	$1,600,000
Average revenue from each of the 1,000 initial customers = expected revenue by Year 2 divided by 1,000 = $1.6M/1,000 or		$1,600

Simple Example 2: Measure the Financial Profit from increasing Customer Retention

The customer value model can be used to value customer retention. Customer lifetime value is defined as the profit you earn from a customer over their lifetime. This is the net present value (NPV) of the expected value of the profits you earn on sales to that customer in each of the years the customer remains a purchaser. Assume each customer delivers $1,000 in profit to you each year that they are a customer. We'll use expected value to project the expected profit from a new customer in Table B-2.

Table B-2: Example of Expected Profit Derived from Customer Retention

Customer retention rate	50%	
NPV discount rate	**25%**	
	Year 1	**Year 2**
New customers	1,000	
Expected number of customers = 1,000 × retention rate of 50%		500
Average profit for each customer	$1,000	$1,000
Profit	$1,000,000	$500,000
Discount rate 25%. Factor	100%	80%
NPV profit	$1,000,000	$400,000
Expected profit from 1,000 new customers, cumulative	$1,000,000	$1,400,000
Average profit over 2 years from each of the 1,000 initial customers = expected profit by Year 2 divided by 1,000 = $1.4M/1,000 or		$1,400

Customer care activities can change the retention rate and satisfaction. If improved customer care increases retention rate, profits will go up. If activities decrease retention rate, profits go down. Use the model shown in Table B-2 to determine the breakeven point of customer care costs compared to increase in revenues due to loyal customers.

Balancing Responsiveness and Profits: Customer Value Model Case Study

As we consider the technology available for handling email, return on investment (ROI) is always an issue. The business process within which we consider such an investment is not fixed. We can decide to invest in technology that supports a business process offering varying degrees of responsiveness to customer email. In Table B-3, we look at four examples of that process.

Table B-3: Example of Cases Addressing the Email Avalanche of 5,000 Emails per Day Received by ACME Company

	Case 1	Case 2	Case 3	Case 4
Automated		100%	95%	90%
Personal handling	100%	5%	10%	
Retention rate	50%	50%	40%	60%
Escalation	5% 1-800	8% 1-800	6% 1-800	4% 1-800
Email handling	Handled individually	Fully automated	Partly automated	Part of integrated customer response
Response time	Received after 2–3 days delay on average	Less thorough but immediate	Equally thorough as Case 1; 1 day delay	More responsive, with timely personal touch; 1 day delay
Customer email process		Minimal customer research performed prior to design	Greater investment in design	Greatest investment in design
Ongoing research				Design improvements
Net result: customer lifetime value	−$104	−$100	−$3	$32

Net Result: Customer Lifetime Value

Table B-4 details how the results were obtained, invoking expected value and net present value. If you have questions, email Mei Lin Fung at mlf@resourceful.com.

Table B-4: Detailed Breakdown of CLV Derivation (Reprinted with permission of Mei Lin Fung.)

	Case 1	Case 2	Case 3	Case 4
Number of emails per day	5,000	5,000	5,000	5,000
Time frame	2 to 3 days	Immediate	Average 1 day	Average 1 day
Receipt confirmation	No	Yes	Yes	Yes
Customer email process	None	Self-service	Forms-based	Forms-based
Call center integrated email program	No	No	No	Yes
Response center business analysis investment	$–	$200,000	$100,000	$200,000
Response center technology cost	$–	$200,000	$100,000	$200,000
Relationship enhancement program	$–	$–	$–	$100,000
Response center human involvement	100%	0%	5%	20%
Number of emails handled per rep per day	120	None	100	50
Number of emails requiring rep involvement	5,000	0	250	1,000
Number of reps required	41.7	n/a	2.5	20.0
Assume annual cost per rep, fully loaded	$50,000	n/a	$55,000	$60,000
Cost per rep per day	$200	n/a	$220	$240
Cost per email handled by a rep	$1.67	$–	$2.20	$4.80
People cost per day	$8,333	$–	$550	$4,800
Assume transactions that convert to 1-800 escalations	5%	8%	6%	4%
Number of 1-800 escalations per day	250	400	300	200
Assume cost per 1-800 escalation resolution	$25.00	$25.00	$25.00	$15.00*

Table B-4: Detailed Breakdown of CLV Derivation (Reprinted with permission of Mei Lin Fung.) (cont.)

	Case 1	Case 2	Case 3	Case 4
Total costs in a year (Assume 250 working days)				
Required investment in email program	$–	$400,000	$200,000	$500,000
Email response rep cost per year	$2,083,333	$–	$137,500	$1,200,000
Cost of 1-800 transactions (escalated resolution)	$1,562,500	$2,500,000	$1,875,000	$750,000
Total costs	$3,645,833	$2,900,000	$2,212,500	$2,450,000
Total emails in a year	1,250,000	1,250,000	1,250,000	1,250,000
Prospects and others; breakout 80%	1,000,000	1,000,000	1,000,000	1,000,000
Customers; breakout 20% *(Assume each customer sends emails/year: 25)*	250,000	250,000	250,000	250,000
Number of Year 1 customers	10,000	10,000	10,000	10,000
Assume profit per customer/year (excluding above costs) *Revenue less COGs and selling costs*	$200	$150	$175	$200
Number of customers Year 1	10,000	10,000	10,000	10,000
Assume customer retention in Year 2	60%	50%	40%	60%
Number of customers Year 2	6,000	5,000	4,000	6,000
Profits from customers in Year 1	$2,000,000	$1,500,000	$1,750,000	$2,000,000
Profits from customers in Year 2	$1,200,000	$750,000	$700,000	$1,200,000
NPV profits from customers in Year 2 (25% discount rate)	$960,000	$600,000	$560,000	$960,000
Gross profit from 10,000 Year 1 customers	$2,960,000	$2,100,000	$2,310,000	$2,960,000
Less cost of email handling Year 1	$(3,645,833)	$(2,900,000)	$(2,212,500)	$(2,450,000)
Less NPV cost of email, 1-800 handling Year 2 *for retained customers only (25% discount rate)*	$(350,000)	$(200,000)	$(128,800)	$(187,200)
Net profit from Year 1 customers over two years; *average expected value per Year 1 customer*	$(1,035,833)	$(1,000,000)	$(31,300)	$322,800
Customer value over two years	$(104)	$(100)	$(3)	$32

Index

A

Accenture, 277, 331–332
account management, 72
ACD (automatic call distribution), 180
ACT!
    contact management with, 63–64
    overview of, 204
administration time, reducing with CRM, 262
advertising, costs of, 104
AgentConnect, InterVoice-Brite, 321
algorithms, use in personalization, 136
Allegis Sales Partner
    content and lead matching by, 158
    ease of deployment, changes, and use, 156
    e-commerce management, 159
    partnering benefits and, 149
    as PRM provider, 158–159
    program and fund management, 159
    territory and channel readiness, 158–159
amazon.com, personalized service by, 133
analytical CRM, 39–40
Andersen Consulting. *See* Accenture
Annuncio
    as EMA provider, 126
    features of, 117–118
    personalization strategy of, 145
application service providers (ASPs), 303–313
    advantages of, 306–307
    defined, 304
    disadvantages of, 307–308
    future of, 312–313
    history of, 304–305
    NASPs and, 308–309, 311–312
    overview of, 303–304
    PASPs and, 308–310
architecture
    PRM and, 156
    standards basis for, 259
ASPs. *See* application service providers (ASPs)
automated intelligent call routing, 186–187
automatic call distribution (ACD), 180
AV Electronics, EMA case study, 121–124
Avaya, as call center provider, 195–196

B

B2B. *See* business-to-business (B2B)
B2C. *See* business-to-consumer (B2C)
back-office solutions, 41–42
backend code, for Web-enabled CRM, 52
The Balanced Scorecard (Kaplan), 189

baseline marketing operations, 125
benchmarks. *See* metrics
beta testing, 295–296
bottom-line
    role of CRM in, 31–32
    role of SFA in, 67
Broadbase Software, Inc., 127
browser interfaces, "feel" of, 52
business analysts, 286–287
business analytic tools, 113–115
Business Relationship Network, 18, 21
business-to-business (B2B)
    customers of, 4
    estimated market for, 47
business-to-consumer (B2C)
    customers of, 4
    estimated market for, 47
    marketing and, 107

C

call centers. *See* customer interaction centers
    (CICs)
call routing, automated and intelligent, 186–187
CallCenter@nywhere, 187
CCR (customer contact representative), 185–186
CDW. *See* customer data warehouse (CDW)
cellphones
    personalization and, 143
    statistics on use of, 317
centralized computing, 305
CEOs, selling CRM to, 251–254
    competitive advantage, 254
    customer participation, 253
    vendor relationships, 252–253
CFOs, selling CRM to, 254–262
    executive ownership of project, 258
    measured effectiveness, 256–257
    planned execution, 260–262
    reasons for investing, 255–256
    strategic consistency of project, 258–260
change management
    consulting companies and, 279
    timing of agreement for, 282
channel management
    EMA and, 118
    PRM and, 151–152
CI (Customer Intelligence), 29
CICs. *See* customer interaction centers (CICs)
Clarify. *See* Nortel/Clarify
CLM. *See* customer lifecycle management (CLM)
closed-loop feedback, market analysis and, 120